The Foreign
Relations
of the United
States

Comparative Foreign Relations Series
Edited by David O. Wilkinson and Lawrence Scheinman,
University of California, Los Angeles

Comparative Foreign Relations: Framework and Methods
David O. Wilkinson, University of California, Los Angeles
The Foreign Relations of the United States
Michael H. Armacost, Pomona College
The Foreign Relations of China
Robert C. North, Stanford University
The Foreign Relations of France
Lawrence Scheinman, University of California, Los Angeles

forthcoming:
The Foreign Relations of the United Kingdom
Michael R. Gordon, University of California, Santa Barbara
The Foreign Relations of Russia
Morton Schwartz, University of California, Riverside
The Foreign Relations of Germany
Peter H. Merkl, University of California, Santa Barbara
The Foreign Relations of Japan
Hans H. Baerwald, University of California, Los Angeles
The Foreign Relations of India
Sudershan Chawla, California State College at Long Beach
The Foreign Relations of the U.A.R. and the Arab Middle East
Jivan Tabibian, University of California, Los Angeles

The Foreign Relations of the United States

Michael H. Armacost
Pomona College

Dickenson Publishing Company, Inc.
Belmont, California

To my mother and father

Contents

Foreword

The COMPARATIVE FOREIGN RELATIONS SERIES is designed for foreign policy courses that employ a comparative approach, as well as for courses in comparative politics and international relations that survey the foreign relations of key states. Because the basic literature is lacking, few courses today are able to make a genuinely comparative examination of national actors in the international system, in the manner increasingly adopted for the study of domestic politics. This series has been prepared to fill the need for such a basic literature.

The series presents an analytical model and case materials for beginning a comparative study of foreign relations. As a method of studying foreign relations phenomena, comparison allows us to investigate the differences and similarities among states in relation to the international system, and thereby generate or test propositions about the external relations of states.

In order to compare cases, an analytical model or framework should be used—that is, the same set of subjects and questions should be used to arrange and present information about each case. The analytical model of the series is presented in the core volume, *Comparative Foreign Relations: Framework and Methods,* which outlines a framework for describing the international situation and foreign policy of a state, explaining its current policy, analyzing its current problems, and projecting its future problems and policy alternatives. The case materials are presented in the various country volumes, which, following the analytical model, describe and explain the foreign relations of specific important states since 1945 and sketch their main current and anticipated problems.

The books in the series make comparison possible by presenting material of the same nature about each case; however, the actual comparisons must be made by the reader. Some ways in which the series might be used to further the comparative study of foreign relations are presented in the preface to the core volume.

David O. Wilkinson
Lawrence Scheinman

Preface

So many books have been written about American foreign policy that some justification is demanded of those who choose to add further to the number. This book was written primarily for undergraduate students of foreign policy. It was prompted by the conviction that they might find it useful to have accessible, in a single, reasonably slender volume a description and analysis of the multitude of forces that inform the substance and shape the style of American policy. Since this book possesses a certain unity of approach with other volumes in the COMPARATIVE FOREIGN RELATIONS SERIES, it is hoped that comparative analysis of the foreign policies of the important states in world politics may thereby be encouraged.

By its nature, this book is a work of synthesis. In preparing the manuscript I relied heavily on the perceptive books and articles of a host of diplomatic historians, economists, sociologists, and political scientists. In addition, I consulted the writings of numerous journalists and the memoirs of many officials who have participated with varying degrees of enthusiasm and success in the making of American policy. The highest tribute one author may pay to others is to borrow extensively from their ideas. The chapters of this book are studded with such tributes. Since the book is intended for students and interested laymen rather than specialists, footnotes have been held to a minimum.

I should like to express publicly my appreciation to Professor Reginald D. Lang, Professor of Government and International Relations at Carleton College, and to Professor William T.R. Fox, Professor of Public Law and Government at Columbia University, for stimulating and encouraging my interest in the relationship between domestic and foreign politics. To Professor John A. Vieg, Chairman of the Department of Government at Pomona College, I am indebted for numerous personal kindnesses as well as his indulgence of my requests for teaching assignments that expedited the completion of the manuscript. To Professor Russell Edgerton, of the Department of Political Science at the University of Wisconsin, I am grateful for many helpful comments on an earlier draft of Chapters 5 and 6. Professors David Wilkinson and Lawrence Scheinman, the co-editors of this series, read the entire manuscript and made many useful suggestions. The usual proviso applies in this case. For having been spared embarrassing errors, thanks are gratefully extended. I naturally assume full responsibility for those that remain.

In the preparation of the manuscript, Mrs. Shirley Martin rendered invaluable service as a typist. Excellent editorial assistance was supplied by Mrs. Elaine Linden and Mrs. Wanda Conger of Dickenson Publishing Company. Joseph Dana of Dickenson Publishing Company originally prevailed upon me to undertake this project. With him, therefore, I am prepared cheerfully to share the blame as well as any credit for the final result. Needless to add, I greatly appreciate the encouragement he offered throughout. My wife, Bonny, has more important things to do, thankfully, than edit my prose. Without her patience, however, and the grace with which she and my sons— Scott, Tim, and Chris—accepted IOUs for family outings repeatedly postponed, this book would never have been completed.

1

Introduction

"Foreign policy," President Lyndon B. Johnson once asserted, "must always be an extension of our domestic policy. The reason for this is very simple. Politics are the means by which men give collective voice to their hopes and aspirations." [1] The essential truth of this statement is all too often overlooked, particularly by students of foreign policy.

Foreign policies are shaped, of course, by both domestic and external influences. On the one hand, they express the reactions of a sovereign entity to the dangers and opportunities implicit in the international milieu. Whatever the character of a state's regime, its policies will always be governed to some extent by a calculation of forces and a sensitivity to its power relative to friends and foes. On the other hand, one cannot go very far toward an explanation of a state's purposes, its preferences among alternative strategies, its allocation of scarce resources among competing objectives, its willingness to shoulder onerous burdens or grave risks, or its friendship toward some states and enmity toward others, without detailed analysis of the domestic political community.

It is the purpose of this book to describe and analyze the myriad forces that shape the content and method, the substance and style of American foreign policy. Particular emphasis is devoted to the domestic sources of foreign policy, because they have been

[1] *Time* (September 2, 1966), p. 13.

neglected so often in other studies.[2] That emphasis is all the more appropriate in view of the present "international pecking order." Among the leading states, the United States, the Soviet Union, and the People's Republic of China all possess territories of continental dimensions and have long enjoyed a relative self-sufficiency on the periphery of the European state system. Consequently, they each display not only a generous degree of ethnocentrism but express in their foreign policies attitudes and values deeply rooted in their domestic experiences.

During the past decade the study of major foreign governments has been transformed into a genuinely comparative study of political systems. For years specialists in comparative politics were engaged primarily in the description of formal institutional structures. Recently they have begun to develop a much more analytic discipline. Comparisons have been facilitated by delineating those political activities that are universal and by directing attention to the formal and informal methods that various societies have devised to perform them. A substantial literature has developed around the concepts of interest articulation, interest aggregation, political socialization and recruitment, the art of political communication, the styles of political authority, the varieties of political cultures, the relationships between society and the state, and the quality and roles of political ideologies and political beliefs. Terms have been invented and more or less rigorously defined. Data have been systematically collected. Empirical studies abound. Efforts have been made to revise the rather static bias of structural-functional analysis in order to permit a more developmental or dynamic mode of analysis.[3] That progress has been made in the discipline during the past decade is undeniable. The utility of various new concepts and methods remains a matter of controversy among specialists.

Curiously, however, the reformation of comparative political studies has not yet occasioned an intimate synthesis of the disciplines of comparative politics and international politics. The interrelationships between domestic and foreign policy have rarely—and then only partially—been subjected to systematic analysis.[4] One of the motives for this volume, as for the larger series of which it is a part, is the desire to make more relevant for foreign policy analysis recent developments in comparative politics. Insofar as possible, therefore, those concepts and terms are employed that have acquired some

[2] For an appraisal of the extent of and reasons for that neglect, see James N. Rosenau, "Pre-Theories and Theories of Foreign Policy," in *Approaches to Comparative and International Politics*, R. Barry Farrell (ed.) (Evanston, Ill.: Northwestern University Press, 1966), pp. 27–92.

[3] See, for example, Gabriel Almond and Bingham Powell, Jr., *Comparative Politics: A Developmental Approach* (Boston, Mass.: Little, Brown, 1966).

[4] Two notable exceptions have been relied upon heavily in the preparation of this volume: Zbigniew K. Brzezinski and Samuel P. Huntington, *Political Power USA/USSR* (New York, N.Y.: Viking, 1965); and Kenneth N. Waltz, *Foreign Policy and Democratic Politics* (Boston, Mass.: Little, Brown, 1967).

currency and utility in the latter discipline. To be sure, the bias of the author is implicit in the selection of materials and concepts for discussion. In this respect the approach is eclectic; those concepts have been employed that seem to explain important features of American foreign policy and that permit comparisons with the foreign policy behavior of other prominent states.

It is necessary to acknowledge at the outset that an attempt to discover causal connections between various features of a domestic political system and the conduct of foreign policy is an enormously hazardous enterprise. Conclusions will necessarily be tentative, and should be understood as hypotheses warranting further investigation. Indeed, the obstacles encountered in attempting to isolate the influence of individual variables may be insurmountable. One cannot, after all, render the behavior of a single individual intelligible by merely referring to elements in his genetic make-up. Behavior is a result of heredity and environment—"predisposing factors confronting routine or novel situations." Likewise in explaining foreign policy behavior, attention must be directed to both the structure of world politics and the character of the domestic polity. Since the former has persistently shaped American choices since 1940, it is well to begin with a brief discussion of the international environment and the American security position. Perhaps the most important determinant of American foreign policy is America's power position in relation to the contemporary international system.

The security position of the United States

Foreign policy is properly understood as "a means by which the social organism defends itself against encroachments and seeks to achieve the international environment within which it can prosper." [5] The challenges a nation confronts, the responsibilities it shoulders, the role it plays in fashioning a favorable international milieu reflect the extent of its power and the nature of its security position in the world. In recent decades American diplomatists have had to acknowledge— as they had not for much of the nation's history—the compelling necessities of international politics. This experience has not fundamentally destroyed the voluntarism that is characteristic of the Anglo-American tradition in foreign affairs, but it has rendered more visible the constraints upon choice and the limits on American power that are implicit in the contemporary structure of world politics.

Through the first half of the twentieth century American security rested essentially upon a set of extremely advantageous external conditions. America's remote geographic location and the relatively primitive and static character of military technology made it inconceivable that any possible foe could prepare and unleash from within its own borders a knockout blow against the United States.

[5] Edmund Stillman and William Pfaff, *Power and Impotence* (New York, N.Y.: Vintage, 1966), p. 185.

Meanwhile, the European balance of power tended to neutralize the military potential of all possible adversaries on the continent. Britain, whose power was freed during periods of continental equilibrium for exploits at home and within its overseas empire, did not deploy the type of force that threatened the United States directly. In any event, the British entertained commercial rather than territorial ambitions in the Western Hemisphere.

The security of the United States could be gravely jeopardized only if one state managed to establish hegemonial control over the continent and mobilized all of its resources for combat against the New World. In normal times the European balance of power either deterred ambitions for, or posed obstacles against, such hegemony. Efforts to overcome those obstacles, on the other hand, were time consuming and insured the United States an interval in which to arouse itself to latent dangers and to exploit the power potential of its vast resource base. In a protracted conflict, the United States could mobilize a military potential exceeding the capabilities of any possible combination of enemies. Thus, as Professor Warner R. Schilling has observed, the American security position was doubly insured: "By virtue of its superior potential, the United States had no need to fear any nation; by virtue of the character of military technology and the balance of power abroad it could afford to leave that potential largely unmobilized." [6]

The external conditions of this enviable security position began to disappear in the early twentieth century, and they were undermined in the course of World War II. The development of atomic bombs and the promise of delivery capabilities of intercontinental range destroyed former buffers of time and space, posing the prospect of "war in an instant, devastation in a flash." The ravages of war left Europe in a state of political collapse. The Western European economies had been shattered, their peoples were morally and physically exhausted, and old nations were exposed to the very real threat posed by the Red Army, whose power had been thrust into the center of the continent. If countervailing force was to be mustered to contain Russian ambitions, only America could mobilize the requisite resources.

This dramatic transformation of America's security position actually occurred gradually, and the implications of the outcome of World War II were not immediately apparent to most United States officials and citizens. What eventually became clear, however, was the fact that, as the Soviet Union harvested the fruits of nuclear technology, it could launch a possibly decisive attack against the United States from within its own territory. Mastery of Western Europe would not be a necessary prerequisite for such an attack. The Atlantic Ocean would not prevent it. Unmobilized military potential would not deter it. The so-called "great debate" of the early

---

[6] Warner R. Schilling, "The Politics of National Defense: Fiscal 1950," in *Strategy, Politics, and Defense Budgets*, Warner R. Schilling, Paul Y. Hammond, and Glenn H. Snyder (New York, N.Y.: Columbia University Press, 1962), p. 6.

postwar years focused precisely upon the ramifications of this novel situation.

Some—though only an insignificant minority—argued that the magnitude of the threat justified preventive war. Others contended that the urgency of the situation demanded any concessions necessary to achieve a general settlement of all outstanding issues with the Soviet Union. Still others preferred to retire to Fortress America to prepare a hemispheric defense system. Ultimately the advocates of a middle course prevailed. Whereas, previously, defensive power had been mobilized only when direct and unambiguous threats presented themselves, after 1945 American policy was directed toward the management of *potential* as well as *actual* challenges. A traditional *defensive posture* was transformed into a *precautionary policy* akin to Great Britain's instinctive sensitivity to threats to the Low Countries. After 1947 America acknowledged the overriding importance of maintaining superiority in a technological arms race with the Soviet Union, and the necessity of denying its principal adversary access to the industrial potential of the United Kingdom, Japan, and the Ruhr district of West Germany.

As new tasks were assumed, former freedoms were eschewed. No longer could the United States dogmatically forego peacetime alliances. No longer could the mobilization of war potential be postponed until hostilities broke out. No longer could foreign and military policies be divorced from a careful consideration of their economic and military requirements. Ratification of the Rio Treaty and the NATO Pact signified a reversal of the first tradition. The establishment of the Strategic Air Command disclosed a commitment to permanent preparedness. Passage of the National Security Act in 1947 authorized the creation of those institutions necessary for synchronizing domestic resources, military requirements, and foreign policy initiatives in the postwar world.

Despite the claims of some revisionist historians,[7] this transformation of America's relationship with the world was not a manifestation of a lust for power. Necessity rather than ambition enjoined the United States to participate in world politics on a grand scale. The appearance of power vacuums rather than ambitions for hegemony provided the occasions and identified the locales of American interventions. The carefree recklessness of neutral status was exchanged for the reluctant acceptance of responsibilities that appeared unavoidable.

Dominant features of the postwar international environment

The international system has undergone continuous change since 1945, but two features of that system have demonstrated their re-

[7] See, for example, D. F. Fleming, *The Cold War and Its Origins* (Garden City, N.Y.: Doubleday, 1961) 2 vols.; and David Horowitz, *The Free World Colossus* (New York, N.Y.: Hill & Wang, 1965).

silience throughout the period and have had a decisive impact on American policy: (1) strategic bipolarity in a nuclear world, and (2) the heterogeneity and revolutionary character of world politics. Both are subject to significant modification at the present moment.

Strategic bipolarity

The United States and the Soviet Union exceed all other states by a substantial margin in their economic potential, their military capabilities, the mobility of their power, and the range of their interests. Between them they produce and consume more than 50% of the world's energy resources, control virtually all the strategic forces currently deployed, and alone among the great powers can afford to maintain balanced arsenals of nuclear and conventional military forces. Both states face toward the Atlantic and the Pacific. Each possesses a broad range of instrumentalities with which to convince as well as to coerce other states. If Russian and American leaders were animated by a common vision of world order, they could perhaps impose their dominion on the world. But the "fatality of position" and a fundamental ideological animosity have propelled them into prolonged and pervasive cold war.[8]

Strategic bipolarity has had two very significant effects upon United States policy. In the first place, it has simplified somewhat the calculus of American security policy. In a multipolar balance-of-power system, dangers tend to be ambiguous, responsibility for maintaining an equilibrium diffuse. In a bipolar world, perils are concentrated, the responsibilities of the superpowers clear. Only the Soviet Union possesses the mobilizable force to constitute a direct threat to the United States. The first and foremost prerequisites of American policy are consequently a persistent sensitivity to changes in Russian capabilities and continuing efforts to shape their intentions.[9]

The logic of bipolar competition encourages swift adjustment to any significant changes in the preparedness posture of the "enemy-partner." In one sense, the United States has inherited Britain's former role as the more or less self-conscious manipulator of the equilibrium, the custodian of the balance of power. In a bipolar world, however, diplomatic dexterity is not the essential art. Allies contribute essential increments to American strength, but their recruitment and management are less critical than domestic efforts to raise, lower, and reallocate the national security budget. The critical choices are made within the context of budgetary politics, in the decisions related to industrial mobilization, in the innovation of novel weapons, in the

---

[8] In a bipolar world, as Raymond Aron has observed, the two largest states almost inevitably assume postures of distrust, rivalry, and mutual suspicion, since only through their countervailing power can equilibrium be maintained. See Raymond Aron, *Peace and War* (New York, N.Y.: Doubleday, 1967), Chap. 5.

[9] For a detailed analysis of this point, see Kenneth N. Waltz, "Stability in a Bipolar World," *Daedalus* (Summer 1964), pp. 881–909.

extension of commitments, and in the manipulation of deterrent threats.

The interdependence of American and Soviet strategic decisions is evident in the way the level of United States preparedness has fluctuated regularly in response to perceptions of a heightened or diminished Soviet threat. The early postwar demobilization was arrested in response to manifestations of Stalin's truculence in the Mediterranean and the Near East. The formulation of the Marshall Plan and the negotiation of the North Atlantic Treaty grew out of the anxieties fostered by the Berlin blockade and the Czechoslovakian coup d'état. Approval of a more substantial rearmament was spurred by the Korean war, as were the establishment of SHAPE (Supreme Headquarters Allied Powers Europe), the decision to rearm Germany, and the development of operational thermonuclear warheads. A sense of urgency in American space and missile efforts was prompted by reports of Soviet activity in this field. Widespread fears of an anticipated "missile gap" led to an acceleration of missile procurement in the early 1960s. The decision, announced in September, 1967, to deploy a "thin" antiballistic missile (ABM) defense system was made partly on the basis of evidence of an apparent Soviet commitment to an ABM system.

Each of these actions has had obvious implications for the Soviet Union, feeding a cycle of challenge-response. American policy is, of course, more than merely a mechanical adjustment to Russian moves. The point is, however, that for those responsible for American foreign and security policy, the most basic reality is the policy of the Soviet Union. Competition with this rival has been the central preoccupation of American policy-makers for more than two decades.

A second consequence of strategic bipolarity is to be found in relationship to America's allies.[10] The very nature of the cold war propelled the United States into a global competition with the Soviet Union for political influence. Among the stakes in that competition, the recruitment of allies ranked high. In a nuclear era, however, allies may both contribute to a nation's strength and multiply the risks it may be required to run. With the advent of intercontinental missiles, the military necessity for a globe-encircling network of alliances has declined. Since most of the military force buttressing these alliances has been American, United States alliance policy has involved the relations among equals less than the management of associates and clients. The increment of strength provided by such associates has been less crucial to the United States than the maintenance of America's access to various regions of the world for purposes of influencing the local balance of forces.[11]

The margin of power between the United States and its allies

---

[10] See Kenneth N. Waltz, "International Structure, National Force, and the Balance of World Power," *Journal of International Affairs*, XXI (1967), pp. 215–232.

[11] George Liska, *Imperial America: The International Politics of Primacy* (Baltimore, Md.: Johns Hopkins University Press, 1967).

is such that the United States has retained a substantial margin of freedom from allied influence on the most basic strategic and diplomatic choices. To be sure, if the benefits of association are to be evident to allied states, their interests may not be consistently ignored. On the other hand, there are obvious limits to American indulgence. Little encouragement or assistance has been granted allies seeking to fulfill nuclear ambitions. Revisions in American strategic doctrine have been introduced unilaterally, often without prior consultation with major allies. Allies have been disciplined or restrained if they embark upon adventures threatening to provoke an East-West confrontation. Nor has the United States accommodated French reservations about the strategy and organization of the Western Alliance. On the contrary, it has adjusted to the withdrawal of France from the integrated command and planning structure of NATO with a certain degree of equanimity. In short, unlike the alliances among equals of the pre-1914 vintage, America's contemporary alliance system has not mortgaged United States freedom in the realm of diplomatic-strategic action to the whims or indiscretions of associates.

As the East-West antagonism has been moderated in recent years, American policies have been complicated by new problems: above all, the need to reconcile diverging roles. The United States remains the chief competitor of the Soviet Union for power and influence. It also shares with its "enemy-partner" some common responsibilities and common dangers. Developments in the Middle East since June, 1967 suggest the extent to which America is a "rival pitted against a resourceful foe in a spirited competition." At the same time, the United States is the chief partner of its Russian adversary in the effort to stem the proliferation of nuclear weapons and periodically investigate the possibility of resolving some stalemated issues of the cold war. These two roles conflict; neither can be entirely abjured.[12] As a "rival in a contest" the United States is thrust into the position of bloc leader, active participant in the arms race, articulator of deterrent threats, protector of peripheral allies, and provider of assistance to those facing external aggression or internal insurrection. These are the tasks associated with the policy of containment.

Behind the containment thesis, however, there has always been the hope for reconciliation, the vision of Russia's conversion to a more liberal political philosophy, the expectation of a general diplomatic settlement of the cold war. Such hopes have been reinforced by the recognized dangers of a nuclear world. Prompted by hope as well as fear, the United States has sought tacitly to coordinate its military policies with the U.S.S.R. through limited forms of arms control. It has internationalized some crises in order to avert a direct confrontation. Methods of establishing direct forms of communication have been devised to prevent gross miscalculations of one another's intentions in moments of mutual danger. Relations with allies

[12] See Stanley Hoffmann, "Restraints and Choices in American Foreign Policy," *Daedalus* (Fall 1962), pp. 668–704; and his *The State of War* (New York, N.Y.: Praeger, 1965), pp. 247–251.

are understandably complicated by the exploration of areas of agreement with the primary foe; the prospects of reconciliation and an end to Europe's partition are in turn hampered by the necessity of constantly reaffirming American fidelity to nervous allies fearful of another Yalta agreement.

The waning of bipolarity

In moments of grave international crisis when general war threatens, strategic bipolarity may continue to exert its controlling influence on world politics and on the calculations of statesmen. When the prospect of war is considered very remote, however, allies no longer feel compelled to humbly acquiesce in American initiatives.[13] The European states have regained their economic vitality and along with it a growing political self-assertiveness. The liquidation of colonial commitments has left them freer, moreover, to direct their energies and resources to continental objectives. The new states that have emerged from the destruction of the imperial system have in turn demonstrated an unanticipated capacity to sustain their independence in the face of occasional subversive pressures and a notable scarcity of those qualities usually deemed essential to the exercise of genuine sovereignty. The consequence of these two developments, in conjunction with the substantial neutralization of American and Soviet strategic power through mutual deterrence, has been a pronounced trend toward multipolarity in world politics. Intermediate and small states have acquired an increased margin for maneuver. The degree to which the United States can control or discipline the domestic or foreign policies of its associates has been correspondingly diminished. Evidence for this is to be found in the disarray apparent in the Western camp with respect to the structure and strategy of the NATO Alliance.

A contrary tendency is also evident; namely, American ascendancy in an increasingly polycentric world. In the early 1960s one could plausibly anticipate industrial and military parity between the superpowers within the foreseeable future. Impressive Soviet economic growth rates and their apparent headstart in the production of military missiles and space satellites prompted anxious soul-search-

---

[13] This is to suggest that whether the world appears bipolar or multipolar depends upon the issue and the circumstances. The Soviet Union and the United States possess the dominant share of military and industrial power in the world. The Cuban missile crisis of 1962, in which the possibly imminent prospect of thermonuclear war directly shaped the calculations of the participants, was resolved *à deux*. On many issues, however, the power of the United States and the U.S.S.R. may be either not directly relevant or neutralized by the East-West competition. As Roger Fisher has observed: "Rather than perceived as the poles of a magnet, the economic and thermonuclear power of the two big states might be considered more like two jokers in a deck of cards, each joker capable of trumping any card except the other joker. Political factors may so shuffle the deck, or even change the game, that in many important . . . plays these powerful cards will not be involved; in others they may end up in the same hand." Roger Fisher, "Perceiving the World through Bipolar Glasses," *Daedalus* (Summer 1964), p. 912.

ing in the United States even as they nourished great power chauvinism in the U.S.S.R. In the past seven years Soviet hopes and American fears have been proved unfounded—or at least premature. The Russian bid for industrial parity has been lost for the indefinite future. American economic and military power has grown more rapidly in both relative and absolute terms than that of the Soviet Union in the 1960s. So great have these margins of power become that some even speak of a "monopolar" world or a "unifocal" international system.[14]

Although one may discern these disparate trends, their significance is less perceptible. Suffice it to say that they have stimulated contradictory interpretations. Many critics of contemporary American foreign policy dwell on the possibilities implicit in polycentrism and the potential dangers of American ascendancy. Defenders of recent Administration policies have been more inclined to warn against the possible dangers of multipolarity and are more eager to exploit the possibilities of ascendancy. These rival interpretations are useful reminders of the fact that foreign policy is not *determined* by the structure of the international system. Statesmen may see the international environment as a set of forces to be molded to their own ends rather than simply a reality to which they must adjust.

International relations in a revolutionary system

The conduct of foreign policy is influenced by ideas and emotions as well as by the relationships of forces. The character of an international system is controlled by the aims and objectives of the great powers as well as by the distribution of power among them. A distinction of critical importance thus exists between *revolutionary* and *stable* international systems. Some scholars have preferred to distinguish between *homogeneous* and *heterogeneous* international systems, but in either case the significant difference is whether the principal states are organized according to similar or different principles, appeal to contradictory or congenial values, and obey common or mutually exclusive conceptions of policy.[15]

Since 1945 the nature of the means of policy available to the Soviet Union and the United States—that is, weapons of unprecedented destructive power—has induced a measure of moderation in the behavior of these rivals who have regarded one another with hatred rather than mere hostility. The competition between those two states has been the principal relationship of tension within a system appropriately designated revolutionary. The Russians and Americans have appealed to antagonistic values, and each has purveyed an

---

[14] See, for example, Liska, *op. cit.*

[15] For discussions of these differences, see Aron, *Peace and War*, Chap. 4; Henry A. Kissinger, *A World Restored* (Boston, Mass.: Houghton Mifflin, 1957), Chap. 1; and Hoffmann, *op. cit.*, Chaps. 4, 6, 8, and *passim*.

ideology or a set of principles considered anathema to the other. As the United States viewed the Soviet Union after World War II, the latter's behavior appeared neither traditional nor oriented toward the achievement of limited objectives. At the time when the cold war was joined, the Soviets were openly denouncing the basic framework of international order and expressing their dissatisfaction in foreign policies whose purpose seemed to be the transformation of that order into a monolithic global society of totalitarian regimes. The revolutionary character of the international system followed from the absence of agreement upon aims, values, and ideas that could limit the competition, confine the scope of conflicts, and encourage mutual respect and forebearance between the superpowers.

American estimates of Soviet intentions have been persistently complicated by the suspicion that Stalin, Khrushchev, and their successors took seriously their responsibilities as custodians of the revolutionary pretensions of Marx and Lenin as well as their obligations to achieve the enduring national objectives of the Russian state. Fearful that the Russians aimed to demonstrate that they were in truth the "wave of the future," anxious lest the slightest advance by the Soviets be interpreted as evidence of the "inevitable collapse of the West," and scrupulous in applying the presumed lessons of the 1930s (*viz.,* "appeasement leads inexorably to war"), American statesmen regularly have concluded since World War II that the balance of power itself was at stake whenever a local Communist success might significantly undermine the ability of the non-Communist world to deter the Communist states from further advances. But attention has not been focused exclusively on the balance of power. On the contrary, many Americans have defined the Soviet challenge as ideological in character. Consequently, more than Europeans, they have been inclined to consider *communism* rather than *Russia* (or more recently, China) to be the object of containment.[16]

Confronted by an adversary that professed its aims in the rhetoric of revolution, the United States frequently has yielded to the temptation to fortify itself through the elaboration of a counterideology, featuring variously the themes of Free Worldism, Liberation of the Captive Nations, Atlantic Partnership, Peaceful Engagement, or the Great Society for Asia. Since, moreover, the emergence of a dynamic Communist bloc coincided with the demise of European colonialism in many parts of Africa, the Middle East, and Asia, it has been especially difficult to dissociate domestic developments in the new states from superpower rivalries. Whatever the ideological formula of the moment, the United States, as the more conservative of the superpowers, has been thrust into the role of defender of existing regimes, promoter of piecemeal reforms, and opponent of radical movements of social change. These circumstances and perceptions have contributed to a consistently interventionist posture by the

[16] For evidence that this was not the original assumption behind the containment policy, see George F. Kennan, *Memoirs 1925–1950* (Boston, Mass.: Atlantic–Little, Brown, 1967), Chaps. 13–17.

United States toward the newly developing countries. The methods and means of such interventions have varied widely in response to changing circumstances and changing premises of policy.

The waning of revolutionary politics
in the 1960s

The containment policy vaguely anticipated a "mellowing" of the rigid totalitarianism of Soviet political life. In truth the Soviet Union has undergone a substantial political metamorphosis since the death of Stalin in 1953. Recent developments have apparently stabilized the Soviet regime, moderated Soviet ambitions, and fragmented the Soviet bloc. Marxism-Leninism still provides an aura of legitimacy to the Soviet government and a set of criteria for administrative decisions, but it seems to have become less significant as an inspiration for an expansive foreign policy design. The unity of what was once considered a monolithic world Communist movement has been irreparably destroyed. As a secular faith, communism appears to be in an advanced state of disintegration. In Western Europe it is, in Richard Lowenthal's apt phrase, "more gauche than threatening." In the Balkans Soviet influence is at a discount. In Eastern Europe Soviet domination is yet a reality. But their brutal invasion of Czechoslovakia revealed their failure to maintain control in their camp with more subtle methods. Nor can it conceal the fundamental dilemma confronting industrialized Communist states: the harsh rule of monopolistic parties is increasingly incompatible with the requirements of economic rationalization and the yearning of peoples for more popular participation in government. In Latin America, Africa, and Asia nationalism generally has triumphed over all competing ideologies, and local Communist parties are beset by factionalism, reveal a marked autonomy from either Chinese or Russian domination, or are ignored by the local population. To the extent that the Soviet Union or China has served as a model in the Third World, the leaders of emerging nations have been attracted more by the efficiency of the monopolistic party than by the vision of a Communist utopia. To be sure, the Chinese have attempted to revolutionize the peasantry in the "rural" areas of the world. But the violence of Mao Tse-tung's rhetoric scarcely veils the essential weakness of this overpopulated and under-industrialized state, and the excesses of the Cultural Revolution threaten the authority of his regime at home as well as its influence abroad.

The implications of these developments are both profound and encouraging. The experience of the past two decades makes it increasingly evident that the external manipulation of indigenous revolutionary movements is an almost impossible political accomplishment. It is certainly one at which neither the Russians nor the Chinese have achieved any notable success. Consequently it becomes increasingly possible to deal with revolutionary movements in the non-Western areas outside the context of cold war considerations.

Every challenge to the status quo in the emerging regions need not be invested automatically with symbolic importance in the East-West struggle. Neutralization can resume its former honorable place as a plausible technique for defusing dangerous conflicts and removing certain areas and issues from the arena of competition. Unilateral initiatives to relax tension may be undertaken without such grave apprehensions that they will signal imminent retreat. Spheres of influence may reemerge as a legitimate feature of great power relations.

A significant normalization of relations with the Soviet Union has already occurred. This is evidenced by the rather extensive fabric of tacit understandings and formal agreements developed with them in recent years. In diplomatic parlance and political discourse the Soviet Union is increasingly referred to as a formidable industrial power rather than merely a "Communist menace." "Peaceful engagement" has joined confrontation and containment as basic themes in United States policy in Europe. To an increasing extent the United States must evaluate political initiatives in other areas in terms of their repercussions upon the Soviet-American détente.

Although American statesmen no longer expect that the non-aligned states will soon be converted to either Soviet or Chinese forms of communism or will easily be subverted through the manipulative genius of foreign Communist parties, this is not to say that the United States is free to ignore the developing regions. Nor can the United States entirely resist the developing regions' efforts to promote some rearrangement of world patterns of resource allocation and consumption. The United States' growing need for imported raw materials and its self-image as the world's "first developing nation," as well as the organized influence the fledgling states can exert on it through the United Nations and other international forums, insures the developing regions a courteous, if far from indulgent, hearing in Washington.

One might, to be sure, cite additional environmental constraints upon United States policies. The more polycentric the structure of world politics, the more complex have American calculations become. But while the responsibilities that the United States must assume appear enormous, so, too, are the margins of opportunity and error afforded by an abundant material base. Small states characteristically pursue modest objectives. They attempt to safeguard their security, protect their territorial integrity as best as they can, avert suzerainty or subordination, minimize the risks of international involvements, and sustain some diplomatic autonomy if possible. The United States, as perhaps the world's only genuine global power, operates on a different scale, pursues a broader range of interests, and is tempted to undertake tasks of an imperial dimension. In the international environment of the late 1960s it is increasingly possible for the United States—its narrow security interests being well protected—either to define its objectives with a greater modesty and self-restraint or to interpret the successful achievement of the basic objectives of the containment policy as the basis for an attempt to assert even more ambitious goals, such as the establishment of a more tolerable world order. America's vast power establishes for it an impressive framework of possibilities. Other factors, however, condition its choice of objectives and its selection among alternative means.

The American political culture and foreign policy

The objectives and methods of a state's foreign policy are more likely to be rigorously determined by the nature of its government if it possesses an *ideological* political system. The American system, however, is *instrumental* rather than ideological. That is to say, it tends to reflect and sustain the existing society rather than provide a vehicle for determined men to radically transform societal institutions.[17]

The prevailing political beliefs in America constitute a smattering of liberal "views on things," as Stanley Hoffmann has observed, rather than a systematic body of doctrine incorporating a critique of the existing social and international order, a utopian vision of the future, and a detailed action program. Since no formal, officially authorized, generally accepted ideology exists in America, foreign policy objectives can hardly be derived by painstaking exegesis of an orthodox dogma. On the contrary, foreign as well as domestic policies generally emerge from the interplay among rival intellectual traditions and political beliefs, which are themselves somewhat amorphous. There is, for example, the familiar tension between "realist" and "idealist" modes of thought about foreign policy.[18] The former reflects concern with narrow security interests and is intellectually akin to the traditions of a civilized Machiavellianism; the latter has its roots in the Enlightenment and expresses a fervent desire to establish patterns of a "new diplomacy." [19] Nor do these American intellectual traditions always conform to a neat dichotomy. The pragmatic internationalism of Walter Lippmann mirrors neither the nationalistic egocentrism of Admiral Mahan nor the utopian schemes of William Jennings Bryan, though his qualified voluntarism owes something to both.[20]

There is plenty of room for argument about the intellectual merit and the political significance of these various traditions. The

[17] For a definition and analysis of these terms, see Brzezinski and Huntington, *op. cit.*, pp. 71–76, and Chap. 3 of this work.

[18] See Robert E. Osgood, *Ideals and Self-Interest in America's Foreign Relations* (Chicago, Ill.: University of Chicago Press, 1953).

[19] Felix Gilbert's little volume, *To the Farewell Address* (Princeton, N.J.: Princeton University Press, 1961), provides an excellent analysis of the intellectual roots of American foreign policy concepts.

[20] See Charles D. Tarlton, "The Styles of American International Thought: Mahan, Bryan, and Lippmann," *World Politics*, XVII (July 1965), pp. 584–614.

nature of the American political culture is revealed, however, by the fact that no single set of beliefs or perspectives has achieved a monopoly of acceptance, none has been approved without qualification and pressed to its logical conclusions, and all rest upon a common bedrock of ideas enjoying general acceptance. The American tradition in foreign policy is Lockean or liberal insofar as that implies an enduring acceptance of the sovereign equality of states, a commitment to the virtues of self-government and self-determination, a marked affinity for legal procedures, and a fundamental respect for human rights and civil liberties. These represent convictions from which precise foreign policy objectives are not easily deduced. But liberal principles clearly influence the pattern of American aims, delimit the framework of means, and condition the perception of the international situation. Differences quite naturally arise over the way in which such principles may be translated into policies.

America's domestic experiences have provided the crucible in which the Lockean tradition has gained acceptance. The application of liberal ideas to international affairs has been subjected to modifications by the harsh facts of international competition since 1945. Still, the heavy imprint of historical memories, traditional beliefs, and a pragmatic and optimistic national style is to be found on contemporary policies, as will be demonstrated in Chapters 3 and 4.

Political beliefs are translated into programs by political leaders. It is through such leaders that a national style in foreign affairs is disclosed, through them that the lessons of the past are selectively applied. Recruited from a mobile society, American political leadership is socially homogeneous but politically pluralistic. In a variety of ways the character of American political leadership is manifested in foreign policy. Both the substance and style of policy are conditioned by the extent to which leaders are recruited from the legal and business professions. The quality and the continuity of policy is shaped by the degree to which novitiates in the craft of diplomacy occupy the highest policy-making posts in the federal government. The timeliness and coherence of policy is influenced by the bureaucratic setting in which political leaders must operate. Hand in hand with the expansion of scope in America's relations with the world has come an increasing specialization of personnel for managing military and strategic problems, allocating foreign economic assistance, disseminating foreign propaganda, conducting secret political operations overseas, developing programs of cultural exchange, and extending commercial intercourse. This brings in its wake the problems of meshing a number of instrumentalities of policies, harmonizing conflicting perspectives and advice, and compromising jurisdictional clashes.

The impact of America's liberal tradition on its foreign policy is as readily discernible as is the impact of Marxist-Leninist ideology upon Soviet foreign policy behavior. So, too, America's "pragmatic-bureaucratic" leadership leaves its mark upon foreign policy as vividly as does the "ideological-bureaucratic" leadership of the Soviet Union, or the "charismatic-revolutionary" leadership of many of the new states.[21]

Political institutions and processes

"Democracy," de Tocqueville observed in a classic statement, "appears to me better adapted for the conduct of society in times of peace, or for a sudden effort of remarkable vigor, than for the prolonged endurance of the great storms which beset the political existence of nations ... Foreign politics demand scarcely any of those qualities which are peculiar to democracy; they require, on the contrary, the perfect use of almost all those in which it is deficient ... [A] democracy can only with great difficulty regulate the details of an important undertaking, persevere in a fixed design, and work out its execution in spite of serious obstacles. It cannot combine its measures with secrecy or await their consequences with patience ..." [22] Others, like Walter Lippmann, have more recently echoed this critical refrain.[23]

It is interesting in this connection that few of the traditional reservations about democracy's effectiveness in the area of foreign policy enjoy the status of contemporary "conventional wisdom." Disclosures of the activities of the Central Intelligence Agency have confirmed a long-suspected ability of the United States government to carry out covert operations abroad through well-concealed financial arrangements at home. The hastily contrived military intervention in the Dominican Republic in 1965 indicated an ability to act with dispatch, though, some would contend, not with discriminate judgment. The durability of congressional support for the Johnson Administration's policies in Vietnam in the face of mounting casualties, prodigious expenditures, and meager results bespeaks an extraordinary patience in awaiting the outcome of even those policies whose wisdom and efficacy are widely questioned. Many critics are concerned less by the inconstancy of American foreign policy than by the massive continuity of this policy in a world undergoing revolutionary transformations.

American foreign policy is obviously influenced by the peculiar pattern of its representative institutions. One defining characteristic of American democracy is to be found in the wide diffusion of power among separate yet interdependent branches of government. The result is an extraordinarily complex institutional scheme in which autonomous branches, departments, and agencies must voluntarily coordinate their activities in order to accomplish functions for which

[21] See Henry A. Kissinger, "Domestic Structure and Foreign Policy," *Daedalus* (Spring 1966), pp. 503–529.

[22] Alexis de Tocqueville, *Democracy in America* (New York, N.Y.: Vintage ed., 1954), Vol. I, pp. 237 and 243–244.

[23] Walter Lippmann, *The Public Philosophy* (Boston, Mass.: Little, Brown, 1955).

they bear joint responsibility. Problems created by the constitutional doctrine of "separation of powers" have been compounded by the vast expansion in the size of government and by the specialization and bureaucratization which have accomplished this increase in scale.

The process of developing political support for a specific policy within the executive branch alone—let alone within Congress—can be exhausting, enervating, and time consuming. The result may be policies out of phase with the international situations for which they were designed; policies whose efficacy has been compromised by political maneuvers consciously designed to win essential governmental or public support; policies that reflect the low common denominator of intragovernmental bargaining rather than the requirements of sound foreign policy; or policies that become undesirably inflexible simply because officials are reluctant to challenge the assumptions upon which they rest for fear of having to negotiate the policy anew.

American foreign policy is shaped not only by the extent of institutional pluralism, but by the "openness" of political competition within and without the government. Competition among governmental elites rarely occurs within the ambit of "closed politics." The prerogatives of the Congress, the traditions of the American press, the cultural norms that govern political in-fighting among executive branch agencies, and the activities of lobbying groups all insure that the arena of policy-making is at least "quasi-public" at almost all times. To an extent unknown either to totalitarian governments like the Soviet Union or to more centralized democratic forms of rule à la Great Britain, the pulls and tugs of societal pressures are reflected in foreign as well as domestic policies, and the public-relations aspects of policy-making become themselves one determinant of the substance of policy. These matters will be examined more thoroughly in Chapters 5 and 6.

Comparisons with other political systems

These brief introductory comments suggest the uniqueness of that chain of causal factors that conditions the formulation and implementation of American foreign policy. Since foreign policy is influenced by such a multitude of factors, it is difficult not only to isolate the influence of individual variables but to establish the relative merits or disadvantages for foreign policy of a specific pattern of institutions, a particular set of ideological convictions, a single method of selecting political leaders, or a special set of policy-making procedures. With whom, then, can the United States be most relevantly compared?

There are obvious reasons for comparisons with the Soviet Union. Like the United States, it possesses vast space, an impressive resource base, a modern economy, and military and diplomatic instruments to support an extensive range of foreign policy interests. The differences are equally obvious and no less consequential. Since they are especially marked in patterns of political leadership, political culture, the procedures for policy-making, and the nature of political ideas and beliefs, the impact of such differences on the foreign policies of the "enemy-partners" ought to be the more easily perceived.

In terms of political culture, the United States is most readily compared to the United Kingdom, with its competitive parties, civic culture, apolitical civil and military bureaucracies, profusion of lobbying groups, free press, and generally democratic style of authority. Since the United States and Great Britain possess similar political cultures, the influence of the parliamentary and presidential systems, respectively, upon British and American foreign policy can be more readily isolated. Needless to add, the exigencies of the international situation appear differently to a state like Britain that has impressive resources and wide interests but that, nevertheless, is unable either to compete with the superpowers of the present or to forget its own past ascendancy.

Continental states like France and Germany are more fruitful referents for contrasts than for comparisons. Possessing fragmented political cultures, emerging from traditions of multiparty politics, fraught with the remnants of bitter ideological divisions, and plagued by the discontinuities of their own recent historical experiences, they possess different dimensions of power, more confined ranges of interests, less homogeneous political cultures, and more elitist institutional and bureaucratic structures.

To summarize, American foreign policy is framed in response to developments in the international milieu. American power is sufficiently vast, however, that the United States has the capacity to shape the international system even as its behavior is constrained by it. The psychological environment of American policy-making is marked by perceptions of the world and of America's responsibilities in it that are firmly rooted in a heritage of beliefs and instincts. These reflect the fortuitous experiences of "a people of plenty," which inherited the principles of constitutional government and was able to apply them in a land of opportunity. Yet, historical habits of thought and action are increasingly being modified by the equally unique character of the world's first postindustrial society, increasingly differentiated even from the Atlantic world by the novelty of its social and economic organization and the political perspectives and attitudes to which these give rise. If American society is revolutionary, American political institutions are archaic. The content of foreign policy decisions is naturally influenced by the distribution of power and the procedures of policy-making that characterize the presidential-congressional system.

2

Economic and military capabilities

In an anarchical world, sovereign states must fend for themselves. Their prospects for survival, security, and the achievement of their more ambitious goals are thus conditioned by the space they occupy, the resources at their disposal, and their capacity for collective action. Those fond of analogies between politics and card games will understand that in both the outcome is related to the distribution of the cards as well as the prevailing rules of the game and the skill of the players. Declarations of high purpose are one element of a state's foreign relations, but, ultimately, foreign policy is a science of means. Statesmen must ask themselves what course they wish events to take. They must, however, also ask whether they have the power to channel the course of events in the preferred direction.

Power is an elusive element. It is not precisely measurable, for it depends to some extent upon intangibles such as the quality of political leadership, the efficiency of administrators, the cohesiveness of a people, and the authority of a government. Since power is defined here as the capacity of one political entity to impose its will upon other entities, it is a *relational* and *instrumental* concept. It is not helpful to attempt to specify the absolute power of the United States. One can but ask: Under what circumstances has the United States the power to achieve which specific objectives in relationship to which constellation of friends, neutrals, and adversaries?

If power defies quantification, its constituent elements, for example, military, economic, and even moral force, are more susceptible to comparative analysis. The purpose of this chapter is to identify and describe the material resources that the United States possesses on paper, and the extent to which it has mobilized (or is able to mobilize) those resources for the conduct of its international relations.

Material resources are the means of force. Dominion over additional resources may be an objective of policy—the stake of interstate rivalries. Whatever the objectives of a state may be in relationship to the external environment, its material resources are constraints upon the operational feasibility of its policies. Resources are thus to be seen both as inducements to action and constraints upon policy. Nature's caprice in distributing the means of force, hence the ingredients of power, has proved providential for some states, merciless to others. The United States falls into the former category. The resources available to the United States for the conduct of diplomatic-strategic action surely permit Americans to aspire to first rank among the world's powers. Some contend that nature's munificence imposes correlative obligations to create and sustain a new international order.

Contemporary demographic and geographic influences on foreign policy

The United States is the world's fourth largest state in both territorial extent and size of population. Occupying a continental domain of some 3,615,211 square miles, its population of some 200,000,000 presses neither upon the available land nor upon the residual raw materials of the nation. Population density is a low 55 persons per square mile, and agricultural productivity is extensive. Americans may consequently anticipate a broad margin of demographic and economic growth without additional increments of territory.

In its share of raw materials the United States is richly blessed. It enjoys a degree of resource security that only the Soviet Union can begin to approach. Virtually all of the critical resources essential to industrial and military strength are available within or close by the United States. The size of the land and the diversity of basic resources permit a degree of self-sufficiency to which few states can aspire.

In the supply of basic foodstuffs, this self-sufficiency is particularly manifest. A vast acreage of arable land, a fortunate combination of mild weather and excellent soil conditions, efficient soil and water management, the incentives of the family farm system, and the application of science and technology to commercial farming have contributed to such a level of agricultural productivity that less than 7 percent of the population can produce not only enough food for the domestic market but a substantial food surplus for export, despite production controls at home. In 1966 the United States accounted for some 60 percent of the combined grain exports of the net exporting regions. More than 176 million metric tons of food, valued at $15.7 billion, have been shipped abroad under the concessional terms of the Public Law 480 Food for Peace program between 1954 and 1966.[1]

At a time when the population growth in non-Western areas, the rising incomes in the more established states of Europe, and the chronic crisis of agricultural productivity in the Communist states accentuate world demand for foodstuffs, America's agricultural surpluses are an important asset. Grain shipments may permit the United States to express disinterested friendship toward one state, to acquire a measure of diplomatic leverage against another. By becoming the major agricultural supplier of Japan in the postwar period, the United States is bringing about a more thoroughgoing integration of the American and Japanese economies, undergirding already-firm diplomatic ties. The persistent agricultural surpluses of the United States dramatize by comparison the endemic weakness of this aspect of the Communist economies, and to some extent diminish the attractiveness to the newly independent states of the Communist model of economic growth. Such abundance poses its own set of problems, to be sure, as frictions with France over the United States' right to maintain a privileged access to the European market attests.

The United States is also abundantly endowed with those raw materials essential to industrialization. It is particularly fortunate in its possession of ample sources of inanimate energy, in known reserves of which it exceeds all states.[2] Russian production of electrical energy is only 40 percent of the American production level. Although the Soviet Union exceeds the United States in its production of cement, lumber, and coal, output figures for 1964 reveal that it produces only 63 percent as much crude petroleum, 29 percent as much natural gas, 39 percent as much sulfuric acid, 27 percent as much chemical fiber, 65 percent as much chemical fertilizer, and 75 percent as much steel. In 1963 the United States alone accounted for more than 12 percent of the world's production of coal, copper, iron ore, crude petroleum, potash, sulfur, tin, tungsten, and zinc. All of these materials are essential to significant industrial potential.

As American supplies of raw materials are gradually depleted, dependence upon imports will grow. Such dependence already exists for industrial diamonds, quartz, chromite, nickel, strategic grade mica, and long-fiber asbestos. The United States also imports most of its platinum, manganese, mercury, cadmium, tungsten, and cobalt,

---

[1] Orville Freeman, "Malthus, Marx and the North American Breadbasket," *Foreign Affairs*, 45 (July 1967), pp. 579–593.

[2] There has been a surprising correlation between the availability of sources of energy and the power potential of states. In known sources of energy the United States and the Soviet Union are followed by China, West Germany, the United Kingdom, Poland, Canada, India, the Union of South Africa, Australia, and Japan. It is astonishing how closely this comes to an intuitive ranking of the power positions of the world's leading states.

as well as substantial amounts of bauxite, lead, zinc, and copper. Many of these raw materials are available within the Western Hemisphere, particularly the metals and ores. Access to tin, rubber, and other raw materials provided by more distant suppliers seems assured through international trade. If necessary, most such materials could be foregone through the use of substitutes or the development of synthetics.

America's size and its material abundance offer a framework of possibilities; its location contributes to this framework and enhances American security. Located on an island in relation to the Eurasian land mass, the United States has no need to seek more defensible frontiers. Neighbors on the north and south are relatively weak and traditionally friendly. Distance from extrahemispheric centers of power has been rendered a more equivocal advantage in an age of globe-encircling rockets capable of almost instantaneous attack. Nevertheless, the Atlantic will continue for a time to protect the United States from the bulk of Russia's strategic nuclear forces: medium-range ballistic missiles (MRBMs) deployed against Western Europe from the center of the continent. Distance also promotes a sense of psychological security that has even survived the darkest days of the cold war. The American and Russian people have not succumbed to the sense of the inevitability of military conflict that is characteristic of incipient conflicts between contiguous nations and between neighbors who have become sworn enemies. Moreover, the unambiguous "homeland separateness" that the United States enjoys by virtue of its well-defined boundaries, friendly neighbors, and ocean barriers makes it unlikely that small wars might spill over into California or Vermont as the Korean war threatened to expand into China or as any military hostilities in Central Europe would pose dilemmas of geographic limitation in relation to the Soviet Union.[3]

Territorial extensiveness also continues to contribute to American security by providing space for the dispersal of strategic forces, by making more remote the possibility that society could be annihilated should general war occur, and by permitting the underground testing of nuclear weapons in the empty deserts of the Southwest without occasioning diplomatic incidents or necessitating interference with the rights or compromising the health of other peoples.

Dimensions of American economic strength

The industrial potential implicit in the American resource base has been realized to an extraordinary degree through the application of technical know-how and skilled labor. It requires, in fact, a considerable effort to fully comprehend the magnitude of American wealth. Whatever the standard for comparing material strength, be it weight

[3] For an analysis of the relationship between geography and the problems of limiting military hostilities, see Thomas Schelling, *Arms and Influence* (New Haven, Conn.: Yale University Press, 1966), Chap. 2, esp. pp. 56–60.

of resources, scale of industrialization, or standard of living, the preeminence of the United States is palpably manifest. It is this economic supremacy that has led some observers to suggest that world politics is tending to develop a "unifocal" or "monopolar" character, dominated by a single superpower to such an extent that the state has acquired a degree of hegemony.[4]

The most general index of United States economic power is its gross national product (GNP); that is, the dollar value of the nation's final output of goods and services at market prices over the period of one year. The GNP, or total national income, delineates the broad economic constraints upon foreign policy, the size of the "national security fund" or the "cold war chest" from which deposits may be drawn to respond to threats or exploit opportunities. Economic strength is significant because it enables the United States to afford more of those things considered essential to national security. Short-range economic constraints upon policy depend on the degree to which resources have been mobilized in the service of national objectives or may be rapidly converted to such purposes. Over the longer haul, the major resource limitations consist of general monetary constraints whose costs are most easily measured in dollars, and whose dimensions are revealed in the general size of the GNP. Depending upon the time frame, specific constraints may also be removed through planning, investment, and the application of technology.[5] Table 1 shows comparative gross national products for 1965 for the United States, the Soviet Union, and other major states.

Table 1.

**Comparative national income
statistics (1965)**

state	amount (in US$ billion)	% of U.S. GNP
United States	692.3	
Soviet Union	297.0	42.9
West Germany	112.4	16.3
United Kingdom	98.5	14.2
France	94.1	13.5
China	60.0	8.6

Source: U.N. Monthly Bulletin of Statistics and U.S. State Department, Indicators of East-West Economic Strength 1965, Table 1. U.N. Definition of GNP is employed.

[4] The accuracy of the conjecture is for present purposes less significant than the fact that it may seriously and plausibly be entertained. For such an interpretation see, for example, George Liska, *Imperial America: The International Politics of Primacy*, and Maurice Duverger, "America the Superpower," *Interplay*, X (October 1967), pp. 12–14.

[5] For an elaboration of this approach, see Charles Hitch and Roland McKean, *The Economics of Defense in the Nuclear Age* (Cambridge, Mass.: Harvard University Press, 1960).

With but 7 percent of the world's population, the United States regularly produces more than 30 percent of the gross world product.[6] Its national income is more than twice that of the Soviet Union, and outdistances by a slightly larger margin the combined national products of the six member states of the European Economic Community, that is, France, Germany, Italy, and the Benelux countries.

Several years ago a number of American economists expressed concern about the differential rates of economic growth in the Soviet Union and the United States. By projecting those growth rates into the future and emphasizing the capacity of a totalitarian state to devote a larger proportion of its resources to national security expenditures, some anticipated an early closing of the economic gap between the two superpowers. More recent developments suggest that the Soviet Union has lost its bid for industrial parity with the United States for the indefinite future (see Table 2).

Table 2.

Comparative trends in U.S. and U.S.S.R. GNP (in US$ billion at 1964 market prices)

	1950	1955	1958	1960	1962	1963	1964
U.S.	387.0	477.0	487.0	531.0	577.0	599.0	628.7
U.S.S.R.	124.0	174.0	215.0	237.0	265.0	272.0	293.0
Difference	263.0	303.0	272.0	294.0	312.0	327.0	335.0
U.S.S.R. as % of U.S.	32.1	36.5	44.2	44.6	45.9	45.4	46.7

Source: U.S. Congress, Joint Economic Committee, New Directions in the Soviet Economy, Committee Print, Part II-A, 89th Congress, 2nd Session (Washington, D.C., 1966), p. 109.

Since 1958 the absolute dollar gap between the American and Soviet economies has been steadily widening, while relatively the Soviets have made but marginal gains. Nor is this development attributable to extraordinary circumstances. Rather, there has been a leveling off of the Soviet rate of economic advance as their structural problems have continued to accumulate. In the United States, more sophisticated management of monetary and fiscal policy has produced an uninterrupted expansion for more than seven years. For the period 1960–65 the Soviet Union achieved a 4.9 percent annual rate of growth compared with 4.6 percent for the United States. Assuming that the Soviet rate of growth continues to fluctuate

[6] By the fourth quarter of 1967 the absolute dollar value of the United States gross national product had reached a level of $807.3 billion (the seasonally adjusted quarterly total expressed at the annual rate). See Committee or Economic Development, The National Economy and the Vietnam War (New York, N.Y.: April 1968), p. 72.

between 4.5 and 5.5 percent and that of the United States remains at about 4.5 percent, the absolute margin between the American and Russian national incomes would widen further by 1975 to between $415 and $438 billion. The ratio of Soviet to American output would range from 47 to 49 percent, an incremental advance at best. Even if one projects a conservative 3 percent growth rate for the United States and a generous 5 percent rate for the U.S.S.R., the United States would not be overtaken until well into the twenty-first century.[7]

It is true, to be sure, that the United States economy is consumer- and welfare-oriented. A substantially higher percentage of employment is to be found in service occupations than in the Soviet Union. Nevertheless, industrial production still remains roughly twice that of Russia. This is significant in that factors of production may be more easily reallocated between branches of industry than within the economy as a whole. For this reason, military potential is perhaps more directly related to industrial production than to the gross national product. Soviet rates of growth in industrial production have been substantially higher than comparable rates in the United States, but here, too, the Russians have run into severe problems, and it is unlikely that the gap will soon be closed.[8]

America's wealth naturally has important foreign policy implications. It has permitted expenditures of more than $800 billion since World War II on defense and mutual security programs. Another $100 billion has been spent abroad in foreign economic and military assistance. In FY 1967 alone more than $70 billion was expended for national defense. This figure was larger than the entire national income of Mainland China, yet constituted less than 10 percent of the American gross national product.[9] The approximately $2 billion regularly requested for Agency for International Development grants and loans appears a modest expenditure when considered as a percentage of America's national income. Nevertheless, in 1966 only four states (Britain, France, the Soviet Union, and China) spent more than that on national defense, let alone economic aid programs.

Nor does American wealth impinge on foreign societies only through public economic and military assistance programs. A prime importer of capital during the nineteenth century, the United States is now the world's largest source of capital exports. In 1940 the United States government and private American citizens possessed $2.3 billion in overseas assets. In 1965 it was estimated that the inter-

---

[7] U.S. Congress, Joint Economic Committee, *New Directions in the Soviet Economy*, Part II-A, 89th Congress, 2nd Session (Washington, D.C., 1966), p. 109.

[8] In 1962 United States industrial production was four times that of the United Kingdom, five times that of Germany, nine times that of France, and eighteen times that of China. Alexander Erkstein, *Communist China's Economic Growth and Foreign Trade* (New York, N.Y.: McGraw-Hill, 1966), Table 7–2, p. 250.

[9] Los Angeles *Times* (January 30, 1968), p. 19. Planned expenditures for FY 1969 approach $77 billion. For comparative statistics on the military budgets and force structures of the principal states, see Institute of Strategic Studies, *The Military Budget 1967–1968* (London, 1968).

national production of American companies located outside the United States approximated $80 billion. This enormous sum exceeded the total GNP of Italy, France, or Japan that year. In 1964 manufacturing companies in Western Europe, of which Americans owned at least 25 percent and that were for the most part controlled by American management, enjoyed sales of more than $16 billion, a figure twice the value of American exports to Western Europe. In 1966 Americans contributed 41 percent of the total national investment in Canada. The figures for the Netherlands, United Kingdom, and Belgium were 11.2, 9.8, and 8 percent, respectively. In France, although the relative percentage of American investment was somewhat smaller (5.5 percent), it was highly concentrated in the critical electronics industry.[10]

Almost 75 percent of these foreign assets and investments are privately owned. They do not constitute a weapon of economic warfare easily manipulated by the United States government. Indeed, the very magnitude of American interests in foreign economies is often a source of minor irritants and major embarrassments to the State Department. The ever-present possibility of expropriation of American property poses sensitive diplomatic problems. The concentration of American investment in critical sectors of foreign economies —for example, in defense-related electronics and aircraft industries in Europe and in extractive industries in developing countries—may give rise to incipient fears of foreign domination and may prompt anti-American sentiment in the most improbable places. At times the hands of public officials in foreign countries have to be greased with foreign aid in order to insure a favorable climate for direct private investment in the same country. This is but one facet of the "inverse imperialism" of foreign aid.

Despite these qualifications, one must not lightly dismiss the importance of such investments to America's power potential. They have contributed to such an interpenetration of the American and European economies that military conflict between the two regions is all but unimaginable. The contribution of private investment to the growth of developing economies in the non-West and in Latin America will continue to grow as these countries increase their capacity to absorb venture capital. Coproduction arrangements in Eastern Europe, joining American capital and managerial techniques with low-wage Eastern European labor for the manufacture of goods for export to the West, may constitute a most promising means of "building bridges" to the East. Moreover, even though such assets are most frequently controlled by private citizens, the government may exercise surveillance and influence through the manipulation of tax advantages, credit facilities, and other more direct controls.

Supplementing direct private investment overseas, the United States government authorized and obligated a grand total of $116.1 billion upon other states in loans and grants between 1946 and

[10] For a detailed analysis of these investment patterns, see Christopher Layton, *Trans-Atlantic Investments* (Boulogne-Sur-Seine, 1966).

1965: over $83 billion in grants; $20 billion in loans, generally with low interest and generous repayment terms. Of this total, $81.4 billion was authorized for economic aid and $34.7 billion for military assistance programs. More than 120 states have been the recipients of American aid. The level of assistance has fluctuated over the years in response to external conditions, and priorities as between grants and loans, economic and military assistance, and so forth, have varied from one year to the next; but a program of impressive dimensions has been sustained throughout the postwar period. The magnitude of the postwar aid program is indicated in Table 3.

Table 3.

**Obligations and loan authorizations
in U.S. aid (1946–65)***
(in US$ billion)

Region	Military	Economic	Total
Near East and South Asia	6.3	17.3	23.6
Latin America	.9	9.4	10.4
Far East	9.9	16.2	26.1
Africa	.2	3.1	3.3
Europe	16.2	30.5	46.7
Oceania and Canada	.1	.2	.3
Nonregional	1.1	4.7	5.7
	34.7	81.4	116.1

* The figures include monies expended by the United Nations Relief and Rehabilitation Administration, the Export-Import Bank's long-term lending program, Food For Peace, and many other miscellaneous programs. Source: John D. Montgomery, Foreign Aid In International Politics © 1967 (Englewood Cliffs, N.J.: Prentice-Hall, Inc.), p. 28.

It is not possible to establish with any precision the amount of diplomatic influence secured through foreign aid outlay. Such programs do, however, serve a variety of purposes. Grants or loans may be employed to assist other peoples in overcoming the effects of natural disasters; they provide a means of maintaining an American "presence" in other countries, a vehicle for demonstrating the sophistication of American technology or for gaining access for American corporations to foreign economies. In addition, they may buy more tangible returns. Aid has also been employed to sustain friendly elites in power, to cement alliances, to reinforce the neutrality and independence of the uncommitted, to obtain influence over foreign military establishments, to finance local defense forces, and to promote economic stability and growth in friendly states. There is little doubt that at times such programs have provided substantial leverage over foreign regimes. In Laos, for example, by supplying commodities to the regime, the United States furnished the means of financing the Royal Laotian Army in the late 1950s and early 1960s.

Even the threat to withhold supplies could pose a parliamentary crisis in Vientienne. Such leverage is the more marked in poor societies where American grants and loans constitute a very large percentage of governmental revenues.

If the general dimensions of American wealth are one source of strength to American foreign policy, the absolute increments to national income regularly yielded by even modest rates of growth are another. During the past four decades, the distribution of national income among personal consumption, gross private investment, national security, and other expenditures reveals a remarkable stability. The pattern of American income distribution among these uses is shown in Table 4.

Table 4.

Distribution of national income
(% of GNP)

Components	1930	1940	1944	1950	1953	1957	1964	1965
Personal consumption	71	68	49	66	62	65	63	63
Gross private investment	15	15	4	19	15	15	14	16
National security	1	1	46	7	15	11	9	8
Other	13	16	1	8	8	9	14	13

Source: U.S. Bureau of the Census, Statistical Abstract of the United States, 1966, 1967, 87th and 88th editions (Washington, D.C., 1966, 1967).

The fixed character of these allocations reflects in part the difficulties encountered in the American governmental system in attempting to alter, particularly to increase, existing tax rates. With those rates fixed and reasonably progressive, it is relatively easy, however, to finance additional levels of effort in international affairs on the margins of growth, for the yield in tax revenues increases even more rapidly than the growth of the economy as a whole. Federal tax revenues in 1955 totaled $67 billion. The national income at that time was $477 billion. Tax revenues thus equalled 14 percent of the GNP. In 1964, with no change in the tax rate, revenues exceeded $114 billion, while the GNP had grown to $628.7 billion. The ratio was then 18.2 percent. To be sure, there is no absolute freedom to commit new tax revenues to foreign policy purposes. A substantial percentage of new revenues are committed in advance to social security financing. Nevertheless, it is evident that the United States has the means to maintain, and even increase, its national security expenditures without jeopardizing either personal consumption or domestic investment. This is the more significant in a country in which the tolerable living standard is that which one has either already attained or to which one aspires. In neither World War II nor in the Korean war was civilian austerity the complement to increased defense expenditures. An expansion in spending for both "guns" and "butter" was achieved by capitalizing upon the "fat" and "slack" in the economy, that is, resources whose availability depends merely upon activation, such as the unutilized capacity of steel plants.

In the 1960s adequate financing of foreign programs may be assured through continuing economic growth or deficit financing, the latter having achieved the status of a legitimate technique for promoting the former. It is noteworthy, in this connection, that the United States is currently conducting one of the most extravagant wars in history in Vietnam. The annual cost of this exercise in counterinsurgency was in excess of $30 billion by 1967, yet no national emergency had been declared, no price controls had been imposed, no mobilization of industrial resources had been ordered, and inflation had been held to moderate levels. Nor was the war financed, at least prior to 1967, at the expense of domestic health, education, or poverty programs, in each of which areas public expenditures were trebled in the three preceding years. As the scale of American assistance to South Vietnam has grown, the ability to finance both guns and butter has been more insistently challenged. Programs, such as the Model Cities program, have been victims of budgetary constraints. In order to contain inflationary pressures, moreover, the President belatedly requested a 10-percent surtax, and congressional leaders responded with demands for cuts in domestic spending programs early in 1968. The war also has compounded strains on America's international financial position, accentuating a chronic balance-of-payments problem, diminishing foreign confidence in the dollar, and prompting widespread speculation in gold in the spring of 1968.

Prior to World War II, the United States economy was both robust and erratic. Fluctuation of the business cycle produced rather frequent recessions and one devastating depression, beginning in 1929 and lasting nearly a decade. The latter event had significant foreign policy implications, reinforcing isolationist instincts on the one hand, stimulating interest in reciprocal trade agreements on the other. In the postwar period, economic growth has been steady, if not always spectacular. Equally important is that, except for the mild recession of 1958, the economy has been remarkably free of recessions or damaging inflation. The growth of the government sector of the economy and the general acceptance of Keynesian economics have provided the means and the method for disciplining the business cycle rather successfully. Moreover, since the structural problems in the American economy reflect the uncertainties of demand rather than the insufficiencies of supply, temporary recessive trends are the more plausibly met by increases in government spending and in the level of federal deficits. Here the tactics of economic management divert additional expenditures into public programs, and defense or space programs are obvious potential recipients of such additional largesse.

All of these features of the American economy suggest the relative self-sufficiency of the United States in a world of sovereign states. The abundance and diversity of American resources and skills do permit an unusual degree of economic autarchy. International trade accounts for less than 7 percent of the gross national product, even though the United States alone accounted, in 1964, for 10.3 percent of the world's imports and 15.2 percent of world exports. In 1966 the United States enjoyed a favorable balance of trade of more than $5 billion, exporting more than $37.9 billion while importing but $32.6 billion of merchandise.[11]

One can think of virtually no important resource for which the United States is dependent upon a single supplier. Almost two-thirds of American trade is currently conducted with Canada and Western Europe; that is, with "permanent friends" rather than mere "temporary allies." Until very recently, trade with members of the Warsaw Pact states and Asian Communist countries was consciously limited. It presently constitutes a minuscule fraction of total trade. It is arguable how much impact the United States trade embargo on strategic materials has had on economic growth in Communist states. It is quite clear that neither camp possesses substantial economic leverage over the other.

Table 5.

The structure of United States trade
(1967)
(exports and imports of merchandise)

Area	Exports (in $ million)	Imports (in $ million)
Canada	7,173	7,099
19 American Republics	4,126	3,853
Other Western Hemisphere	595	785
Western Europe	10,099	8,055
European Economic Community	5,646	4,457
European Free Trade Area	3,270	2,882
Near East	961	308
Japan	2,696	2,999
East and South Asia	3,557	2,058
Oceania	1,016	581
Africa	1,116	890
Communist areas	195	180
TOTAL	31,534	26,816

Source: U.S. Department of Commerce, Overseas Business Reports (Washington, D.C.: U.S. Government Printing Office, May 1968), pp. 17–23.

The strength as well as the structure of America's trade position is indicated in Table 5. The basic strength of America's position as a creditor nation veils one source of potential bargaining weakness

[11] U.S. Department of Commerce, *Overseas Business Reports* (Washington, D.C.: U.S. Government Printing Office, Aug.–Sept., 1967).

vis-à-vis other states. Since 1949 the United States has run a deficit in its balance of payments in every year except 1949. The cumulative deficit through 1964 amounted to $34 billion in gold sales and an increase of $22 billion of liquid dollar liabilities to foreigners, private and official. This continuing deficit is a consequence of America's global responsibilities. The problem consists most fundamentally of an inability to offset with a very favorable balance of trade the outflow of dollars required to support American military and economic commitments throughout the world.

Since 1945 the United States has served as the world's banker, providing the primary source of long-term capital with which to finance the expansion of world trade. In this respect, continuing deficits have been the means of increasing international liquidity and financing trade from which we, along with others, have benefited.

The overall financial position of the United States is very strong. In December, 1966 it possessed foreign assets valued at more than $110 billion and a gold reserve of $13.2 billion over against foreign claims of approximately $60 billion. Included in its liabilities, however, were more than $33 billion in short-term liabilities—a figure substantially in excess of the United States gold supply plus America's short-term claims abroad. Under no foreseeable circumstances would all claimants on United States reserves demand payment simultaneously. Nevertheless, continuing balance-of-payments deficits do pose restrictions on America's freedom of action and limitations on America's ability to pursue its international objectives.

The deficits have increased domestic pressures to cut foreign aid expenditures, or to transform such programs essentially into export subsidy programs through the application of "Buy American" restrictions. They render the United States vulnerable to pressures from those states that have accumulated substantial volumes of dollars in American banks. They have shaken the confidence of some foreign central banks in the United States' financial position. Most importantly, the need to discourage requests for payment in gold has prompted a manipulation of interest rates that, at times, has threatened domestic objectives of credit expansion. In short, the fact that the dollar is both a domestic and an international reserve currency has posed difficult problems of synchronizing policies that will simultaneously sustain domestic economic growth and promote further expansion of international trade.

American military capabilities

It is frequently asserted that a sound dollar and a healthy economy are the basis of United States military might. This contention contains an abiding truth and an important omission. In the nuclear age, the decisive phases of general wars are likely to occur in the initial hours or days of hostilities. Consequently, only that portion of a nation's resources that have been transformed into forces-in-being are likely to weigh heavily in the more or less precarious balance of terror.

Economic war potential no longer possesses the significance it once enjoyed. In general nuclear wars, unmobilized potential cannot affect the outcome; in smaller, local conflicts, for example, the Korean war, the scale and tempo of limited war does not place as severe demands upon economic potential and the result is not likely merely to reflect industrial power. In the ambiguous guerrilla warfare becoming so familiar in the newly developing countries, poor societies have discovered a mode of warfare that tends to offset the advantages of industrial nations—extracting advantages from apparent weakness and offsetting modern technology with political cunning and the capacity for collective action.

Nonetheless, economic strength remains important to a state's military potential. It determines the range of contingencies for which the state can afford to be prepared, the amount of insurance it can secure against an uncertain future, the number of military options it can obtain for itself in the face of a variety of possible threats. These decisions are revealed by the size and allocations of the nation's defense budget. The American defense budget discloses the maintenance of vast and immensely flexible military power (Table 6).

Table 6.

Defense expenditures, 1964–1966

	Total expenditures (in $ million)	% of GNP
1964	51,213	8.8
1965	51,935	8.4
1966	67,950	9.2

Sources: Institute of Strategic Studies, The Military Balance 1966–67; 1967–68; House Appropriations Committee, Hearings, DoD Appropriations, 1968, p. 521.

By comparison with those of other states, these expenditures appear truly enormous. Russian defense spending for 1966–67 has been estimated at $29,800 million in equivalent United States purchasing power, or about 44 percent of American spending over the same period. In 1966 the United States spent nearly three times as much on national defense as did all of its NATO partners combined. Expenditures for the production and deployment of strategic forces alone in 1962 and 1963 exceeded the combined total of British and German defense spending in those years. Although such costs have declined slightly in recent years, they remain higher than the entire defense budgets of every other state except the Soviet Union. Spending for military research and development likewise exceeds the total level of defense spending of every European ally. Outlays such as these have required significant and sustained sacrifice. The stability of the effort is indicated by the fact that at no time since 1950 has the United States spent less than 8 percent of its GNP on defense. In 1966–67 only Iraq, Israel, Jordan, Saudi Arabia, Syria, the United Arab Republic, China, and Vietnam devoted a higher percentage of their national incomes to national defense.

Nor is the size of the present defense budget an indication of the level of expenditures that could be endured in a national emergency. It reflects rather a "climate of opinion" regarding current military requirements and the level of spending most consistent with the achievement of other objectives, such as domestic welfare, fiscal responsibility, and future economic growth. Experience suggests that the margin for additional mobilization is substantial. In 1950 many economists thought that a defense budget of more than $14 billion would destroy the economic health of the country. Within the next three years, during which the United States was involved in the Korean war, Congress appropriated $129.6 billion for defense. Far from producing adverse effects on the economy, the increase in spending had the effect of extricating the economy from a mild recession.

Again in 1961, after four years in which annual defense expenditures had averaged $45 billion, the spending plateau was significantly increased to finance the missile buildup of the 1960s. Since 1961, defense spending has averaged more than $50 billion annually and is gradually increasing in response to the steady escalation of the Vietnam war. In addition to the procurement of a massive missile striking force, combat-ready Army divisions have been increased by 45 percent; combat helicopters by 45 percent; airlift capabilities by 100 percent; Air Force fighter squadrons by 51 percent; naval ship construction by 100 percent; special forces training by 1000 percent; and tactical nuclear weapons pre-positioned in Europe by 67 percent. These increases in the size and diversity of American military power have been achieved without serious deleterious effects on the domestic economy, and a steady and impressive level of economic growth has continued since early 1961.

The basic policy of the United States, that is, containment, is essentially negative in character. Accordingly, the appropriate military strategy has emphasized deterrence; that is, the ability to prevent threats or actions from being executed by posing equal or greater threats of counteraction. The maintenance of an adequate deterrent posture is without doubt the highest priority military task of the United States. For more than two decades American political leaders have proved willing to spend any amount deemed essential to sustain a capability to inflict intolerable damage upon any potential attacker. Billions of dollars have been spent to guarantee the survival of a substantial portion of American strategic forces even in the face of a surprise attack. Since deterrent pledges have been extended to assure the integrity of many other states from external aggression, additional billions have been spent in an effort to perpetuate the credibility of such commitments. Heretofore, this has required a substantial numerical superiority to the Soviet bloc in strategic forces. And since the United States has been increasingly reluctant to invoke threats of nuclear reprisal in response to every challenge, however ambiguous, conventional forces recently have been bolstered to permit a strategy of "flexible response"—a discriminate application of force in the light of the specific conditions surrounding any particular conflict.

Table 7.

U.S. versus Soviet intercontinental strategic nuclear forces (October 1, 1968)

	U.S.A.	U.S.S.R.
ICBM * launchers (excluding test launchers and Soviet IRBM/MRBMs * targeted against European sites)	1054	900
SLBM * launchers	656	80
Total intercontinental missile launchers	1710	980
Intercontinental bombers	646	155
Approximate number of warheads	4206	1200

Source: *The Japan Times* (October 27, 1968), p. 1.

* ICBM—intercontinental ballistic missile; IRBM—intermediate-range ballistic missile; MRBM—medium-range ballistic missile; SLBM—submarine-launched ballistic missile.

At present, American strategic forces consist of 1054 hardened Minuteman I, Minuteman II, and Titan missiles, plus 41 nuclear-powered submarines each carrying 16 Polaris SLBMs. In addition, the Strategic Air Command still retains 697 manned bombers at its disposal and is procuring 210 FB-111A supersonic bombers to become operational in 1968–69.[12] So imposing is this force that the Secretary of Defense has estimated that the detonation of but one-fifth of the American force that would in all probability survive a direct surprise attack by all missile forces available to the Soviet Union through 1972 could destroy the Soviet Union as a modern society, devastate one-half of its industrial capacity, and kill 30 percent of its population.[13] Effective command and control of these forces in the face of a grave international crisis has been reinforced by establishing, in addition to the central command center, an airborne command post maintained aloft at all times in a KC-135 aircraft.

[12] Initial combat tests of these planes in the Vietnamese war were not entirely successful, and they were temporarily grounded on April 23, 1968.

[13] Statement of Secretary of Defense Robert S. McNamara before a Joint Session of the Senate Armed Services Committee and the Senate Subcommittee on *Department of Defense Appropriations on the Fiscal Year 1968–72 Defense Program and 1968 Defense Budget* (January 23, 1967), p. 43.

The deployment of even a significant Soviet antiballistic missile defense system would not materially alter these calculations. Such defenses as may be deployed by the Soviet Union will be more than offset by accelerated development of an advanced submarine-launched missile (Poseidon), the rapid replacement of Minuteman IIs by the more powerful and more accurate Minuteman IIIs, and the procurement of more sophisticated penetration aids. On September 18, 1967, the Secretary of Defense announced a decision to procure a limited antiballistic missile defense system. The proposed Sentinel ABM system, designed to offset a Chinese threat in the 1970s, consists of Perimeter Acquisition Radars, Missile Site Radars, long-range Spartan area-defense missiles, and Sprint local-defense missiles. The initial investment costs of this system are estimated to be $5 billion. For the moment, proposals to deploy a more ambitious system to provide for the defense of American cities against Soviet attack have been rejected. Such a system would require an investment for development, procurement, and initial operating expenses of approximately $40 billion over a period of ten years. These are enormous expenditures for a defense whose efficacy is subject to grave doubts. Yet they would constitute less than one-half of the average annual expenditures for strategic forces during the past five years and less than .7 percent of the GNP. The probable superfluity of such expenditures rather than their general magnitude has heretofore prompted skepticism in the Office of the Secretary of Defense regarding the wisdom of such an investment.

American strategic forces have accomplished more than simply deterring a direct attack on the United States or upon valued allies. They provide a measure of insurance that escalation in local challenges may be controlled. Many would attribute China's circumspection in the Vietnam war to the implicit threat of American retaliation. More dramatically, in the Cuban missile crisis of 1962, American strategic superiority seemed to prevent the Soviet Union from attempting to force concessions in Berlin in exchange for a removal of IRBMs and MRBMs from Cuba. Both the magnitude and flexibility of American military power were revealed in that crisis. Both were crucial to the success of that venture. America's retaliatory forces were sufficiently invulnerable to render a direct attack by the Soviet Union suicidal; substantial numerical superiority in strategic forces posed the threat of a counterforce attack against the Soviet Union should they attempt to extend the arena of bargaining by initiating provocations in the center of Europe. Control of escalation was complemented by local military superiority: 100,000 men were deployed in the southeastern portions of the United States, thus implying the possibility of an invasion of Cuba, should the Russian missiles in the Caribbean not be withdrawn. These units included paratroops, armored divisions, and infantry. One hundred eighty-three ships with 85,000 sailors aboard were moved to the vicinity of Cuba to constitute the quarantine force. Several thousand warplanes were deployed to provide air cover for an amphibious assault on Cuba if that contingency arose. Reserves were called up. This ominous display of diversified military power indicated the breadth of American power. Its measured application in the service of precise objectives demonstrated a capacity to successfully manage a grave international crisis.

The range and mobility of American power

In addition to the size and diversity of its own supply of men, equipment and weapons, the United States is the leader of a globe-encircling network of alliances and military bases. This system was created in the first postwar decade when the United States was invulnerable to direct attack. Today these alliances entail a multiplication of risks as well as benefits, but on balance represent a cardinal element in American military power. At present the United States is formally tied to forty-two sovereign states in mutual defense arrangements through the Rio Treaty, the North Atlantic Pact (NATO), the Southeast Asia Treaty Organization (SEATO), the ANZUS military accord, and bilateral agreements with Japan, South Korea, Formosa, and the Philippines. The United States possesses observer status in the Central Treaty Organization (CENTO) covering the Middle East. When one compares the total military strengths of the Western and Communist alliance systems, a quite favorable picture emerges. Equally evident is the fact that the United States is the principal supplier of security in the Western system, the other forty-one states being principally "consumers" of such security.

The motives and the purposes of these various alliances vary. NATO is incontestably the most important. Its initial purpose was to provide a shield behind which the Western European states might regather their strength and restructure their politics. The North Atlantic Treaty transformed a tacit interest on the part of the United States in the security of Western Europe into a formal obligation to provide assistance in the face of aggression. It represents a contract affirming coincident interests in the face of a palpable threat. It has served to associate the destinies of North America and Western Europe and add the forward bases of the latter to the strategic arsenal of the former. The promise of United States retaliation in the event of a Soviet attack on Europe gives to the alliance the character of a unilateral guarantee. The stationing of American troops in the center of the continent enhances the credibility of such a pledge. The rearmament of Europe and the deployment of tactical nuclear weapons, for the most part under United States custody, permits a rough parity in ground strength in Central Europe. These forces promise to be adequate to the tasks of dealing with incidents arising out of miscalculations, meeting a Warsaw Pact mobilization with an approximately equal expansion of forces, and denying an Eastern European adversary any possibility of military success in anything less than a full scale, all-out attack with all of its attendant risks of nuclear escalation.

The United States continues to contribute a disproportionate measure of strength to the alliance. Strategic forces are almost entirely controlled by the United States. It possesses the most powerful naval force, the largest army, the best equipment, most of the tactical nuclear weapons, and the bulk of the tactical air forces of the alliance. An American has commanded NATO forces since the inception of SHAPE. It is this imbalance in material contribution to the military power of NATO that makes possible, and perhaps encourages, France's disenchantment and withdrawal on the one hand, and the capacity of the alliance to absorb the French withdrawal without altering its strategy or mobilizing additional forces on the other.

Other alliances are less aggregations of strength than means of giving note of American intentions, thus influencing the calculations of adversaries. SEATO was negotiated in the mid-1950s largely in order to obtain a platform for expressing America's continuing concern for the future of various Southeast Asian nations. CENTO represented a means of closing the ring around the Soviet bloc and an apparatus through which military assistance could be channeled to participant states in the Near East. The Rio Treaty is another means of expressing the United States' traditional interest in the security of the Western Hemisphere. These alliances permit the United States military access to every region of the globe, with the exception of Eastern Europe. To this extent they contribute to the mobility of American power.

The mobility of American power is further enhanced by the pre-positioning of men, material, and weapons on advance bases. Army units are deployed in exposed positions in Berlin and South Korea, for example, as an earnest of America's intentions to stand by public commitments to those areas. Air Force units stationed in England, Spain, West Germany, Japan, Korea, Thailand, and Okinawa provide air support for these alliances, allow for more economical operations, and establish a continuing presence in far-flung areas of the world. The presence of the 1st Fleet in the eastern Pacific, the 2d Fleet in the Atlantic, the 6th Fleet in the Mediterranean, and the 7th Fleet in the western Pacific further reinforces this impression of mobile power in support of global commitments.

The range of American commitments in conjunction with the increasing fluidity of international political developments has contributed to the diversification in the kinds of units, capabilities, weapons, equipment, supplies, and training provided to United States General Purpose Forces. It has also encouraged a substantial expansion in the numbers of those forces. A further development has been the effort to improve capabilities for moving forces rapidly to distant theaters. The creation of forward floating depots of arms and materiel and the dramatic expansion in airlift and sealift capabilities are among the concrete steps under way to implement this objective. In Operation Big Lift in 1963, 15,000 troops, an entire combat division, were moved from Texas to Europe in sixty-three hours. When the massive C-5 cargo transport aircraft becomes available, the same feat will be possible within thirteen hours. In a few years, the United States will presumably be able to move most of its central reserve of active ground forces anywhere in the world within a period of from thirty to sixty days. It is this combination of massive military potential with the range of American power that insures America's status as perhaps the only truly global power in the world today.[14]

In addition to being able to participate in defining the local balance of forces in every region, the United States has demonstrated a desire to develop capabilities relevant for every major form of contemporary military or paramilitary combat. The most formidable form of contemporary conflict has been variously called subversive warfare, sublimited war, subterranean warfare, or guerrilla insurgency. It substitutes political organization, selective terror, and assiduous indoctrination for the technology of modern warfare. It challenges the United States' capacity to assist foreign regimes in the establishment of their authority and the promotion of cohesion among frequently disparate peoples within newly formed borders.

Although espionage and subversive techniques are not sustained easily by a democratic state with a tradition of noninterference in the internal affairs of other states, the United States has expended considerable energy and effort in acquiring some capabilities in the realm of political warfare. The exploits—and the misadventures—of the Central Intelligence Agency have been more and more widely reported in recent years. It was instrumental in bringing down the Arbenz government in Guatemala in 1954, in the planning and execution of the ill-fated Bay of Pigs debacle, in gathering remnants of the Chinese Nationalist army and placing it in the remote jungles of Burma (presumably to harass the border areas of China), in providing abortive assistance to military officers seeking to overthrow the Sukarno government in Indonesia in 1958, and in various political-military operations in Southeast Asia.

The overall picture of American military power is, then, one of imposing force capable of adaptation to a variety of forms of conflict and capable of being applied with great flexibility and great mobility. American military might provides the capacity for coercion that complements the instruments of persuasion so abundantly provided by American industrial strength, the force to deter and coerce that complements the diplomatic power of the United States to persuade and cajole.

Nonmaterial factors in the power inventory

The diversion of resources into foreign aid programs and military spending presupposes a willingness on the part of the public to forego some consumer benefits. The transformation of potential power into actual programs requires administrative ability. Focusing the con-

[14] For an analysis of developments in transportation and communication technology and their implications for American foreign policy, see Albert Wohlstetter, "The Illusions of Distance," *Foreign Affairs* (January 1968), pp. 242–255.

stituent elements of national power upon those points in the international situation which directly affect important national interests tests a nation's diplomatic skill. The credibility of national commitments depends not upon capabilities alone, but upon the nation's reputation and its prestige. Prestige depends in turn upon the historical record of a nation's performance in foreign affairs and the integrity and determination of contemporary leaders.[15] If a nation is to achieve its objectives with an economy of means it must possess moral authority as well as the resources of force. But moral authority is contingent upon a reputation for magnanimity, respect for the rights and interests of others, and regular adherence to the norms of civilized conduct. To be the source of others' hopes, the object of their respect, and a model for their emulation is likewise contingent upon the effective combatting of domestic problems. President Kennedy's anxiety to "get the country moving again" was grounded, above all, in his concern for American prestige in the world and his conviction that progress in eliminating the squalor in America's cities, injustice from America's race relations, crime in America's streets, and the deficiencies in America's educational system would simultaneously help to redress unfavorable elements in the international balance of power.[16] None of the above-mentioned factors lend themselves to precise measurement. All significantly condition the nation's "capacity for collective action."

In subsequent chapters those factors that condition the ability of the American government to marshall its resources, mobilize its manpower, and employ ideas in the pursuit of concrete diplomatic or strategic objectives will be analyzed. At this point broad generalizations must suffice. The moral unity of the American people is impressive, but historically that unity has frequently been sustained by averting controversial international entanglements. American political institutions are among the most durable in the world. They were fashioned, however, with an eye to their *representativeness* rather than their *efficiency* or their capacity to respond to foreign crises with dispatch. America's record for generosity is surely unmatched, but poor recipients are rarely as grateful as rich donors might anticipate them to be. Nor has the assumption of responsibilities as a custodian of the balance of power inspired universal approbation or affection. Still one may echo George Ball's conclusion that the United States and the Soviet Union, alone among the world's powers, possess both a resource base of continental dimensions *and* the "internal cohesion and unified political will to deploy those resources around the world." [17]

---

[15] C. B. Marshall once defined prestige by alluding to the genetecist who crossed a panther and a parakeet. Regarding the results of that experiment, he observed: "When it talks, I listen!"

[16] See Seyom Brown, *The Faces of Power: Constancy and Change in United States Foreign Policy from Truman to Johnson* (New York, N.Y.: Columbia University Press, 1968), Chap. 12.

[17] George Ball, *The Discipline of Power: Essentials of a Modern World Structure* (Boston, Mass.: Little, Brown, 1968), p. 14.

The limits of American power

One consequence of America's incomparable power position is the broad margin of error permitted to American diplomacy. Even gross miscalculations need not be irreparably damaging to a nation so amply endowed with the resources of force. No other state can afford so much insurance against so many contingencies. In an earlier age a great power was a state that could plausibly contemplate war with any other power. In the nuclear age, only the United States and the Soviet Union retain traces of this former status by being able to deter all other states from launching war against them. The risks of initiating war induce caution in both. In the economic realm, super-power status implies an approximation of that self-sufficiency that is increasingly beyond the power of any modern state to sustain. The United States enjoys more relative independence than any other state.

This description of the sources and dimensions of American strength is, however, apt to be misleading. If the United States has the resources with which to attempt to shape the international order, it is also subject to numerous constraints of international competition, as noted in Chapter 1. How is one to resolve the apparent paradoxes of America's unparalleled power and her seeming lack of freedom, of her unprecedented resources of influence and the alleged immobility of her diplomacy? Why, if the world is indeed acquiring a "unifocal" character with the United States playing the role of the single truly global power, is the predominant mood in America one of frustration? Why is the accomplishment of declared objectives so elusive? Allies defy American advice with impunity, a small primitive state in Southeast Asia maintains a military stalemate with the West's most impressive military power, and specifically American efforts to promote the evolution of milder forms of authoritarianism in Eastern Europe appear largely superfluous.[18] A number of possible explanations suggest themselves.

1. The currency of expectations is terribly inflated. Americans frequently succumb to what C. B. Marshall has termed the "illusion of perfect efficacy" in foreign affairs.[19] This is less a desire for supreme and overweening power than the expectation that all initiatives will be crowned with success. Such illusory notions are rooted in a fortuitous and extremely favorable set of historical experiences. Bismarck once shrewdly remarked that a special providence must look after "drunks, fools, and Americans." While representing a small, peripheral, frontier state, American statesmen kicked the British out of the Northwest frontier area, bargained the French out of the

---

[18] The Eastern European states that have received the bulk of America's economic assistance, for example, Poland, have been the most conspicuous recent backsliders; those with whom the United States has had virtually no formal relationships, for example, Czechoslovakia and Rumania, have been the most vigorous in their self-assertiveness against the Soviet Union.

[19] Charles B. Marshall, *The Exercise of Sovereignty* (Baltimore, Md.: Johns Hopkins University Press, 1965), pp. 47ff.

Louisiana Territory, dislodged the Spaniards from Florida, evicted the Mexicans from Texas and the American Southwest, bluffed and blustered the British out of Oregon, and purchased Alaska at bargain-basement prices. Later the Spanish were expelled from Cuba and the Philippines, and the Germans and Russians were restrained from imposing their hegemony on the European continent.

To be sure, hardships at home have been encountered, but the experience of tragedy has been conspicuously absent. As someone has observed, even from occasional traumatic experiences have come happy results. From the Civil War emerged a more durable federal union. As a consequence of the Depression, the President acquired new powers to manage the potentially dangerous fluctuations of the business cycle as well as the resources to sustain other political initiatives. Decisive intervention in two world wars brought not invasion and civil strife but global leadership—even if the United States was neither desirous of it nor particularly well prepared for it.

The conditions of America's initial engagement in the trials of post-1945 world politics were especially favorable. At war's end America was virtually unscathed by the conflict. Its homeland had escaped attack. Its economic and military resources were more fully mobilized than ever before. It had become the world's greatest creditor nation. The authority of its government and the integrity of its institutions had been reinforced by the successful conduct of general war. It had established a temporary monopoly on nuclear weapons. The challenges the United States confronted at this time were unprecedented. So, too, were the opportunities and capabilities for creative response. The advantages may have been transient, but they encouraged expectations that have persisted even though the conditions for American initiatives have undergone continuous and dramatic transformations. The experiences of the early postwar years encouraged that peculiar form of conceit that assumes, when something has gone wrong somewhere, that it must be attributable to official failure—to the incompetence of the State Department, or the malfeasance of American policy. Much contemporary frustration is a result of exorbitant expectations rather than inadequate power.

A corollary of this tendency to excessive expectations is the temptation to underestimate the magnitude of American achievements. American power is generally "most effective where it is least visible." During the past two decades, the primary American objectives have been negative in character. Containment has been achieved. In retrospect it becomes more and more difficult to establish beyond the shadow of a doubt that "enemies-turned-adversaries" once harbored aggressive designs. Deterrence has been largely successful. To the extent that it succeeds, however, nothing happens. Subsequently one cannot prove that a specific level of preparedness did indeed ward off potential threats. In the developing areas, stability has most frequently been the American goal. Stability is not only ephemeral; it is difficult to attribute to specific, especially external, sources.

2. The possession of great power is not to be confused with freedom of action. America's material resources of force have been multiplied even as her *situational power* has been eroded. As long as the United States carefully assumed a posture of nonalignment, the decision to intervene could have immediate and significant results in redressing a disjointed equilibrium, as the experience in two world wars readily attests. But since World War II the freedom of nonalignment has been exchanged for the responsibilities of engagement. Permanent involvement entails the loss of occasional opportunities to drastically alter the international situation through a dramatic entrance onto the world stage.[20]

The extensive range of American commitments hampers American flexibility in several ways. First, the assumption of a commitment always implies a correlative self-denial of some options.[21] To align oneself with others eliminates the alternative of remaining negligent of their interests. Being aligned with some forty-two sovereign nations, the United States cannot but have its diplomacy shaped by the myriad interests of allies and their perspectives on contemporary problems.

Second, as the range of American commitments widens, available power is dissipated over a broader area. Small states may focus their efforts and direct their resources toward the accomplishment of one or several primary objectives. A global power like the United States must allocate its resources among a much greater variety of competing aims. It discovers regularly, as do the most amply endowed philanthropic foundations, that resources, however substantial, are forever being outrun by both expectations and demands.

Third, the breadth of American commitments also prompts a continuous extension of disposable power available to honor them. The annexation of the Philippines in 1898 made it necessary to increase the size and mobility of American naval power in order to provide protection for these distant colonies. The extension of mutual security agreements to a host of states during the past two decades has correspondingly encouraged the maintenance of strategic and conventional forces sufficient to prevent provocations against even marginal allies. Furthermore, many of America's commitments were undertaken precisely in order to reduce its freedom to disregard the interests of others. Success in bargaining is often a product of inflexibility; thus, a tying of one's hands, a staking of the nation's honor, and the formalization of tacit interest into contractual responsibility are among the means through which the United States has sought to enhance the credibility of its deterrent threats. Moreover, a reputation for the reliable acquittal of commitments is essential

---

[20] This point is forcefully expressed in C. B. Marshall's slender volume, *The Limits of Foreign Policy* (New York, N.Y.: Holt, 1954).

[21] As Mr. Irving Kristol observed of the United States, "A great power is imperial because what it does *not* do is just as significant, and just as consequential, as what it does. Which is to say, a great power does not have the range of freedom of action—derived from freedom of inaction—that a small power possesses." *Foreign Affairs* (July 1967), p. 602.

to deterrence; failure to honor an explicit pledge may diminish one's prestige, and thereby one's actual power. Hence a state is bound by its previous commitments, however prodigal they may appear in retrospect.

Fourth, the marked tendency of the United States to inflate specific obligations into more general responsibilities further serves to expand the kinds of power required to achieve declared objectives. The specific pledge to offer assistance to Greece in 1947 was phrased in the universal language of commitment to the principle of self-determination. Assistance to an embattled regime in South Korea was transformed into a more general commitment to honor the principles of collective security—even unilaterally if necessary. The attempt to assist the South Vietnamese government in putting down an ambiguous insurgency has been justified in terms of a more general obligation to frustrate "national liberation wars." Power adequate to deal with specific objectives may appear terribly inadequate for the achievement of more universal purposes.

3. One may also question the appropriateness of American power to the novel challenges of the day. Nations that aspire to the possession of nuclear weapons are likely to exaggerate their efficacy for diplomatic and political purposes. To those nations that have accepted sacrifices to obtain them, their value is more apt to appear at a discount. Nuclear weapons are highly serviceable as defensive or deterrent weapons. They do not, however, self-evidently extend the flexibility and versatility of a nation's diplomacy. Those brandishing such weapons as counters in a political contest are apt to find them as difficult to translate into diplomatic influence as "changing a $1000 bill in a country drug store on Sunday." President Kennedy once observed with regret, "We possess weapons of tremendous power, but they are least effective in combating the weapons most often used by freedom's foes: subversion, infiltration, guerrilla warfare, civil disorder."

With regard to such phenomena, there are very real limits to American capabilities. Insurrections and civil disorders such as those confronting South Vietnam pose, by definition, a challenge to the authority of a regime, to the capacity of its government, and to its ability to inspire cohesion among its people. Success in countering insurgency is contingent upon antecedent qualities of the government through which supporting assistance is to be channeled. A capacity to provide advice and assistance should not be confused with the power to control political developments in the unfavorable terrain of a foreign society. Nor should the power adequate to the task of insulating small states from external interference be equated with the ability to reform their governments or establish their identity with an indigenous constituency.

4. When one seeks the limits of American power, it is prudent to recall that force tends to generate countervailing force. American power is to some extent neutralized through competition with the Soviet Union. Small states have always obtained a margin of maneuverability in the interstices of the balance of power. Historically many

of America's successes were products of Europe's distress. In the recent past, non-Western states have been able to obtain supporting assistance from both protagonists in the cold war without accepting the advice of either. More recently, as fears of the Sovietization of the newly independent states have subsided and the clear industrial ascendancy of the United States has been increasingly established, there has been a perceptible groping toward countercontainment. This is best symbolized by the growing parallelism of French and Soviet foreign policy on a wide range of issues.

5. The resources of force are not synonymous with an ability to persuade or the power to control. Much of America's foreign policy is, in fact, shaped by reactions to the unintended consequences of American wealth, American power, and the American presence. With an air of resignation and no little regret, James Reston once commented that the United States was just "too damned rich and too damned big." Like Gulliver in the land of Lilliput, it can produce by its every inadvertent movement unintended and frequently unfortunate consequences, for which amends must subsequently be made. The vast extension of American responsibilities has brought in its wake the more or less graceful acceptance of correlative social obligations to the peoples upon whom American power impinges. The assumption of responsibilities, however, by no means guarantees the efficacy of official acts.

Despite these qualifications, it is clear that the United States is a global power of the very first rank. Since World War II its aid, investments, bases, trade, military deployments, and security guarantees have been extended throughout the world. The size of America's material base permits it to devote more resources to diplomatic-strategic action than any other state. The mobility of American power enables the United States to influence the local balance of forces in virtually every region of the world. The variety of American resources allows for attempts at persuasion where coercion promises to be risky or costly. An ample supply of financial capital, technicians, commodities for trade, and so forth, makes it possible to offer a variety of emoluments in order to reaffirm friendships, solidify alliances, sustain clients, confirm the independence of neutrals, grease the wheels of compromise with potential or real adversaries, and provide incentives for the relaxation of tensions with enemies.

The United States cannot destroy its antagonists with impunity; it can demonstrate the futility of general war, indicate clearly its own intention of averting it, and seek to influence the Russians and Chinese to forego efforts to expand their own territorial base. The United States may have difficulty enforcing its will upon allies; but it can unilaterally formulate strategy and even adjust with a certain equanimity to the defection of even a major ally like France from the machinery of NATO. The United States cannot determine the course of political developments in the Third World; it can fortify the capacity of some new states to sustain their independence and it may upon occasion intervene forcibly to prevent outcomes of local political strife that are deemed unacceptable.

3

Political beliefs, historical traditions, and American foreign policy

Political communities are shaped by their historic experiences. Through those experiences the principles of a people—their accepted or professed rules of political conduct—are formulated and tested. Over time national traditions—those bodies of doctrines and practices habitually adhered to—are established and sanctified by usage.

Intellectual foundations of American foreign policy

Throughout the history of the United States, certain ideas have continuously informed American perspectives on foreign policy. For several decades an argument has raged among scholars regarding the relevance and the realism of the American tradition in foreign relations. That there is an essential continuity in the ideas and political beliefs that have inspired that tradition is hardly a subject for dispute.[1] The heart of the American tradition is to be found in the conviction that personal and political conduct are indissolubly

---

[1] See especially Francis Loewenheim, *The Diplomat and the Historian* (New York, N.Y.: Harcourt, Brace, 1966). In his essay, "A Legacy of Hope and a Legacy of Doubt," pp. 1–71, the author convincingly disputes the views of prominent scholars, diplomatists, and commentators such as Hans Morgenthau, George Kennan, and Walter Lippmann, who have denied the continuity of American thinking on foreign affairs. He does not entirely put to rest some of their reservations toward contemporary American perspectives on international politics.

linked, even as are the conduct of domestic and foreign policy. "We certainly cannot deny to other nations," Thomas Jefferson wrote to Thomas Pinckney, "that principle whereon our government is founded, that every nation has a right to govern itself internally under whatever form it pleases, and to change these forms at its own will; and externally to transact business with other nations throughout whatever organ it chooses . . ." [2]

On the validity and relevance of certain basic principles, then, there has been general agreement. Government, it is agreed, should be derived from the just consent of the governed. Peoples should be allowed to exercise choice over their forms of government. States should refrain from engaging in meddlesome interference in the affairs of other sovereign entities. Each of these ideas has found a hardy echo in the policies of Jefferson, Lincoln, Wilson, Truman, Kennedy, and Johnson. At times, to be sure, one or another principle has been neglected to exploit an irresistible opportunity, as in the annexation of the Philippines in 1898, or to confront unpleasant realities, such as those that emerged in Europe after 1945. Even then, however, the principles of self-government, self-determination, and noninterference remain to haunt those who disregard them, for these principles provide the criteria by which their actions are subsequently judged.

While the relevance to foreign policy of these ideals is casually assumed, several distinct intellectual styles are apparent when it comes to translating general principles into specific policies. Indeed, two contradictory attitudes are implicit in the two most basic documents in America's history: the Constitution and the Declaration of Independence.[3]

The Constitution was an essentially conservative document. The purposes it proclaimed were almost exclusively domestic in character. They were deemed unique to the American situation, and they reflected a preoccupation with the establishment and limitation of power at home. No concrete social program, no foreign policy design, no vision of the ideal world order is to be found there. The enduring purposes of the state were prescribed in the Preamble. Justice was to be established and maintained, domestic tranquility assured, a more perfect union forged, the general welfare provided for, and the blessings of liberty secured for all. A narrow definition of foreign policy was implied by the single goal related to foreign policy, that is, the maintenance of a "suitable establishment for the common defense."

The Declaration of Independence, on the other hand, while specific in its application to the conditions of America, proclaimed principles presumably general in their validity. Framed in language that was messianic, it proclaimed the virtues of self-government, the

---

[2] Quoted in *Ibid.*, pp. 7–8.

[3] See C. B. Marshall, "Our Noble Dream," *The Key Reporter* XXIX (Spring 1964), pp. 2–5, for an elaboration of this point.

right of self-determination, and the evils of intervention. The United States, as C. B. Marshall once commented, was, according to the Declaration, to take "the lead in a new order of things, portraying for others what their future [was] to be like, setting an example for all to follow." [4] America was to assume the mission of demonstrating the universal relevance of Lockean conceptions of natural rights, the sanctity of private property, and the virtues of Jeffersonian democracy.

These disparate approaches reflect rather accurately the rival premises of the "realist" and "idealist" schools of thought. Each tradition in turn expresses a different intellectual temperament, a different conception of international relations, and a different understanding of the uniqueness of the American nation.

Political realists

Realists have generally sounded a note of skepticism regarding the direct applicability of liberal principles in the world beyond America's borders. Anticipating, along with Alexander Hamilton, that the United States would "likely ... experience a common portion of the vicissitudes and calamities which have fallen to the lot of other nations," many prominent American statesmen have instinctively appreciated the rudiments of power politics in a world of sovereign states. The Founding Fathers, William Seward, Theodore Roosevelt, Elihu Root, or Dean Acheson, for example, readily acknowledged the persistence of struggle, the latent risk of war, and the role of force in the relations among sovereign political collectivities. For men of such temperament national security has been a preeminent concern, the husbanding of national strength an abiding preoccupation. Understanding war to be the product of a multitude of possible causes, such realists have generally been dubious of proposals heralding the elimination or prohibition of violence in world politics. They have sought neither to evade the imperatives of participation in international affairs nor to exorcise the practitioners of strategy and diplomacy through a willful neglect of foreign relations or their transformation into purely commercial relations.

This is not to suggest that so-called "realists" invariably agree on policy questions, for political realism represents a disposition toward politics rather than a doctrine from which policies may be readily deduced.[5] The common currency of their style of thought is to be found in their rather dour attitude toward human nature, their limited expectations of human progress, their concern for interests and facts, and their conception of politics as a method of resolving conflicts of interest through the interplay of power. Anxious to prevent vain interventions in Europe's quarrels, Hamilton concluded

---

[4] *Ibid.*

[5] See, in this connection, Kenneth Thompson, *Political Realism and the Crisis of World Politics* (Princeton, N.J.: Princeton University Press, 1960).

that "our situation invites and our interests prompt us to aim at an ascendant in the system of American affairs." Similarly in the changed situation of the 1940s Dean Acheson was less impressed by the potential of a global collective security system centered in the United Nations than by the necessity of creating a specific alliance, NATO, to protect a specific portion of mankind, the Atlantic community, against a specific foe, the Soviet Union. Neither denied the significance of liberal principles in foreign policy, principles such as self-determination, self-government, or noninterference. Both, however, acknowledged the claims of prudence and were guided in their efforts to implement such principles by the realities of power. What is perhaps significant in this connection is that the American tradition of political realism is not one that romanticizes the virtues of *Realpolitik*. Among American realists the exercise of power has normally been accompanied by counsels of moderation, restraint, and forebearance, and the imperatives of strategy and diplomacy accepted as a necessary evil.

Political idealists

An attitude quite different from the realists' toward international politics may be discerned in the writings of James Madison or Woodrow Wilson. This tradition—influenced by the philosophical ideas of the Enlightenment, reinforced by the sectarian Protestant and English origins of America's early colonists, and confirmed by the favorable domestic experiences of a liberal political community—is marked by an ebullient optimism, a certain apolitical bias, and overtones of millenarianism. The "idealist" school of thought is grounded in a generally shared belief in the uniqueness of the American experiment and the universal validity of those principles that inspired the American Revolution.

To the "Enlightenment idealists," from Madison to Wilson, certain ideas were axiomatic. The balance-of-power system was considered to be one of resistances, shocks, disturbances, violent explosions, uncertainties, and wars; alliances were seen as "preparations for treason"; treaties were viewed as mere "temporary armistices"; diplomats were dismissed contemptuously as spies or devious practitioners of even oilier arts. Politics, with its presumed emphasis upon power, struggle, and strife, was juxtaposed with the principles of commerce, where a natural harmony of interests was alleged to prevail, mutual profits were considered the rule, and a "marvelous and intricate division of labor" constituting a new and comprehensive principle would place isolated sovereignties into a higher system of community.[6] Power politics was to be abandoned, for its practice threatened the peace; its practitioners—diplomats and soldiers— threatened republican principles. "Consuls," Jefferson said, "would do all the business we ought to have" with foreign societies. An

[6] See Felix Gilbert, *To the Farewell Address* (Princeton, N.J.: Princeton University Press, 1961), pp. 44–76.

equally intense distaste for "power politics" was disclosed later by Woodrow Wilson in his efforts to transform a "balance of power" into a "community of power" and to replace a security system organized around constantly shifting alliances with a collective security system organized within a legal framework.

This basic commitment to reform the international system is a familiar theme in American diplomatic history. Secretary of State Kellogg was eager to outlaw war "with a stroke of the pen." Secretary of State Stimson sought to thrust aggressors into social ignominy by refusing to acknowledge that conquest brought its own rewards. Sumner Welles called for an international conference to discuss an ethical code of international conduct in the late 1930s, at a time when the "lamps were going out" on the continent. The desperate search for organizing principles for a new world order has continued since World War II, though in recent years it has been consistently accompanied by a greater sensitivity to American security interests.

Instinctively, adherents of this set of perspectives have considered economics a more fundamental reality than politics. Some saw free trade as the solvent of international animosities; more recently the creation of a European continental market through the application of supranational principles has been grasped as a panacea for the recurrent strife on the continent, or economic development held up as a cure-all for the strife and turbulence of the new nations. There is also an abiding confidence that power relations can be transformed if they are successfully disciplined by legal principles; thus the effort to codify international law, to negotiate arbitration and mediation treaties, and to organize international cooperation institutionally. There is, finally, a tendency among political idealists to emphasize ideas at the expense of interests. The common currency of this intellectual style is an abiding optimism, a disposition not to consider conflict endemic in the human condition, and a faith that where differences among sovereign entities arise they may be reconciled by intellectual give-and-take, by referring them to the adjudication of third parties operating within strict legal procedures, or by overcoming them through a search for mutually profitable commercial transactions.

Among those believing in America's unique mission and the superiority of the American political community, a fund of common assumptions has not insured identical policy preferences. One schism in particular is worthy of mention. "Liberal isolationists" have been content to perfect political arrangements at home with the expectation that others would eagerly emulate them. Distaste for the "power politics" allegedly practiced "over there" has been translated into the attempt to avoid contamination by having as little foreign policy as possible. The example of a "moral and upright nation foreswearing relations with corrupted and power-seeking nations, pursuing policies of neutrality, and abstaining from the morally ambiguous exercise of influence or coercion in world politics," many thought, would ultimately suffice to abolish Machiavellianism. Others, however, have displayed a greater willingness to intervene abroad in order to guarantee a more general application of principles of political conduct that have been tried and tested at home. To the "liberal interventionists" America's involvement in world politics was, of course, contingent upon a reformation of the rules of international conduct. In the absence of basic reforms, the United States would presumably revert to its traditional isolationism. Common to both outlooks is a profound distaste for power politics, an equally profound sense of America's special responsibilities for reforming the international order, and a determined refusal to accept the world on the world's own terms.

At each crossroad in America's "rendezvous with destiny," the dialectic between the so-called realists and idealists (of both isolationist and interventionist inclinations) has been resumed in a vigorous public debate. The similarity of the arguments in 1796, 1898, 1916, 1937, 1945, and even today is eloquent testimony to the durability of these intellectual styles. Invariably, too, the resolution of conflicting perspectives has emerged in the form of policies that constitute a defensible conception of American security interests cloaked in the language of high principle. From 1789 until 1888 the synthesis of security requirements and principled instincts was expressed in a general policy eschewing involvement in European political quarrels. As American power waxed, so, too, did enthusiasm for participation in world politics. Initially this instinct found expression in the quest for hemispheric ascendancy, later in the extension of American commercial activity throughout the world. In the twentieth century the United States has been drawn ineluctably into the struggle for mastery in Europe and the world. One consequence has been the need to thrash around for a new synthesis of security interests and high ideals. Another has been the need to adapt and modify attitudes and perspectives toward world politics that were formed in a more serene era. This in turn has occasioned a basic revision of traditional policies that had acquired the force of habit and the status of legitimacy.

Traditional policies

The foreign policies of a state evolve in response to the exigencies of the international situation. The legacy of the past is apparent, however, in the general and particular objectives of policy and in the friendship or enmity nourished toward particular foreign societies. Today, as in the past, there exists a tension in American foreign policy between the desire to remain true to a sense of national mission of a liberal character and the natural instinct to safeguard the substantial security interests of a global power. This tension is not so easily resolved today as it was during the nineteenth century through the development of a set of "introversive" policies that acknowledged the priority of internal development and reserved foreign policy to an instrumental role only in the quest for prosperity, industrial expansion, social cohesion, and peace.[7] The traditional policies may be briefly outlined.

"No entangling alliances"

By the end of the nineteenth century the isolationist impulse had hardened into an instinctive rejection of involvement in European quarrels. Isolationism was an article of faith, a hallowed dogma, a natural condition. Originally, however, the decision to eschew "entangling alliances" was a shrewd adjustment to the imperatives of America's domestic situation and the opportunities latent in the international situation.

There were obvious reasons for the United States, as a "new nation," to express its autonomy, integrity, and independence in the realm of diplomacy. The motives were comparable to those that induce the new nations of the 1960s to studiously assume postures of nonalignment or "positive neutralism." Convinced that the Old and New Worlds had peculiar constellations of interest that by no means automatically converged, the Founding Fathers were eager to focus American resources on the preservation of uniquely American interests. Recognizing the fortuitous conditions that seemed to guarantee American security and promised ascendancy in the hemisphere, George Washington asked: "Why forego the advantages of so peculiar a situation? Why quit our own to stand on foreign ground?" There were also eminently practical reasons for abjuring specific commitments to one or another European state at a time when the British, French, Spanish, and Russians all continued to retain imperial footholds on the North American continent.

Isolationism was surely a posture that suited the requirements of America's domestic situation. In an overseas settlement colony counting among its citizens partisans of Republican France as well as Loyalists of pro-British sentiment, an activist policy with regard to European wars and disputes obviously threatened domestic solidarity. Washington, as the architect of an American national consciousness, was convinced that a moratorium of perhaps two decades on international entanglements might suffice to insure the integrity and identity of the United States. The surge of immigrants to America in the mid-nineteenth century and continuing through World War I contributed to both the durability and the relevance of the isolationist impulse.

Equally important, isolationism was consistent with the American security position, particularly after 1815. A remote location, relatively static and primitive military technology, the European balance of power, and the generally felicitous tone of Anglo-American relations after 1815 provided adequately for America's security with-

---

[7] The distinction is Jean Baptiste Duroselle's. "Extroversive goals result in the primacy of foreign affairs and are associated with the quest for power, security, glory, or grandeur." See his essay, "Changes in French Foreign Policy Since 1945," in Stanley Hoffmann et al., *In Search of France* (Cambridge, Mass.: Harvard University Press, 1963), p. 306.

out explicit measures of preparedness other than a modest program of coastal defense. Formal alliances could have added little to this security position. With its security assured at modest expense, the United States could afford to husband its resources and focus its energies upon the opening up of a vast continent and the exploitation of nature's abundant largesse. Indeed, self-abnegation as far as European involvements were concerned was the corollary of continental expansion.

Based on more than these prudential concerns, a policy of isolationism was consonant also with that striving for high purposes that has always been associated with the American's sense of nationhood. Psychologically, the one generally shared experience among Americans was escape from Europe. Immigration to the New World was prompted by a variety of motives, but among them was the fervent wish to leave the arena of the European state system with its attendant strife and warfare. America sought emancipation first *from* Europe. By fashioning a new diplomacy that rejected alliances, emphasized commercial relations over military and political relations, and explicitly repudiated the "primacy of foreign policy," American statesmen also believed they were experimenting with methods of statecraft that might later emancipate Europe from the heavy hand of its own traditional practices.

In short, alliances were considered neither necessary nor desirable. Active intervention in European difficulties promised unpalatable domestic consequences and was believed to be inconsistent with the national sense of mission in the world. To be sure, American statesmen never aspired to the solitude of hermit nations like Japan prior to 1856. The corollary to the widely accepted strictures against "entangling alliances" was an active effort to promote "peace, commerce, and honest friendship with all nations."

Continental expansion

The American appetite for additional land was prodigious. Aside from the Soviet Union, the United States acquired more real estate during the nineteenth century than any other state. Fortunately, the restless energies of a pioneer nation could be largely dissipated in virtually unpeopled areas. Expansion was permitted the United States without the necessity of imperialism and the collision of cultures experienced by European states as they established colonies in Latin America, the Near East, Africa, and Asia. Admittedly, the American Indians were consigned to their own form of apartheid, but their numbers were small and the experience of expelling them from the land had little effect upon the national psyche.

Expansionism required considerable diplomatic finesse, an occasional display of political demagoguery, and now and then the threat of coercion or the actual use of force. Foreign powers had to be neutralized, territorial claims patiently sustained, and divisions among the colonial powers exploited. Doubtless the United States had extraordinary good fortune in all this, yet luck alone cannot be credited with the remarkable string of diplomatic triumphs represented by the Louisiana Purchase, the Pinckney Treaty (which ratified the acquisition of Florida from Spain), the incorporation of Texas into the Union by joint resolution of Congress, the cession of the present Southwestern United States by Mexico in the Treaty of Guadalupe Hidalgo, the favorable settlement of the Oregon question, the Gadsden Purchase, the successful negotiations with Russia for the purchase of Alaska, and the annexation of Hawaii. When one recalls that America was initially ringed around with European imperial powers harboring little affection for the upstart republic, the record is even more impressive. Diplomatic miscalculations were pregnant with potentially calamitous results, yet with but one exception—in 1812—the American continent was secured without war with the European states.

The continental character of American expansion is noteworthy, for it gave rise to an unprecedented system of "imperial" administration. In the Northwest Ordinance adopted by the Congress of the Confederation in July, 1787, a regular set of stages was anticipated through which new territories could pass from colonial status to full equality with the oldest members of the Union. Unlike existing imperial systems, therefore, the Americans experimented with the "coordinate-state" principle, which honored the full equality of all members of the Federation, provided for a normal progression from external control to self-government, and promised ultimate assimilation into the Union. It was a system neatly adapted both to the principles of self-government and self-determination and to the desire to promote national growth.[8]

In 1898 expansionism gave way to a more overt imperialism in the annexation of the Philippines. This produced a break in the American tradition, since control was asserted over a remote and alien people for whom assimilation into the Union was not contemplated. Acquisition of the Philippines provoked a passionate public debate and prolonged agitation. The Treaty of Annexation was ultimately ratified by a margin of but a single vote in the Senate. Manifest Destiny held sway, but precariously and temporarily. The imposition of colonial control over another people against their will was a decided aberration. It occasioned a crisis of conscience for many Americans who feared that the act of annexation amounted to a repudiation of the principles of the American Revolution. Rarely have the burdens of empire been shouldered so reluctantly or preparations for self-government of the colonies been so early initiated.

The Monroe Doctrine

President Monroe's declaration of opposition to European colonization of the Western Hemisphere expressed anew the familiar American

[8] See Daniel Boorstin, *The Americans* (New York, N.Y.: Random, 1965), pp. 391–430.

belief in the existence of two spheres—an Old World and a New World—each possessing its unique and separable constellation of interests. Fashioned with an eye to keeping the American and European political system as "separate and distinct from each other as possible," the doctrine was articulated in response to the threat of intervention by the Holy Alliance in the independence movements of Spanish America. Since the British had already indicated their opposition to any such intervention, the United States could adopt a bold rhetorical policy without assuming substantial risks.

Rather like the American Constitution, the Monroe Doctrine as originally asserted was brief, ambiguous, and sufficiently flexible to permit later adaptation to unanticipated circumstances. Although it expressed resistance to European interference in the Americas, it left for the future more precise determination of the forms of interference that were specifically to be prohibited. In President Monroe's declaration there was no mention of the transfer of existing colonies among European powers, or of the voluntary cession of territory by American republics to European powers, or of the special interest of the United States in the Caribbean. There was likewise no hint of the American attitude toward the forcible collection by Europeans of public debts owed them by the American republics, United States prerogatives to arbitrate boundary disputes in the hemisphere, or American tolerance for this or that form of governmental system in the region. There was no pledge to uphold the doctrine by force, no request for congressional acquiescence to legitimatize it, and no unqualified promise to abstain from European politics as the price for European forebearance in the New World.

All of these matters were subject to subsequent clarification (or occasional obfuscation) in response to the restless surge of events. If there has been a thread of consistency in American policy within the hemisphere, it is to be found in the acute sensitivity to developments in the Americas; in the resistance displayed consecutively toward Spanish, British, French, German, and Russian designs in the hemisphere; in the assumption that the hemisphere provided a broader arena in which the principles of self-determination and self-government ought vigorously to be applied (even though their implementation at times required neglect of another cherished principle—noninterference); in the aspiration to assert a benevolent American ascendancy in the hemisphere.

Nonintervention and neutrality

The small and relatively weak American state, on the periphery of the European state system, had an obvious interest in erecting obstacles to the interventionist policies of European powers. Such expediential concerns were buttressed by a commitment to the principle of nonintervention as the vital link between America's devotion to self-government and to self-determination. If either of these latter principles were to be realized, states had to refrain from meddlesome interference in the affairs of other sovereign entities.

Born in a revolutionary act of secession, America felt a natural sympathy with liberal revolutionaries in other lands. Throughout the nineteenth century, however, American policy was guided by the self-denying ordinance of noninterference. Again and again political leaders expressed their regret at seeing men's natural rights and civil liberties extinguished by foreign despots. Popular enthusiasm for revolutionary causes in Spanish America, Greece, France, Hungary, and Poland led to repeated demands for overt assistance in the 1820s, 1830, 1848, 1849, and 1863, respectively. On each occasion sympathy for the revolutionaries was eloquently expressed, but material assistance was withheld. As John Quincy Adams commented on one such occasion, "It is our duty to remain, the peaceable and silent, though sorrowful spectators of the sanguinary scene."

This prudent concern to avert interventionism in others' internal affairs was manifested in the policy of extending diplomatic recognition on the basis of de facto control of a given territory. In the traditional doctrine, recognition did not imply approval; it merely acknowledged a factual situation. To fail to extend such an acknowledgment was considered in itself intolerable interference.

This traditional doctrine was not without one temptation to ambivalence. The tendency to extend de facto recognition to regimes effectively in control of a populace was accompanied by an insistence that in order to win de jure recognition from the United States, regimes had to enjoy "popular support." This was later to lead to the substitution of "democratic legitimacy" for "effective control" as the criterion for recognition.

In return for a scrupulous regard for the integrity of other states, the United States insisted upon European respect for the legal rights of states assuming a neutral attitude toward their quarrels. Such demands were the natural corollaries of an isolationist policy, and they were designed to insulate American citizens from the effects of European wars and to protect American commerce from excessive interference by belligerent states. Throughout the nineteenth century, and well into the twentieth, the United States was the foremost proponent of the codification of the rights of neutrals, a tireless advocate of principles such as "free ships make free goods," of the narrowest possible definition for contraband goods, and of the right of neutrals to freely transport noncontraband goods from one unblockaded port to another. In return, America attempted a fastidious observance of neutral obligations.

Recognizing that "a nation despicable by its weakness, forfeits even the privilege of being neutral," the United States was forced to maintain naval power sufficient to enforce its claims to neutral rights. Corsairs were sent to deal with the Barbary pirates when the nation was still in its infancy. Four of the six grievances prompting a declaration of war against Great Britain in 1812 were related to maritime incidents. Flagrant violations of American neutral rights and raids upon American commercial vessels played a prominent role in provoking Amercan intervention in World War I.

The promotion of commerce

The promotion of commerce was not constrained by anxieties about entanglement. As John Adams warned his colleagues in Congress, "Our business with them, and theirs with us is commerce, not politics, much less war." American traders had begun to seek markets in the Orient before the formal establishment of the Union. Among the very earliest acts of Congress, in July, 1789, was the construction of a large merchant fleet. The negotiation of a commercial treaty with Great Britain was among the highest priority objectives of Washington's Administration. This was accomplished in 1794. An important motive for westward expansion was the desire to obtain inviting ocean ports to improve the avenues of American commerce to the Far East. The United States contributed significantly to the opening up of China and Japan to Western trade. American statesmen actively championed the principle of the "most favored nation treatment" and the Open Door principles in order to enjoy the commercial privileges and extraterritorial rights exacted from China by the European powers. Commercial interests likewise were among the motives for the acquisition of Hawaii, coaling stations in Samoa, and Dollar Diplomacy in the Caribbean.

Contemporary adaptations

The dominant "introversion" of foreign policy aims that marked American diplomacy throughout much of the nineteenth century has been eroded from two sides in the twentieth. On the one hand, the instinct to champion more actively in the wider arena of world affairs the liberal instincts and principles that animate American domestic political life has grown apace with the expansion of American power. The scope of American liberal interventionism has thus been extended progressively from the American continent, to the Western Hemisphere, to the Atlantic and Pacific basins, and finally to the global diplomatic system in the post-1945 period. On the other hand, the external conditions of American security began gradually to disappear after 1914, as suggested in Chapter 1. The result of these two developments has been the necessity of defining a new relationship to the European and Asian balances of power, and of devising a new set of policies that synthesize the prudential requirements of United States security interests with the American need to strive for lofty moral purposes in international politics.

Various attempts at such a synthesis have been made since 1898; none has proved as satisfactory or as durable as isolationism. Manifest Destiny was an aberration of but temporary appeal; Dollar Diplomacy a passing fancy. "Democratic interventionism" quickly gave way to a return to "normalcy" in the twenties and an even more firmly held commitment to "neutrality" in the thirties.

After 1945 a new synthesis became the more imperative as Western Europe and Eastern Asia collapsed and exposed the United States more directly to Soviet power. This situation challenged the relevance of most of the traditional doctrines and policies. What William Carleton has called the "revolution in American foreign policy" was in essence an adjustment of the traditional reflexes of policy to the novel circumstances of the postwar world.[9]

At war's end it was still widely assumed that the United Nations would provide a forum within which dangerous disputes might be resolved through peaceful discussion. If hostilities broke out, it was anticipated that the continued amity of the wartime allies would insure that effective sanctions were organized against international lawbreakers. Soviet actions in Iran, Greece, Turkey, and Central Europe rendered those premises increasingly dubious. They consequently gave way to a new set of assumptions which continue even into the late 1960s to provide guidance to American policy-makers. It was concluded that the Soviet Union was actively seeking a position of supremacy in world politics and that only American resistance could insure the maintenance of a global balance of power. It was also recognized that in future general wars, the United States would not likely escape massive destruction threatening the lives of a substantial portion of the American populace. Thus the avoidance of war as well as the containment of Communist expansion became a prime aim of policy. To avert these twin dangers, it was considered essential to make American power available to arrest the extension of Soviet influence into contiguous areas. In practical terms this led the United States to make its primary objective of foreign policy the restoration of an equilibrium of power in Europe and Asia. As Secretary of State George C. Marshall put the matter succinctly in November, 1947, all American actions were to be viewed in the light of that objective.[10]

If these premises provided the intellectual underpinnings of policy, the emotional foundations were constructed out of the bitter experiences of appeasement, war, and the shattering of early hopes for amicable relations with the Soviet Union. The memory of Munich produced by analogy a set of axioms or reflexes which in their crudest form amounted to the generalizations that "dictators' appetites always improve with the eating" and "appeasement invariably provokes new aggression." The conviction that Russia's imperial advance had to be counterbalanced left undetermined, of course, the exact role which the United States might play in seeking their containment.

The "containment" policy that emerged embodied some striking reversals of traditional policies. Isolationism was exchanged for

[9] William G. Carleton, *The Revolution in American Foreign Policy* (New York, N.Y.: Random, 1963).

[10] Walter Millis, *The Forrestal Diaries* (New York, N.Y.: Viking, 1951), p. 341. See also Seyom Brown, *The Faces of Power*, Parts I and II.

extensive involvement. Peacetime alliances were negotiated with almost promiscuous zeal in the 1950s. Private foreign investment was supplemented by massive infusions of public economic assistance into the world economy. A strategy of mobilization was replaced by an emphasis upon forces-in-being and reliance upon the "balance of terror." Instruments for disseminating propaganda abroad were established and generously financed.

In some respects the departure from past policies and doctrines was not so radical. Initially, containment's appeal was as an interim measure that promised to reestablish the more familiar terms of America's relationship with the Old World by restoring the vitality of the "intermediate zones" of Western Europe and Japan and by preventing hegemony over Europe and Asia to fall unchallenged to the Soviet Union. In a sense, containment merely represented a plausible means of "maintaining a suitable establishment of the common defense" under the quite novel conditions of the postwar world. Preventive war was unpalatable, global settlement with the Soviet Union unlikely, and hemispheric defense unresponsive to the conditions in Europe and Asia.

Yet containment was not simply a last resort. As it was originally conceived, it was not only defensive in character but was also motivated by the traditional liberal principles of self-government, self-determination, and noninterference. American power was to be employed in a discriminating fashion on behalf of the independence and self-esteem of established powers in Europe and Asia. The occupation of Germany and Japan was to yield gradually to their resumption of formal powers of governance. The imperial system was to be eroded by persistent American pressure on European states with overseas colonies. Anxieties about Soviet ambitions were fed by the destruction of illusory hopes of applying the principles of self-determination in areas liberated by Soviet armies.

The policy was acceptable, in addition, because it produced initially none of the frustrations that later attended efforts to transfer its precedents to non-Western areas. That is to say, containment was operationally feasible in Europe because it demanded the reconstruction of areas in which the impulse of self-help was highly developed. It did not require the support of feudal leaders, the promotion of defense establishments at the expense of economic development, or the need to arouse an indigenous sense of nationhood as the prerequisite for resistance to external dangers. It required of the United States the extension of a protective umbrella, which a temporary monopoly of atomic weapons rendered both effective and apparently safe. It required that a prosperous country share its material abundance with states seeking to reestablish productivity upon a preexisting economic infrastructure. It required, finally, that the United States apply its technical and scientific ingenuity to the arms race. Thus, in its original form, containment required assistance to peoples with whom Americans possessed ties of blood and civilization, a sharing of resources that were available in ample supply, and the application of

Yankee ingenuity to the military-technological problems of a future war.

If in the first postwar decade the Soviet Union reduced its neighbors to satellite status, exploited its allies for purposes of its own internal reconstruction, and asserted its ideological leadership in a heavy-handed and often capricious way, within the Western world the United States exerted its "hegemony" more generally on behalf of the reestablishment of the autonomy of intermediate and small states, of the greater interdependence of states in various regional ensembles, and of the emergence of a more pluralistic world order.

The policy of containment has proved to be immensely flexible as well as enormously resilient. It has provided a convenient rationalization for a variety of actions of a generally anti-Communist character. Policies supporting the general purposes of containment have undergone continuous evolution in response to the ebb and flow of international developments and to domestic reactions to those developments.

The decision to contain communism was originally implemented in President Truman's declared intention politically to support peoples who were threatened by "subjugation by armed minorities or by outside pressures." Prompted by the British government's inability to maintain its commitments in the eastern Mediterranean in the spring of 1947, the initial actions contemplated under the Truman Doctrine included economic and military assistance to Greece and Turkey, whose governments were threatened by an externally backed insurrection and diplomatic intimidation by the Soviet Union, respectively. Such aid as was provided served to fortify the resistance of non-Communist elements in both countries. It also helped to prevent the kind of spectacular political success by the Soviet Union that might have confirmed the suspicion of many Europeans that they would inevitably be subjected to Soviet imperialism.

Although President Truman employed sweeping language in articulating an American policy of support to "free peoples who are resisting attempted subjugation by armed minorities or by outside pressures," there is little evidence to support the view that the Truman Administration intended indiscriminate American support for any and all regimes confronted by an internal or external Communist threat. As Secretary of State Acheson later made clear in his discussions with congressmen, assistance would be made available only in response to sincere requests by governments in evident need, and only in cases where such assistance could be effectively put to use and would be consistent with other United States policies.

Policy-makers at this time retained a capacity to relate American policy to the external actions rather than the domestic structure of foreign powers. The image of a monolithic Communist world had not yet hardened into official orthodoxy. Tito's defection from the Soviet bloc in 1948 was welcomed, and aid was promptly supplied. The offer of Marshall Plan aid announced in 1947 was initially extended not only to Western European states but to the Soviet Union and her Eastern European clients as well. In part, no doubt, this was a shrewd tactical ploy designed to force the Soviet Union to shoulder the blame for the partition of the continent. The offer, however, also revealed an attempt to modify, if possible, the relationships of dependence that the Soviets had so assiduously cultivated in their sphere of influence. Moreover, although the United States offered substantial economic and military assistance to the Nationalist forces in the Chinese civil war, American patience with and support for Chiang Kai-shek were far from unlimited. Suggestions that American combat forces haul Chiang's chestnuts from the fire were consistently rejected. And when he was forced to retreat to Taiwan, proposals that the United States subsidize a military buildup on the island were vetoed by the President, whose policies were consistently Europe-oriented. The Administration prepared to recognize the Maoist regime in Peking, convinced that if the United States could remain aloof from China's internal struggles while the "dust settled in Asia," the natural antipathies of the Chinese and Russians for one another would reassert themselves and provide a basis for an Asian equilibrium.[11]

To implement its objective of containing a Russian imperial thrust, the United States was prepared to experiment with the novel instrument of economic aid. In the Marshall Plan, the Truman Administration combined a humanitarian concern for the fate of starving millions on the continent with a shrewd appraisal of the American interest in Europe's economic reconstruction. Rapid recovery was perceived as the essential prerequisite of a renewed political vitality that might both undermine the appeal of local Communist parties in Italy and France and bolster Western European self-confidence in their ability to resist Soviet pressures. In addition, Washington officials realized that only a prosperous Europe could provide an adequate trading partner for the United States. In formulating the Marshall Plan, America encouraged European initiative, emphasized the importance of Germany's rehabilitation as an integral element in Europe's restoration, and defined the objective positively as the mitigation of Europe's economic distress and political malaise rather than the combating of communism. In so doing, she was able to avoid overtones of paternalism, establish the basis for felicitous ties with the defeated enemy, and, incidentally, exhibit a considerable maturity of political judgment.

As a portent of the future, a token program of technical assistance to the undeveloped nations was simultaneously initiated. Later it was to become virtually an article of faith that in the developing areas containment was synonymous with the elimination of those conditions of economic backwardness in which communism was alleged to thrive.

Containment acquired more distinctively military overtones

---

[11] For a thorough analysis of the evolution of American policy in the Far East, see Tang Tsou, *America's Failure in China 1941–50* (Chicago, Ill.: University of Chicago Press, 1963), esp. Chaps. 11 and 12.

with the negotiation of the North Atlantic Treaty in 1949. That historic decision marked an abandonment of the traditional policy of eschewing peacetime alliances, and was prompted by two basic convictions. First, it was felt that the likelihood of future European wars could be significantly diminished by indicating unequivocally America's intent to resist Soviet aggression in that region. Second, many believed that the Western Europeans would be prepared to invest in their own future only if they were reassured that the fruits of reconstruction would be theirs to enjoy. As one observer put it, the collective defense treaty bore the same relationship to the Marshall Plan that a fence bears to a cornfield. Initially the substance of protection was provided by the unilateral United States nuclear guarantee rather than by a shield of local defense forces.

During the 1950s the containment policy underwent numerous permutations. The Korean war played an especially significant role in shaping its evolution. The blatant invasion of South Korea by Communist forces presumed to be acting as "proxies" for the Soviet Union convinced many American policy-makers that Russia's intentions were militarily aggressive and that hostilities in Europe might be an imminent possibility. While a limited war was being fought in Asia, NATO was transformed into a genuine multinational alliance engaged in coalition military planning, endeavoring to build up an infrastructure for handling logistic support, and promoting the rapid rearmament of its members. The European economic recovery program gave way to a mutual security program designed to facilitate European rearmament. In its anxiety to share the burdens of the common defense, the United States secured the assent of its partners to the rearmament of Germany, and Congress was persuaded of the necessity to deploy American forces on the continent to demonstrate symbolically the organic connection between European and American security.

Outside Europe, following the Korean conflict, the containment policy was "globalized" in terms of operational commitments.[12] Secretary of State Dulles displayed an almost obsessive zeal in recruiting allies from among the fledgling states located along the periphery of the Soviet bloc. SEATO and CENTO, as well as several bilateral mutual defense treaties, were among the products of his labors. Behind his frenetic diplomatic activity and the anti-Communist convictions that he expressed with a theological intensity lay the conviction that, ultimately, the source of policy guidance and direction for all Communist states was to be found in the Kremlin. Apprehensive about the costs of local defense in remote regions and anxious to avoid being drawn into an endless series of "proxy wars" in which the adversary might remain formally uninvolved, the United States elaborated a new strategic doctrine that vaguely threatened the Russians with nuclear retribution for attenuated provocations in peripheral areas.

[12] Brown, *op. cit.*, p. 59.

The frustrations unleashed by the prolonged stalemate in Korea also prompted the formulation of a new declaratory policy for Europe. The Republican Administration that was elected in 1952 promised not to settle for long-term coexistence with the Communist states but rather to pursue the "liberation of the captive nations." However, despite the desire to "grasp the psychological and political offensive" in the cold war, the economy-mindedness of the new Administration prevented the acquisition of capabilities that might have lent an aura of plausibility to its activist rhetoric. The United States instinctively chose to compete on a global basis with the Soviet Union for bases, allies, raw materials, and prestige, but, confronted by overt challenges, President Eisenhower frequently chose, prudently, to temporize. When the efficacy of the Administration's "massive retaliation" strategy—and Mr. Dulles' announced intention to indulge in the delicate art of brinksmanship—were first put to the test in the French-Indochinese war in 1954, proposals to authorize American airstrikes at Dien Bien Phu were rejected, American intervention was shunned, and a negotiated settlement was accepted.[13]

The propaganda directed at Eastern Europe by the Voice of America may have encouraged Hungarian rebels to revolt in 1956. When Russian tanks appeared on the streets of Budapest to suppress the insurrection, Washington issued vehement denunciations of the Russian intervention but provided no material assistance to the insurgents. Limited-liability commitments were shouldered vis-à-vis the regimes of Ngo Dinh Diem in South Vietnam and Nuri El-Said in Iraq. But when the mounting insecurity in the countryside threatened the authority of the former after 1957 and when a bloody coup ousted the latter in 1958, the Eisenhower Administration adopted a posture of watchful waiting, occasional symbolic demonstrations of American concern, and some limited diplomatic and economic assistance.

American policy, however, was not invariably characterized by such quiescence. As the cold war was increasingly interpreted in ideological rather than geopolitical terms, the United States almost instinctively began to associate its interests with more conservative and moderate governments who assiduously eschewed the rhetoric of revolution, paid homage to the virtues of the market economy, and avoided other than pejorative references to Marxism-Leninism. When the Mossadegh government in Iran appeared to threaten substantial Western interests, Mossadegh's downfall was swiftly manipulated. Later when the Arbenz regime in Guatemala allowed Communist influence to wax internally and welcomed military assistance from the Soviet bloc, the CIA engineered a coup and presided over the establishment of a more deferential government. Sensitivity to challenges within the Western Hemisphere remained acute.

At the same time, as the struggle with the Soviet Union assumed global dimensions, American policy-makers became increas-

[13] The United States refused, however, to be a signatory to the Geneva Accords, although in a separate declaration it announced its intention to abide by the terms of the Accord. See Dwight D. Eisenhower, *Mandate for Change* (Garden City, N.Y.: Doubleday, 1963), Chap. 9.

ingly sensitive to the sentiments of the nationalist regimes in the "third world." Secretary of State Dulles at one time may have lectured others on the immorality of cold war "neutralism." But he also began to adapt American policy in the Middle East and other areas to the reality of the neutralist governments and to develop guidelines for avoiding their alienation. The Suez crisis and its aftermath in the Middle East was especially instrumental in crystallizing the subtle shift in the drift of American policy toward the developing countries.[14]

In the 1960s the containment policy evolved with equivalently conflicting tendencies. On the one hand, the former intolerance for neutralism, nonalignment, socialist slogans, and central economic planning gave way to "reform-mongering," ardent faith in the democratic left in Latin America, and a pragmatic approach to the problems of development planning. Doubts were increasingly expressed about the monolithic character of the Communist bloc. Hopes were initially high for a dramatic redefinition of East-West relationships.

On the other hand, the growing power of China, the strident tone of Mao's diplomatic language, Khrushchev's truculence and his insistence upon the legitimacy of "wars of national liberation," the appearance of a Soviet military presence in the Caribbean, and the transformation of Fidel Castro from a guerrilla hero proclaiming liberal objectives into an avowed Marxist-Leninist calling for revolution throughout the hemisphere all prompted Washington to become more and more preoccupied with the problems of insurgency. Convinced that guerrilla warfare represented the latest instrument devised by the Communist world for the penetration of societies in the process of modernization, the Kennedy Administration assiduously sought to equip itself with the instruments of counterinsurgency. With new capabilities in the hands of an activist Administration, the temptation to intervene proved irresistible on several occasions. Cuba became the target of a counterrevolutionary invasion by Cuban exiles trained and equipped by the United States.[15] Increased military assistance was provided to South Vietnam in 1961. Almost inadvertently, American prestige became associated with the performance of the Diem government, so that disengagement from the internal war being waged in that land proved increasingly difficult to conceive. An attempted coup d'état in the Dominican Republic, led by men suspected of being vulnerable to the influence of shadowy Castroite elements, prompted the intervention of American marines in 1965.

America's growing military involvement in the Vietnamese war has been rationalized in terms of the importance of protecting the Vietnamese people from surreptitious "indirect aggression" by guerrilla warriors supplied and commanded by a neighboring state. Earlier, in the Cuban missile crisis of October, 1962, the requirements

---

[14] Brown, op. cit., Chap. 9.

[15] Preparations for a possible invasion were initiated by the Central Intelligence Agency during the last year of the Eisenhower Administration. See Theodore Draper, Castro's Revolution (New York, N.Y.: Praeger, 1962), Chap. 2.

of containment had been interpreted to include the frustration of a Soviet attempt to qualitatively alter the strategic and political balance dramatically through the clandestine establishment of missile bases in the Western Hemisphere. Aside from the anti-Communist reflex, no single common thread unites these various activities committed in the name of containment. What seems evident, indeed, is that, as the initial objectives of the containment policy were successfully achieved, the desire to define the conditions of a new world order began to inspire American policies—which, however, continue to be justified in the familiar terminology of containment.

Permanent friends and occasional allies

The continuity of American foreign policy is to be seen not only in the bedrock of principles, traditions, and policies that have informed past conduct but in the amity or enmity that Americans have held for particular foreign states. Geopolitical conditions have prompted those special relations with Western Hemispheric states enunciated in the Monroe Doctrine. America's political traditions and cultural legacy have been obtained from Great Britain, and to a slightly lesser extent from continental European countries. The structure of contemporary world politics encourages a special "love-hate" relationship with the two major Communist powers, the Soviet Union and the People's Republic of China.

In the Western Hemisphere the United States became—in the course of the nineteenth century—simply too large, too industrially competent, and too powerful relative to its neighbors to the north and south for a system of equilibrium to be created in the Americas. American land-hunger was largely sated by westward expansion, and the glories of imperial rule over other peoples aroused a notable indifference. American ascendancy has thus been mild; Pax Americana consists of a "combination of hegemony and the good-neighbor policy." [16] The political boundaries of states in the inter-American system have been generally accepted for more than a half century. The United States has been a creditor of substantial leniency. Occasionally (though by no means invariably), confiscatory policies toward the property of American nationals have been tolerated. Institutions have been created that serve to inhibit unilateral intervention by the United States in Latin American politics. At the same time, the Caribbean has been referred to as an "American lake" and has been the location of the most frequent and flagrant exercises of Dollar Diplomacy and the most recent efforts to dispatch unpalatable governments through covert and/or overt military pressures.

The United States enjoys its most congenial relations with states possessing comparable social and political systems, democratic traditions, open societies, and mixed economies. Above all, the British, the Scandinavian states, and the older Dominions in the British

[16] Aron, *Peace and War*, p. 153.

Commonwealth may be considered "permanent friends." Despite occasional conflicts of interest on specific issues, it is virtually impossible to conceive of military conflict with these states. A "special relationship" with the British is the product of shared language, historic memories, and political traditions. It is expressed in the candor of official relations at various levels of government and in the access available to leaders in both states to informed opinion in the other society.

Relationships with the continental European states have been less firmly grounded in emotional affinity and genuine empathy. Relations with the French have been marked historically by misunderstandings and abrasive experiences. Still, France is America's oldest ally. In the twentieth century the two countries have always fought side by side. They remain a part of the North Atlantic security community, within which no plans are laid for the contingency of being at war with one another. Suffice it to say that the political styles of the French and Americans are more difficult to reconcile, and the requirements of their respective roles—the one an intermediate power seeking to reestablish its diplomatic independence and grandeur, the other an imperial power seeking to maintain the integrity of its grand strategy—render more difficult the synchronization of policy than is the case with Great Britain.

America has fought two wars with Germany in the past half century. Since 1945, however, the Federal Republic of Germany has been among its most steadfast associates and deferential partners. Despite a healthy number of German-American immigrants, relations between these two countries reflect geopolitical calculations rather than mutual affection. Although the United States has officially proclaimed its desire to promote the reunification of that troubled country, wartime memories, an awareness of the reservations of other Western European allies, and an instinctive sympathy for those Central European states whose creation owed something to Wilson's enthusiasm for the principle of self-determination (Czechoslovakia, and Poland in its modern incarnation) have affected the intensity with which this goal has been pursued.

With the Soviet Union the United States has been thrust into a relationship of "enemy-partner." Strategic interests have occasionally acquired a congruence that superseded the incompatibility of their ideological principles or differences in sociopolitical systems. A common interest in protecting China from Japanese incursions was manifested in the 1930s. Joint interests propelled them into wartime alliance against the Fascist powers. As the most powerful and the most vulnerable states in a nuclear world, they share the deepest possible interest in peaceful or competitive coexistence. Relative to the major potential or actual revisionist powers—China and Germany —the United States and the U.S.S.R. possess some common interests, as evidenced by their mutual efforts to arrest the spread of nuclear weapons, and their mutual wooing of India and Japan. The spontaneous sympathy that Russian and American people have for one another is hardly matched, however, by candor and trust between their respective governments. This reflects both the previously mentioned "fatality of position" and the legacy of animosity that is the product of ideology and history.

With respect to China the United States retains an even greater ambivalence. Historically, the United States assumed the role of protector of China's territorial integrity. Recognizing Japan as a potential rival, Americans, following the turn of the twentieth century, considered the Chinese as their most promising and natural associate in the Far East. Though Sino-American relations were somewhat superficial through the first half of the century, Americans reacted to the Communist seizure of power in China as though their friendship had been betrayed. Subsequently, the self-conscious effort to isolate China diplomatically and economically has been carried out with all the vengeance of a rejected suitor.

Japan, meanwhile, has ceased to be considered a rival and enemy. Since 1945 that relationship has been transformed into one of firm friendship. Underlying bonds of interest are reinforced by a growing mutual respect and affection. Elsewhere in Asia, the Philippines have a special attraction for America as a result of the transitory experience of colonial rule. Otherwise, relations with Asian powers are more likely to reflect strategic and political calculations than historic ties of friendship or enmity.

The existence of a large indigenous Negro population has complicated America's relations to the African continent, encouraging a persistent policy of abstinence from unilateral engagements there. A vocal supporter of African independence movements, the United States has thus far committed meager funds to African development programs and has shunned unilateral military interventions on that continent, preferring to work through the multilateral framework of the United Nations both for purposes of policing domestic strife and promoting economic development. In the Middle East, America has enjoyed a special paternal relationship with Israel, although some efforts have also been made to cement closer relations with the Arab world.

The legacy of America's past and its political beliefs

To summarize, America's past experiences in world politics have left their indelible mark on its contemporary conduct in the form of peculiar reflexes, habits, perspectives, and axioms of policy. Several generalizations seem warranted.

1. The American concern with the perils of unrestrained power is as evident in foreign affairs as in its domestic political institutions. Isolationism was to some extent a policy of self-denial. In

the Monroe Doctrine, reciprocal restraints upon the European states were enunciated. The Open Door policy revealed, among other things, an unwillingness to participate actively in the despoiling and dismembering of China. Reluctant intervention in World War I was justified in terms of America's desire for "peace without victory" and "a world made safe for democracy." Following the Second World War, the responsibilities of military occupation were exercised in Germany and Japan in a manner designed to hasten the day of departure for the occupational authorities and to reintroduce former enemies to the comity of Western nations. The containment policy discloses a basically defensive posture. The vision of world order implicit in all these policies is pluralistic—a world composed of many sovereign nation-states or regional federations.

2. America's tradition in foreign relations is determinedly liberal. The principles of self-government, self-determination, and noninterference continue to exert their insistent influence on contemporary policies—even if they frequently assume an ironical form. They explain America's reluctance to become aligned against the newly independent states of Asia and Africa, despite security commitments to European colonial powers in the 1950s. These principles suggest as well why relations with the democracies have been generally facile and felicitous, those with authoritarian or totalitarian regimes more tenuous and tempestuous. They suggest why the principal touchstone of American policy in the postwar period has been the desire to implement the guiding principle of collective security, that is, the maintenance of the territorial status quo against forceful disruption, and why the United States has been prepared at times even to implement that principle unilaterally. Even the recent interventions in the Dominican Republic and Vietnam were based upon sincere—if not entirely unchallengeable—suppositions of externally manipulated pressures upon indigenous political movements in those countries.

3. Little in its past could have prepared the United States for political relationships marked by a measure of both amity and enmity. On the contrary, American intervention into world politics has regularly occurred at times when enmities seemed both fixed and total. "Instead of a succession of limited antagonisms and limited cooperation, characteristic of moderate periods, the United States has experienced a succession of unlimited enmities." [17] In two general wars in the twentieth century, Americans viewed themselves as the children of light doing battle with the forces of darkness. After 1945 Russia simply replaced Germany as the enemy, even as Russia is now being displaced by China.

Nor has the United States been prepared by its past experiences for relationships of equality. Within the Western camp, the

[17] Stanley Hoffmann, "The American Style," *Foreign Affairs* (January 1968), p. 366.

United States has dealt primarily with clients or with smaller and less powerful associates.[18] Much less frequently has it had to ponder the problem of getting along with equals. To be sure, the United States has been disposed toward the creation of a continental-sized political entity in Western Europe. Only recently, however, has it had to cope with the hard bargaining that in the future is likely to characterize American relations with the European Economic Community.

4. This brief historical survey is sufficient to identify the pronounced tendency of the United States to invoke universal formulas to justify specific actions. The desire to derive general norms to govern foreign policy behavior is a persistent trait, nowhere revealed more vividly than in the justifications for armed combat. The Spanish-American War was fought "to liberate Cubans," World War I "to make the world safe for democracy," World War II to defend the principles of the Atlantic Charter, and the Korean "police action" to absolve the theory of collective security. American policy in Vietnam has been variously rationalized in terms of the objectives of "frustrating aggression," "containing communism," and preserving South Vietnam's right to self-determination. American historical experience suggests difficulties in basing particular policies on the specific merits and circumstances of individual cases, and an affinity for universalizing the significance of individual policies, though the constellation of circumstances giving rise to them may have been unique. The dangers are obvious. By justifying political activities in terms of moral principles, policies may become rigid, compromise solutions may be more difficult to obtain, the liquidation of imprudent commitments may become the more politically distasteful, and the acknowledgment of the legitimate interests of friends and adversaries may be somewhat obscured.

At the same time American policy-makers have proved themselves capable of identifying a substantial measure of congruence between concrete interests and historic ideals throughout the postwar period. Confronted by Soviet leaders promoting the development of a monolithic, totalitarian world order, the American ideal of self-determination appears to have been an entirely appropriate ideology to fortify the determination of other peoples to resist Communist threats to their independence. The idea that government derives its legitimacy solely from the consent of the governed likewise proved to be a useful instrument of containment at a time when Communist societies were uniformly ruled with a heavy hand by autocratic leaders displaying little responsiveness to public sentiments. More recently the emphasis given to the concept of a "pluralistic world" in the official utterances of American statesmen reflects the shrewd perception that it may contribute to a diminution of Soviet domination of its former satellites in Eastern Europe.[19]

---

[18] Ibid.

[19] Brown, op. cit., pp. 16, 311.

Dogmatic adherence to principles such as self-determination, peaceful change, noninterference or collective security may result in rigid policies yielding disastrous results. When they are adjusted to a prudent sensitivity to balance-of-power considerations and an awareness of the frustrations that invariably attend the application of principles to political situations, they may contribute to the efficacy and success of American diplomacy.

4

Political culture

Political culture is a concept that only recently has acquired currency in the literature of political science. General agreement upon its precise meaning has not yet been reached. Some employ it to describe the "pattern of individual attitudes and orientations toward politics among the members of a political system." [1] Thus it refers to the subjective realm of ideas and perspectives that underlie the actions of participants in a political system. Others use the concept to embrace a wide variety of societal influences on the politics of a nation.

In America both the socioeconomic order and the political system enjoy a measure of relative autonomy. A dialectic of sorts exists between the two, the character of society imposing limits and influencing the character of the political system even as it is being reshaped increasingly by decisions taken within the political arena. In this chapter, attention is directed to those features of the socio-economic system—social structure, economic organization, cultural homogeneity of the populace, and perspectives of the social and political leadership—that have a more or less direct influence on the character of American foreign policy. An attempt is also made to identify the peculiarities of the American "national style." Since hard and fast conclusions are elusive, suggestive or superficially plausible hypotheses are asserted in hopes of provoking further inquiry into this all too often neglected area.

[1] Almond and Powell, *Comparative Politics: A Developmental Approach*, p. 50.

The American political community

The United States is one of the few genuine political communities in the contemporary world.[2] The central institutions of the United States government not only possess autonomy and sufficient authority to enforce legal rules throughout the length and breadth of the country but are accepted as legitimate by virtually all socially and politically significant groups.[3] Political habits and values are widely shared across regional, ethnic, class, and professional lines. Individuals and groups vary with respect to the priority they attach to the importance of security, welfare, fiscal responsibility, unrestricted market transactions, continued economic growth, and so forth, but all are aims that fall well within the social consensus. The political consensus is perhaps even stronger. It rests upon the proposition that conflicts among interests are a natural condition, politics the natural method for reconciling such conflicts. In America, the *public interest* is identified neither with abstract concepts of justice nor associated with the parochial interests of a particular class. Rather it is believed to be discoverable through the process of group politics operating within the limits of accepted procedures and constitutional processes.

This consensus on fundamental political values is undergirded by a firm sense of national consciousness. Crystallized by the Revolution, American nationalism was early expressed in the Declaration of Independence. Subsequently, the restless westward movement of the pioneers added new sections to the American nation and exacerbated sectional loyalties in the South even as other regional particularities were eroded and national feeling reinforced.[4]

The symbolic ties that bind an immigrant people have to be somewhat artifically contrived. And so they were. Partisan leaders were transformed into popular heroes. Legends about the American past were self-consciously created. The absence of any common sense of identity lent special urgency to the quest for a national purpose. Daniel Boorstin aptly has suggested that "the extravagance of Fourth of July rhetoric was . . . a measure less of the depth than of the uncertainties of national patriotism." [5] Nevertheless, this "language of reassurance" produced a national sentiment that proved to be remarkably resilient in the face of additional waves of immigration in the nineteenth century. There were, to be sure, other reasons for this national sentiment. An open frontier provided limitless opportunities, the public schools developed into remarkably efficient socializing

[2] In the sense in which that term is used by Stanley Hoffmann in his essay, "The Fate of the Nation-State," *Daedalus* (Summer 1966), pp. 904–905.

[3] The rhetoric of the New Left, Radical Right, and some militant Black Power groups to the contrary notwithstanding.

[4] See Godfried van Benthem van den Bergh, "Contemporary Nationalism in the Western World," *Daedalus* (Summer 1966), pp. 849–851.

[5] Boorstin, *The Americans*, p. 389.

institutions for millions of "hyphenated-Americans," and the Anglo-Saxon majority remained substantial for some time.

All of these factors facilitated the assimilation of a polyglot people into the American nation. Fortunately, the nationalism espoused by the American people has been political rather than tribal. Fashioned by an immigrant people without a unique culture, a common ancestry, a classical literature and religion, or epic historical experiences, American nationalism could be satisfactorily based only upon a common commitment to certain fixed political ideas. There is no American race to gather into a specific Lebensraum, no superior American culture to impose on inferior peoples. There are, however, certain principles of government whose transmission to others has always been a part of the national mission.

A firm sense of national consciousness dictates no specific courses of action in foreign policy. It has left its mark, however, in the zeal American statesmen display in safeguarding their own sovereign prerogatives. Though Americans are often disposed to prescribe supranational cures to the ills besetting others, not one iota of American sovereignty has been sacrificed in order to build wider political communities in the world.

It has taken considerably longer to nationalize and homogenize society than it did to contrive a national consciousness. Indeed the task is far from completed. Forty million immigrants have been successfully assimilated since 1820. Those include 6.7 million from Germany, 4.9 million from Italy, 4.6 million from Ireland, approximately 3 million from Poland, 3.8 million from Great Britain, 3.6 million from Canada and Newfoundland, and 3.3 million from territories now in the Soviet Union. Restrictive immigration legislation passed in the 1920s cut the flow to a trickle, and in recent decades the numbers of foreign-born Americans has declined dramatically. By 1960 70 percent of the population of nearly 180,000,000 was native-born white of native-born parents.[6]

At one time the ethnic composition of the American population played a possibly decisive role in inclining the United States toward an isolationist posture in world affairs. Resistance to involvement in World Wars I and II was most intense among German-Americans and Irish-Americans—the former because such intervention was to be directed against their former homeland, the latter because they had little enthusiasm about providing aid and assistance to the British. No equivalent restraints inhibit American interventionism today, nor have they since 1945. When virtually all of the countries in Western Europe from whom the American population had been derived could unite to request American assistance against an unequivocal threat, aid was freely and swiftly made available. Indeed, since Germany was divided and exposed to pressures from the East, and since Irish Catholics recognized a common cause with their persecuted co-religionists in Eastern Europe, the groups formerly

[6] Brzezinski and Huntington, *Political Power USA/USSR*, p. 131.

most doctrinaire in their isolationism became the most fervent advocates of cold war interventionism.[7]

In the 1960s tensions between ethnic groups have been superseded somewhat by an incipient polarization of American society along racial lines. The most evident division in the United States is now between the white majority and a twenty-million Negro minority of black citizens who have found full membership in American society elusive, at the very least. Prolonged procrastination in yielding civil rights and social justice to Negroes has caused many black leaders to stridently reject the social and political institutions in America as intrinsically racist. A presidential commission which studied the nature and causes of civil disorders likewise concluded that white racism was one of the root causes of such disorders in urban America. Implicit in the turmoil of America's cities is the ugly threat of racial animosity and communal strife on a wide scale. That threat makes vivid and relevant a martyred President's "acute and anguished sense of the fragility of the membranes of civilization, stretched so thin over a nation so disparate in its composition, so tense in its interior relationships, so cunningly enmeshed in underground fears and antagonisms, so entrapped by history in the ethos of violence." [8]

Nevertheless, no specifically Negro subculture exists on foreign policy questions. With respect to the Vietnamese war, for example, the leaders of the black community express a variety of views, reflecting generally the broad divisions provoked by that conflict in the society as a whole. Some Black Power enthusiasts express a vicarious sense of identity with national liberation movements in the formerly colonial areas, some have adopted the idiom of anti-Western nationalism, and some openly urge their followers to overthrow the "racist power structure" of white America. Others, like the late Dr. Martin Luther King, have been outspoken critics of some elements of contemporary American foreign policy on grounds that resources were being diverted to peripheral enterprises abroad that might more appropriately be devoted to the amelioration of poverty at home. Still others, such as prominent leaders of the National Association for the Advancement of Colored People (NAACP) and the Urban League, have continued to endorse the broad objectives of American foreign policy, and have sought to dissociate the civil rights movement from what they considered imprudent alliances with various groups primarily concerned with foreign policy questions.

The foreign policy implications of the American racial crisis are at best obscure. Evidence of racial intolerance at home complicates American relations with non-Western peoples. The effort to redress injustices at home subconsciously influences American judgments on African issues. Above all, the growing crisis of the ghetto raises anew the question of whether the nation has the resources—

[7] Samuel Lubell, *The Future of American Politics* (New York, N.Y.: Harper, 1951), esp. Chap. 7, for an analysis of the ethnic basis of American isolationism.

[8] Schlesinger, *A Thousand Days*, p. 725.

financial, moral, and psychological—to simultaneously conduct an active foreign policy and cope with the enormous problems associated with the reconstruction of the cities and the assimilation of the American Negro into a full participation in American society.

Two other foreign policy subcultures warrant a brief comment. The Radical Right and the New Left both display a pronounced alienation from many features of contemporary foreign policy and even from the institutions that make and execute those policies. Both profess a belief that the government is managed by a misguided and malevolent "Establishment." Whereas members of the Radical Right fear an "invisible government" controlled by "Eastern Liberals" (and especially by members of the Council on Foreign Relations), the New Left apprehends a sinister conspiracy of military and industrial elites. Both groups nourish certain foreign policy views that are decidedly beyond the margins of the contemporary American consensus. Both share a distaste for the contingencies of politics and a zest for simple solutions to complex problems. Their diagnoses of America's difficulties and their prescriptions for its ills, of course, diverge. The paranoia of the Right continues to focus on fears of a conspiratorial world Communist movement; [9] that of the Left is animated by the foreboding that America has itself become a "reactionary, counterrevolutionary, imperialistic power." The Radical Right demands that the cold war be ended by winning it; the New Left that it be superseded by a "peace race" or by a renewed commitment to revolutionary efforts to overcome poverty and injustice in the world. In this respect both dissenting groups reveal a thoroughly American attitude in what Kenneth Waltz has termed their "passion for victory." [10]

American politics has been marked by the persistence of conflict among well-organized groups. What is truly remarkable, however, is the degree to which such conflicts have been contained by an abiding consensus on principles and upon governmental procedures. The moderation of American politics is at least partly attributable to the pattern of political socialization. In the United States, responsibility for socializing the young into the political system and for shaping the attitudes of individuals toward political institutions, procedures, policy-makers, and established or alternative public policies is widely shared. The family, schools, churches, civic associations, and the mass media all contribute independently to the induction of individuals into the political system. They cultivate a sense of national loyalty and the development of public interest in the political system, the values it preserves, the institutions that embody those values, and the "rules of the political game" that govern their operation. Patriotic sentiments may be evoked or inculcated by some political substructures, partisan instincts developed by others. Reactions toward incumbents in specific offices and guidance on concrete policy issues are likewise shaped by diverse influences.

[9] See Richard Hofstadter, *The Paranoid Style in American Politics and Other Essays* (New York, N.Y.: Vintage, 1967).

[10] Waltz, *Foreign Policy and Democratic Politics*, p. 73.

In America, the principle of separating powers has been applied not only to the "output" structures of government, that is, the legislative, executive, and judicial branches of government, but to the informal political substructures such as parties, interest groups, and the media of political communication as well. With responsibility for political socialization diffused among these substructures, no group is likely to develop more than a partial claim on an individual. Since most individuals belong to a variety of groups possessing diverse outlooks and organized for different purposes, their attitudes may be moderated as a result of the cross-pressures induced by overlapping memberships. The result is a political culture that has been impressively homogeneous.

America's homogeneous political culture contrasts sharply with some continental European states that still possess fragmented political cultures with relatively little overlapping between distinct Catholic, liberal, and working-class subcultures. With the possible exception of an incipient racial cleavage and the Radical Right and New Left foreign policy subcultures previously alluded to, no such conflicts among separate and distinct subcultures exists in the United States. Generally, interest group conflict is moderated by the fact that lobbying groups have overlapping memberships. Conflict between the political parties is moderated by their realization that they must compete for many of the same blocs of voters. Executive-legislative struggles are softened by party competition across institutional boundaries. As the sociologist E. A. Ross once observed, "A society which is ridden by a dozen oppositions along lines running in every direction may actually be in less danger of . . . falling to pieces than one split just along one line. For each new cleavage contributes to narrow the cross clefts, so that one might say that society is sewn together by its inner conflicts." [11] The overlapping memberships that are characteristic of America's homogeneous political culture promote stability and moderation, then, by encouraging the acceptance of limits to political rivalries and the acknowledgment of "rules" to the political game.

In such an atmosphere, policy-making takes on a pragmatic or empirical cast. Political groups confront one another in an adversary system to engage in arm's-length bargaining, trading votes for policies, assent for special dispensations, acceptance of general principles for generous portions of "pork." The general disposition toward policy-making is experimental. Proposals are treated like hypotheses that are framed in order to be tested and perhaps modified. If the intensity of American politics has generally been kept within bounds, this is because the stakes for which groups contend have been generally low. But when the stakes increase, as in the struggles over American policy in Southeast Asia in the mid-1960's, the fabled "consensus" on policy may be shaken and the agreement to accept certain procedures for changing policy may be threatened.

[11] Edward A. Ross, *The Principles of Sociology* (New York, N.Y.: Century, 1920), p. 165; quoted by Huntington, *The Common Defense*, pp. 422–423.

More normally, neither *avant-garde radical dissenters* like the New Left nor *ideologically conservative opposition groups* such as are to be found on the Radical Right exercise more than a slight influence in prompting incremental shifts in the consensus undergirding American foreign policy. The considerable constancy of American foreign policy in the postwar period, as Seyom Brown has contended, is largely attributable to the central emphasis placed upon sustaining policies that guarantee American survival, protect its security, provide conditions in which a liberal constitution may be preserved, and promote the general welfare and economic prosperity of the whole society. Varying combinations of these values may be pursued by different Presidents, but their range of choice is strictly limited by the necessity of avoiding the ultimate choices between security, freedom, prosperity, and welfare. Radical dissenters may invoke one set of American values to promote changes of policy that would give greater emphasis to welfare considerations; conservative dissenters may invoke equally traditional values to support their demands for policies which emphasize national security or which would permit a balanced budget. The resolution of policy disputes, however, depends less on finding an ideological synthesis than upon the mobilization of facts, the analysis of conditions, and competitive efforts to find a mutually satisfactory set of policies which respond to the "least common denominator of political demand, . . . the nation's interest in its own survival and those conditions which allow for the perpetuation of the nation's essential sociopolitical patterns." [12] In short, the outcome of the dialectic between dissenting groups and the *pragmatic middle* generally turns on changes in the international or domestic situation that prompt the moderates to support marginal or incremental changes in policy. In this respect America's political culture is *secular;* bargaining and accommodative behavior are the rule rather than the exception.

The American socioeconomic system

In the extreme fragmentation of power in the American government, one finds traces of the Tudor origins of her political institutions.[13] But though the American political system may possess a somewhat antique character, its society is among the most modern in the world. There is, in fact, a stark contrast between the continuity of American political institutions and the revolutionary pace at which social and economic change are generated and absorbed in the United States. Scientific and technical knowledge is being discovered at an exponential rate. The methods and discoveries of science are applied to practical affairs in America with an enthusiasm unmatched by any

[12] Brown, *The Faces of Power*, p. 8.

[13] For an analysis of the origins of those institutions, see Samuel P. Huntington, "Political Modernization in Europe and America," *World Politics*, XVIII (April, 1966), pp. 378–414.

other society. America is a future-oriented society. It is about to become the first to enter the postindustrial phase of its development.[14] One prominent scholar has even referred to the United States as the world's first *technetronic* society, that is, the first society to be decisively shaped by technology and electronics.[15]

These developments are accentuating many social and economic trends that have long been in evidence. They may be producing a transition as fundamental as the transformation of European society from an agrarian to an industrial basis. America is, at the very least, a mature industrial society. There is an extensive division of labor and a pronounced specialization of economic and social roles. Access to political, social, and economic leadership positions is based upon merit rather than ascription, as befits an advanced, achievement-oriented society. More than half of the labor force is no longer involved in the production of tangible goods; America has become the world's first "service economy." [16] As American society has become more and more complex, the scope of governmental authority has become more pervasive. This in turn has encouraged more and more groups to press their claims to social rights and privileges through governmental channels. While one consequence of this is to promote the organization of associational, institutional, and professional lobbying groups, another is to enhance the government's capacity to define those few objectives that a major portion of the nation's resources are mobilized to achieve.

American capitalism is no longer a laissez faire system dominated by the captains of industry—if indeed that was ever an accurate portrait of the United States economy. Despite the development of extensive governmental regulatory authority over the economy, the means of production are largely in the hands of private or corporate groups. Market forces are still relied upon to discipline prices and stimulate economy growth. Though economic planning is no longer considered anathema in America, it occurs *within* rather than *above* the corporate giants, and is thus neither centralized nor authoritarian planning. Though some redistribution of income is carried out under governmental auspices, equality of condition—as opposed to equality of opportunity—is accorded scant acceptance as a socially desirable goal. In short, America's is a mixed economy in which the private sector retains its resilience and remains in the ascendant.

It is scarcely surprising that private economic interests exercise considerable influence on foreign policy decisions and quite frequently pose problems for the makers of foreign policy. Efforts by

[14] See Daniel Bell, "Notes on a Post-Industrial Society," *Public Interest* (Winter 1967), pp. 24–36.

[15] See Zbigniew K. Brzezinski, "America in a Technetronic Age, *Encounter* (January 1968), pp. 16–26.

[16] Virtually all of the increase in new employment achieved during the past two decades has come in the service industries, for example, banks, hospitals, schools, and retail stores. See Victor R. Fuchs, "The First Service Economy," *Public Interest* (Winter 1966), pp. 7–17.

private groups to gain access to economic opportunities abroad, to avert discriminatory legislation by hostile foreign governments, or to protect their overseas investments often galvanize the government into action. American foreign-policy-makers are surely subject to pressures quite unfamiliar to Soviet officials presiding over a statist economy. Other Western governments encounter such pressures to a lesser degree, but the American commitment to free enterprise renders its officials somewhat more deferential to private business interests than is generally the case elsewhere. Hostile reactions to the nationalization of American property have occasionally been contained, but the reflex to impose strong sanctions is there, particularly in Congress, which aptly has been described as the "thermos bottle of American resentment" to confiscatory expropriation.[17]

Annual *per capita* income in America is approaching $4000. Thus the United States is on the threshold of postindustrial status.[18] Because it is the world's most prosperous society, American patterns of economic organization have become models inspiring emulation. American industry, for example, is characterized by large firms enjoying impressive resources for internal financing and heavily subsidized by the government in the realm of research and development. Control of the large firms has generally passed from the owners to professional managers, whose sophisticated techniques of policy-making and control have been refined in the process of organizing a continental market.[19] Little wonder that subsidiaries of American corporations have been among the prime beneficiaries of the creation of a market of equivalent size in Europe. One French observer has even claimed that the organization of the European market, in the ninth year of the Common Market, is essentially American.[20]

These American corporations are forcefully challenging more traditional patterns of industrial production and management in Europe. Indeed, the challenge they pose to the Europeans extends beyond the realm of industrial management into their educational systems, tax systems, intellectual perspectives, and governmental policies. The so-called "technological gap" is also a "managerial gap," and is becoming a "cultural gap." It is feeding an incipient sense of American superiority, nourishing European apprehensions, and provoking misunderstandings and resentments within the Atlantic world.

American subsidiaries in Europe represent examples of a more general phenomenon, the multinational corporation. Originating largely in the United States, many such corporations are organized to seek out markets as though national boundaries did not exist. In

[17] Hoffmann, *The State of War*, p. 177.

[18] For a discussion of general features of a postindustrial society, see Herman Kahn and Anthony Wiener, *The Year 2000* (New York, N.Y.: Macmillan, 1967), Chap. 4 and *passim*.

[19] See John K. Galbraith, *The New Industrial State* (New York, N.Y.: Houghton, Mifflin, 1967).

[20] See Jean-Jacques Servan-Schreiber's celebrated book, *The American Challenge* (New York, N.Y.: Atheneum, 1968).

some cases products are manufactured in one country, processed and assembled in a second, and marketed in still a third. Siblings are constantly evolving, and they adopt nationalities that appear convenient from the standpoint of tax advantages, labor supply, or available capital. As such corporations acquire multiple nationalities, they come under the effective jurisdiction of several governments. Problems may arise along with opportunities. Reactions by different governments to the problems of East-West trade and military procurement, attitudes toward planning and competition, and balance-of-payments problems may be quite diverse. Diplomatic complications are an inevitable by-product. Nevertheless, such corporations are likely to become significant vehicles for diffusing scientific and technological knowledge to other industrial states and for transmitting to the world the ethos of American business enterprise, the pragmatic spirit of American managers and entrepreneurs, the values of a competitive market, and the importance of boldness in technological innovation strategies. In the underdeveloped world, the appearance of the most modern industrial firms alongside primitive enterprises may merely dramatize more poignantly the increasing differentiation of mankind, thus sharpening the lines between the postindustrial, industrial, and industrializing areas of the world.

Whereas the development of American society may provide new vehicles for the transmission of its influence abroad, the growing complexity of that society may also reduce the flexibility of the nation's diplomacy. In the "technetronic age," the industrial process is no longer the main determinant of science and technology. Universities, research institutions, professional societies, and governmental agencies have been thrust into increasing prominence as the sources of innovative ideas. Knowledge has, perhaps, replaced property or wealth as the renewable basis of power in America. Accompanying this transformation is an accentuation of the dispersal of political power and a reinforcement of social pluralism with respect to both values and interests. The scientific estate has taken its place alongside the political, administrative, and professional estates.[21] Political power is further dispersed. Consequently, the problems of organizing a consensus for a course of action, mobilizing consent for a given policy, or consulting all the relevant experts and assimilating their myriad perspectives into a considered judgment as to what to do or how to act are compounded. The calculations political leaders must make regarding the manipulation of the political costs of alternative policies are likewise complicated. In short, as society becomes more complex and interdependent, it acquires a quasi-corporate character. If such a society is to move at all, its various parts must move together. The effect of this may be a considerable bias in favor of the perpetuation of policies previously adopted, since agreement on a change of course is difficult to arrange. Thus the range of politically feasible choices may ironically be narrowed even as novel technical

[21] See Don K. Price, *The Scientific Estate* (Cambridge, Mass.: Belknap, 1965).

and economic instruments of foreign policy become available for the first time.

A conservative bias may also be built into foreign policy by the general level of affluence enjoyed by Americans. A sated society is naturally more likely to settle for the status quo, less likely to select leaders prepared to run great risks in foreign ventures, less likely to be attracted by the prospects of territorial conquest, and very likely to be perfectly capable of extending its prosperity through the skillful management of its domestic resources.

Political leadership in America

In a democratic system, political leaders tend to mirror the values of their society. They also tend to display in their perspectives on policy the experiences that marked their paths to leadership positions. Thus one may view political leadership as a medium through which the values implicit in the American social, economic, and political order are transmitted into the content and style of American foreign policy.

Access into the elites

Access to leadership positions in politics is as open in America as in perhaps any society in the world. Men of humble and affluent backgrounds have proved equally adept at conquering the heights of American politics. Franklin Roosevelt and John Kennedy enjoyed substantial advantages in terms of wealth, education, travel, and family connections. Harry Truman, Dwight Eisenhower, and Lyndon Johnson all rose out of rather modest middle-class environments to achieve the Presidency. Consequently, politics is justifiably considered a source of social mobility in America.

Heretofore, the bulk of America's political leadership has been supplied by white Anglo-Saxon Protestants (WASPs). Their dominance has, however, been subsiding in recent years. John Kennedy, a Catholic, achieved the Presidency in 1960. A Negro, Edward Brooke, is already widely considered as a future possibility for national office, having been elected to the Senate in 1966. Thus ethnic and religious barriers are being rapidly eroded by electoral realities.

Negroes remain seriously underrepresented in the American government. Although Negroes constitute 10 percent of the total population, Carl Rowan, who served as the Director of the United States Information Agency for several years, is virtually the only member of his race to achieve a prominent position in the foreign policy establishment. Black Americans are equally conspicuous by their absence in the highest ranks of the military bureaucracies.

Although men of low estate but great ambition and talent may rise quickly in politics, the significance of wealth, social position, and education to a political career are revealed by the social origins of America's top political leaders. Roughly 60 percent of the leaders in Congress and the Administration come from upper-class or middle-class backgrounds. Consequently, those who formulate and execute American foreign policy are more than likely to be the sons of professional men, business executives, owners of corporations, and others who have been successful and who possess an active stake in the society.

Nor are there notable differences in the social origins of political and societal leaders.[22] Indeed, the entire leadership stratum in America possesses a considerable homogeneity. Most leaders are comfortably endowed with material possessions, display a somewhat conservative bias, and are equipped by experience to move easily back and forth between the worlds of business, commerce, law, and education on the one hand and government service on the other. Dean Acheson, James Forrestal, Robert Lovett, John Foster Dulles, and John McCloy were all recruited from Wall Street for service in the foreign policy agencies; Charles Wilson and Robert McNamara came to the Defense Department from industry; McGeorge Bundy, Walt W. Rostow, and John Kenneth Galbraith to the White House and the Foreign Service from the university, and Dean Rusk to the State Department from a great philanthropic foundation. This is not to be viewed as evidence of a conspiratorial "power elite" or the existence of an "invisible government." Rather it attests to the diversity of the sources of political recruitment and explains the congruence in the outlooks of political and societal leaders. It also provides a clue to the sorts of perspective political leaders may have acquired by virtue of experience in other professions.

The "bureaucratic pragmatism" of foreign policy leaders

As Henry Kissinger has observed, foreign policy executives tend to operate on the basis of assumptions, attitudes, and perspectives that are rooted in their previous experiences. Insofar as the leaders of America's foreign policy agencies are normally recruited from the ranks of electoral politicians, lawyers, and businessmen, it is scarcely surprising that they reveal qualities of "bureaucratic pragmatism." [23]

Electoral politicians. In America politics is not the province of philosopher-kings deducing the national interest from abstract principles. Rather, it is a craft practiced by shrewd negotiators who generally recognize that the national interest is to be found among the common aims of different people.[24] Above all, American politicians are skillful brokers. They must necessarily deal with a wide range of interests, seeking to balance them against one another to achieve a resolution satisfactory to representatives of rival factions as well as to their own hopes of future electoral success. Typically, prominent

[22] See Brzezinski and Huntington, *Political Power USA/USSR*, Chap. 4.

[23] See Henry Kissinger, "Domestic Structure and Foreign Policy," *Daedalus* (Spring 1966), pp. 514–518.

[24] Charles E. Lindblom, *Bargaining: The Hidden Hand in Government*, The RAND Corporation, RM-1434-RC (Santa Monica, Calif.: February, 1955), p. 1.

politicians shun doctrines and ideologies, preferring the negotiation of concrete interests to the elaboration of philosophical arguments. The logical consistency of the politician's record on public policy issues is less important than his capacity to constantly broaden his base of support by appealing to a number of different constituencies. A variety of ingenious proposals that appeal to one or another group may be contemplated. Trial balloons may be flown almost promiscuously. Party platforms are employed to engender party unity before elections rather than to provide a standard of accountability for the electorate afterwards. Politicians cannot be held strictly accountable for electoral promises anyway, for in a presidential-congressional system it is difficult to precisely assign credit and blame, and in any event one man's ideas rarely survive the policy-making process intact.

Evading firm positions on controversial issues, arguing around unpleasant choices, and denying the unpalatable consequences of one's expressed preferences are all recognized and honorable political gambits. Such tactics are perhaps harmless at home. If practiced in connection with foreign policy issues, they may, however, lead to diplomatic insolvency, for in foreign relations the element of force inevitably intrudes, the margins of tolerance are narrower, and an experimentalist frame of mind may be misconstrued by foreign statesmen as marking the absence of serious convictions. The pragmatism of the electoral politician was evident during the 1961–62 Berlin crisis when President Kennedy apparently interested himself at one time or another in revisions of the 1959 Geneva plan, adjudication of the dispute in the World Court, the creation of a free city, parallel peace conferences in the East and West, a five- to ten-year *modus vivendi*, the use of Berlin as a site for the U.N. Headquarters, a Central European security plan, International Access Authority plans, a 10-point mutual declaration, and several other proposals.[25] Earlier, that callous disregard for the implications of electoral rhetoric to which politicians are peculiarly prone was revealed in the 1952 Republican call for a liberation of the captive nations in Eastern Europe, even as military strategy was being revised in such a way as to render foolhardy any attempt to implement such an objective.

Lawyers. The pragmatic character of American political leadership is further reinforced by the prevalence of legal training among politicians and appointees to important posts in the foreign policy bureaucracies. Fully two-thirds of the leaders in the federal government, and a majority of congressmen, senators, and governors, come to public affairs from the legal profession. "No institutions of political education compete with those of legal education; as a result, legal styles, legal concepts, legal ways of thought and behavior permeate politics."[26] American lawyers are trained in the tradition of common law. The products of such legal schooling typically prefer actual to hypothetical cases and the manipulation of concrete arguments to

[25] Theodore Sorenson, *Kennedy* (New York, N.Y.: Harper, 1965), p. 599.

[26] Brzezinski and Huntington, *op. cit.*, p. 146.

the resolution of abstract issues. Their training may likewise induce confidence that cases can always be decided, even if the grievances giving rise to them are not necessarily thereby removed. Men with legal backgrounds may be inclined to think in terms of victories and defeats, rather than in terms of the management of ongoing relationships. They may be prone to apply principles found appropriate to one situation to another only superficially similar. Theirs may be a "bias toward awaiting developments and toward operating within the definition of the problem as formulated by its chief spokesmen." [27] On the other hand, the breadth of their training, their respect for facts, their regard for precedents, and their notable skills in negotiation may well endow lawyers for diplomatic assignments.

Businessmen. Businessmen, industrialists, and bankers have been conspicuous among the recruits to foreign policy assignments since World War II. Investment bankers have been particularly ubiquitous in the State Department, captains of industry in the Pentagon. James Forrestal, Robert Lovett, Robert Patterson, Louis Johnson, Stuart Symington, Averell Harriman, Clark Draper, John McCloy, Paul Hoffman, William Foster, Chester Bowles, Charles Wilson, Neil McElroy, and Thomas Gates are among the prominent businessmen who have served the government, some with distinction.

From 1942 to 1958 at least forty-six leading businessmen occupied top positions in foreign policy agencies. Recruitment from the business world was most pronounced during the Eisenhower Administration, but it has been a significant feature of all postwar Administrations. In 1954 seventeen of twenty-four officials of secretarial rank in the Defense Department came from business or corporation backgrounds.[28]

Some types of business experience clearly equip men for effective diplomatic service. Those with backgrounds in the banking and commercial worlds of Wall Street have been particularly well served by their previous experiences. Many of those men who helped define America's role in the postwar world demonstrated an evident cosmopolitanism, a notable skill in negotiations, a grasp of the subtleties of complex transactions, a practical realism about the relationship between objectives and means, and an anxiety to avert insolvent commitments. Industrialists serving in the Pentagon, with a few notable exceptions, have disclosed a greater preoccupation with the intricacies of resource mobilization, an emphasis upon economy, an unlimited faith in technology, and confidence that better salesmanship and more effective advertising are a significant part of the remedy for present ills.[29]

---

[27] Kissinger, *op. cit.*, p. 515.

[28] Samuel P. Huntington, *The Soldier and the State* (Cambridge, Mass.: Harvard University Press, 1956), p. 392.

[29] C. B. Marshall once wryly commented that in a nation where it is assumed that a basically dull person can be transformed into a social lion by using the right deodorant, it is perhaps natural to expect success in foreign policy if the commodity is attractively packaged. *The Exercise of Sovereignty*, p. 49.

Men coming to the foreign policy establishments from business are likely to assume that success depends upon experience, intuition, the range of one's acquaintances, and the skillful manipulation of familiar forces.[30] In foreign policy, however, their experiences, hunches, and associates will be less useful. Nor are many businessmen equipped with an adequate appreciation of the deep forces of history. To this extent, their participation in foreign policy may be directed less toward the shaping of historical trends perceived through informed conjecture than toward the effort to hastily contrive technical gimmicks to resolve immediately pressing problems. "The business elite," Kissinger has argued, "is even less able or willing than the lawyer to recognize that the formulation of an issue, not the technical remedy, is usually the central problem." [31]

The American national style in foreign policy

"The performance of nations," Walt W. Rostow once observed, "is like that of individuals in that it combines discrete, fortuitous elements of heredity and environment, interacting effectively, coming to terms with problems (or failing to do so) in a recurrent fashion, building up over time relatively stable patterns of performance." [32] A nation's style is not discernible in the collective personality of its people, but rather in the characteristic ways in which its leaders resolve recurrent problems. The peculiar way in which Americans apprehend the world and their role in it reveals the uniqueness of the American national style. The salient features of that style have been frequently and perspicaciously described. Here it will suffice to comment briefly upon the foreign policy implications of American liberalism, pragmatism, and provincialism.

Liberalism

The uniqueness of American liberalism has been widely and justly celebrated. Liberal ideas flourished in an open land and an essentially unstratified society. Liberal principles were accorded general acceptance by a people whose history produced no violent struggles against the remnants of feudal privilege, no protracted ideological battles, and no open class warfare. An optimistic belief in progress comes easily to Americans, whose domestic experiences were happily free of the struggle and strife that accompanied nation-building elsewhere. Prolonged isolation from the storms of international strife encouraged the illusion that "America's past was prologue to the future of the world." The applicability of the "lessons" of American history to the

[30] Kissinger, *op. cit.*, p. 516.

[31] *Ibid.*, p. 517.

[32] See his pioneering essay, "The American National Style," in *The American Style*, Elting Morison (ed.) (New York, N.Y.: Harper, 1958), p. 249.

plight of other nations has been casually assumed, the exportability of American institutions rarely (and only recently) questioned.

A variety of expressions of America's liberalism are evident in the American approach to foreign policy. Above all, Americans are guilty of what Stanley Hoffmann has termed the "liberal sin of transposition"—that is, the tendency to impose on international politics a vision of public order rooted in the domestic experience of constitutional government.[33] It is the vision of a world in which peace is normal, war an annoying and avoidable aberration. Since an underlying harmony of interest is presumed to exist among states, force is considered a dispensable element in their relations. Although difference among states on substantive issues may abound, it is anticipated that they may either be dissipated through the healing powers of commerce or resolved through compromise and the procedures of peaceful change.

At home the plausibility of such assumptions is assured by the fabric of shared convictions upon which consensual politics is built. In a world of competing military sovereignties, the applicability of those assumptions is questionable. Nonetheless, what frequently passes for the objective of American foreign policy is the acceptance by others of procedures and principles whose efficacy and utility have been demonstrated in domestic politics. Not surprisingly, most of the "one-shot solutions" proposed by Americans to ameliorate the world's ills have had domestic analogues; for example, arbitration treaties in analogy with the methods employed to settle industrial disputes, the League Covenant and U.N. Charter with the American Constitution, the International Court of Justice with the Supreme Court, and supranational schemes with the federal system.

The lens through which American liberals perceive the world is thus colored by an abiding optimism. American political theory remains "relentlessly pre-Freudian." Most Americans remain convinced that a new world can be constructed; fewer ask, as did Carl Becker in an earlier day, "How new will the better world be?" [34] Obstacles to stability and progress may exist, but they can be removed with vigorous effort. Global solutions to problems may be temporarily unfeasible, but faith in supranational schemes can be redeemed through their application on a regional scale. Disarmament may appear unpromising, but hopes may be invested in more modest arms control proposals. Even the most tough-minded realists sustain their hopes by clinging to their own panacea, that is, a rediscovery of the canons of the old diplomacy.[35]

When progressive movements falter, Americans often react

---

[33] See his essay, "American Foreign Policy: Restraints and Choices," *Daedalus* (Fall 1962), pp. 680–691.

[34] This was the title of a book Becker wrote during World War II inquiring into the problems of reconstructing the postwar world. *How New Will the Better World Be?* (New York, N.Y.: Knopf, 1944).

[35] See, for example, Hans J. Morgenthau, *Politics Among Nations* (New York, N.Y.: Knopf, 1966), Chaps. 31–32.

with a sense of betrayal. President Kennedy's pique at General de Gaulle implies the conviction that the French President was responsible for arresting progress toward a grand design whose promise was considered self-evident and whose benefits were to have been universally shared within the Atlantic community. Initial enthusiasm toward Fidel Castro's Cuban revolution gave way to indignant outrage as liberal niceties were neglected and Marxist leanings were acknowledged.

Reformist in its orientation, American liberalism encounters the world with faith in its principles rather than with precise revisionist goals. Liberalism is insufficiently systematic to constitute an ideology from which policies may be deduced. It is too ahistorical to provide an adequate methodology for analyzing international political problems. Nurtured in an isolationist land, moreover, it provides no traditional guidelines or diplomatic rules of thumb that might furnish useful clues to the nation's enduring objectives and suggest plausible courses of action in response to recurrent challenges.[36] Little positive value is attached by liberals, convinced of the open-endedness of history, to systematic doctrines from which social goals might be derived. The central tenets of American belief—the dignity of the individual, the democratic method for resolving political conflicts, the rule of law, the maintenance of a sphere of private economic and social opportunity beyond the control of the state, the positive value attributed to the right of dissent (especially, perhaps, when it is not exercised)—are principles that may be emulated by others. They do not, however, constitute the guidelines of an active foreign policy. Thus American foreign policy frequently seems more preoccupied with principles, that is, rules guiding action, than with goals that are the objects of action.[37]

This may account for the oft-noted imprecision of American diplomatic aims in encounters with the East. The persistent effort to "relax tensions," the casting about for "new approaches," the favorable empathy attributed to "diplomatic flexibility," and the zealous attempts to dissipate misunderstanding through genial gatherings at the summit all reveal a desire to improve the atmosphere of world politics without implying specific revisionist demands.

Some liberal principles, such as the commitment to self-determination and the belief in peaceful change, do constitute veritable moral imperatives guiding conduct and providing criteria for evaluating foreign political situations. Given the legitimacy of the nationalist idea and the evident stake that the world's wealthiest and most powerful state has in nonviolent procedures of change, it is clear that on many occasions such principles will safeguard essential American interests. It is equally clear, however, that when such principles are believed to transcend narrower interests, problems may ensue. For one thing, under some conditions the urge to self-determination may

---

[36] For an elaboration of this point and other insights into the American style, see Stanley Hoffmann, "The American Style: Our Past and Our Principles," *Foreign Affairs*, 46 (January 1968), pp. 362–376.

[37] Brzezinski and Huntington, *op. cit.*, p. 64.

be implemented only through violent means. For another, indiscriminate application of the principle of self-determination may jeopardize other interests. For example, in Africa support for the principle has been restrained by the desire to avert the Balkanization of that continent. Moreover, belief in self-determination has been accompanied by the conviction that under no circumstances would a people voluntarily submit to a communist regime; thus the ambivalence and vacillation apparent in American policies toward Cuba since 1959 and Vietnam since 1946. Commitment to peaceful change has as its corollary an instinctive resistance to forceful changes in the status quo. But again, dogmatic adherence to the principle may engage American power where no concrete interests are at stake.

Not only does liberalism suggest some objectives of policy, but the liberal experience conditions assumptions about social and political change in the world. The series of reassuring premises upon which American efforts to promote development in the Third World have been based is indicative. Confidence that extensive and partially predictable changes in foreign societies may be managed through marginal contributions of external capital assistance, that economic and social change will assure political stability and growth of liberal political institutions, and that liberal polities will invariably pursue pacific foreign policies congruent with American interests constitutes the "theory" of American foreign aid. But such assumptions constitute less a subtle analysis of the situation of most developing societies than "an idealized projection of America's own experience of economic growth which was accompanied by a large amount of social stability, social progress and political democracy." [38]

American liberalism has had particular blind spots with regard to the role of force in world politics. Liberalism encourages no careful relating of ends to means, and in American history military means have only rarely appeared as the preconditions of social peace. Liberalism has, in fact, been associated with the development of what has been termed a "civilian mind." To many Americans the military have historically appeared as a threat to civil liberties rather than a guarantor of national survival. In the opening up of the West, communities sprang up spontaneously in the absence of government. To be sure, soldiers helped to create a nation out of the vast plains and prairies, but they did so principally as engineers rather than as fighting men. Indians were removed from the land with a minimum of force, and, since America's neighbors scarcely posed menacing threats, the comfortable illusion flourished that power politics was a reflection of European despotism rather than the natural condition of involvement in international affairs.

A tendency to dissociate power and policy is apparent in the general aversion to war, the tendency to consider its elimination an integral part of America's emancipating mission, and the frequently evident disparity between the alleged objectives of United States policy in wartime and the actual conduct of military operations. The

---

[38] Hoffmann, "The American Style," *op. cit.*, p. 374.

Clausewitzian doctrine that war and diplomacy are merely different modalities of continuing political relationships is not intuitively appreciated by those steeped in the liberal tradition, though it has had many American converts in recent years. Americans have more typically viewed war and peace as separable phases in which now the skills of diplomats, then those of soldiers, become exclusively relevant.

In World War I, America's professed war aims were so abstract as to defy accomplishment. In World War II, President Roosevelt sought to postpone the resolution of the thorny problems of peace until after hostilities had been brought to a conclusion—and American bargaining leverage had been dissipated by the changing tide of military fortunes among the allies. The corollary of the postponement tactic was the enunciation of unconditional surrender as the central war aim of the United States. Not only did this possibly stiffen German resistance, but also it disclosed a failure to recognize the relationship between the outcome of battle and the resolution of political issues. In both the Korean and Vietnamese conflicts, military operations have to some extent been disciplined by political considerations. In both cases, however, some confusion existed as to the appropriate political objective. In Korea the President vacillated from proving that "aggression doesn't pay," to restoration of the status quo ante, to reunification of Korea under free elections; in Vietnam it is scarcely clear whether the primary aim is to achieve military victory (by successfully pacifying South Vietnam and eliminating Viet Cong influence) or to avoid military defeat (by dissociating American prestige from the fortunes of the South Vietnamese regime in combating a guerrilla insurgency).

Some former tendencies have been modified under the pressure of events since 1945. No longer are Americans so inclined to starve the military in times of peace or to seek unqualified victories in times of war. There remains, however, a residual confusion between force and power, and a residual conviction that force may be legitimately employed only on behalf of the community. There is a world of difference between the Kellogg-Briand Pact designed to end war "with a stroke of the pen" and the Eisenhower Administration's New Look military policy with its premise that the more horrible the prospective retribution the less likely the prospect of war. At the level of doctrine, on the other hand, both policies reflect what Robert W. Tucker has referred to as "the conviction that violence is not an inevitable evil in a society of sovereign states, that the resort to force is instead an entirely avoidable means for effecting change or for resolving conflicting interests." [39] The New Look's replacement by the McNamara strategy with its emphasis upon options and "graduated and flexible response" suggests the growing influence of those who conceive the application of force to be a modified form of political intercourse. Older instincts are still visible, however, as in W. W. Rostow's important speech at Leeds in January, 1967, in which he por-

[39] Robert W. Tucker, *The Just War* (Baltimore, Md.: Johns Hopkins University Press, 1960), p. 68.

trayed the Vietnamese war as a turning point in human history, potentially establishing the principle that forceful transformations of the status quo will not be tolerated by the international community.[40] One suspects that beneath the tough-minded exterior lurks the faith of a Wilsonian idealist.

It is not to be concluded that liberalism represents an entirely negative inheritance. Some of its elements may constitute substantial assets in relations with friends. The positive value attributed to compromise, the facility in operating through international institutions, and the distaste for dogma have been important to the creation of numerous cooperative ventures within the Atlantic community. Liberal instincts are more likely to be at a discount in the management of adversary relationships.[41]

Pragmatism

If an ebullient optimism, a distaste for force, a preoccupation with principles rather than goals, and a casual indifference toward the relationship between means and ends are products of the liberal tradition in America, then an "engineering approach," an improvisational flair, and a short-term outlook are the marks of American pragmatism. As someone has observed, the pragmatist is preoccupied with method rather than judgment, practice rather than theory, action or invention rather than contemplative thought. To the pragmatist, the solutions to problems are assumed to be embedded in the context of events themselves. Problems tend, therefore, to be defined in the light of immediate, pressing concerns rather than in the perspective of longer range relationships that can only be conjectural.[42]

Emphasis upon the immediate and a casual indifference for long-range hypothetical dangers is perhaps natural for a people whose environment has been subject to manipulation and for whom social, economic, and political problems have generally proved tractable. A fascination with the techniques of problem-solving is perhaps equally natural for a nation whose most difficult distributive problems have been generally evaded by concentrating upon the production of more and more goods and services to be divided. Technical innovations have more than once permitted the resolution of intransigent domestic political problems: the growing power of the railroad magnates, for example, was curbed by the invention of cheap automotive transport.

[40] Walt W. Rostow, "Tasks of the First and Second Post-War Generations," *United States Department of State Bulletin* (March 27, 1967) pp. 491–504.

[41] See Fred Iklé, *How Nations Negotiate* (New York, N.Y.: Harper, 1944), esp. Chap. 12, for a discussion of American strengths and weaknesses in diplomatic negotiations.

[42] Numerous illustrations are to be found in the *Memoirs* of George Kennan. He frequently found himself arguing against the impatience that found its release in frantic activity that often compromised future possibilities. See, for example, his discussion of the negotiations of the NATO Treaty and German rearmament. For specific discussions of the impact of American pragmatism on foreign policy, see Hoffmann, *The State of War*, pp. 173–80; Henry A. Kissinger, "Domestic Structure and Foreign Policy," *Daedalus* (Spring 1966), pp. 503–529; Marshall, *The Limits of Foreign Policy*; and Stillman and Pfaff, *Power and Impotence*.

It should scarcely occasion surprise, then, if technical gimmicks pose temptations for policy-makers confronted by troublesome political problems. To those anxious about the cohesion of NATO, the devising of multilateral force schemes or ingenious consultative arrangements seems more attractive than a redirection of strategic concepts to account for European reservations. The American experience with counterinsurgency in Vietnam discloses a combination of sophisticated techniques and faulty political judgments. Efforts to evade the political dilemmas provoked by the allocation of foreign aid have periodically given rise to efforts to elaborate technical criteria, such as "aid absorptive capacity," that would obviate the need for hard political decisions. The necessity for mutual trust in the implementation of various arms control schemes has been eliminated through reliance upon technological means of inspection. "In the political sphere," someone has observed, "modern America harnesses enormous sophistication of technique to goals which are derived largely from unanalyzed tradition."

The virtues of a pragmatic style are obvious. Rather than focusing efforts upon irremediable difficulties, those problems susceptible of solution occupy official energies. If an Atlantic community cannot be arranged by constitutional fiat, a variety of collaborative arrangements may yet be institutionalized. If a global settlement with the Soviet Union seems unlikely, attempts to discover some joint interests may yet bear fruit.

The shortcomings of this style are also evident. The engineering approach is as ahistorical as American liberalism, and it may also reinforce a short-range outlook on international issues. Immersion in the solution of short-run problems may encourage a neglect of longer range dangers, allowing the present to simply overwhelm the future. Even President Kennedy, whose unusual sense of history has been widely acknowledged, was in Robert Frost's phrase "more Irish than Harvard." The temptation to contract out many problems to specialists, whose expertise may be narrow and whose sensitivities for the interrelationships among issues may be conspicuously underdeveloped, may eventuate in shallow analysis and an excessive segmentation of the issues. A passionate quest for certainty—implicit in the methodological emphasis of much contemporary social science research in America—may prompt undue reliance upon those elements of a problem that lend themselves to quantification despite their lack of intrinsic importance. Perhaps the greatest danger of such pragmatism is the possibility that, with the preoccupation in a series of pressing crises, the search for a consistent and intelligible philosophy of foreign relations is forgotten.

Provincialism

A people who have led a sheltered existence, who have been free from foreign invasion, and whose neighbors have been generally friendly and always weak are apt to lack what Lord Vansittart once termed "that sensitive awareness born of uneasy contiguity." Extended isolation produced, not surprisingly, an unusual provincialism. Few Americans have possessed a comprehensive or profound understanding or favorable empathy for foreign societies.[43] Even rarer have been the occasions on which men of such insight have scaled the heights to the pinnacle of the foreign-policy-making establishment. Ironically, the "China hands" and "Soviet specialists" trained by the State Department in the 1920s and 1930s were in the 1940s and 1950s at once widely respected abroad and ignored or maligned at home.

In the conduct of foreign policy two things are essential. One is a sense of perspective or proportion in maintaining balance among a variety of objectives and commitments. This is crucial if scarce means are to be satisfactorily distributed among competing aims. Equally significant, however, is the development of a "feel" or "sense" of the local situations to which specific policies are to be addressed. As George Kennan has observed, "The sources of international tension are always specific, never general. They are always devoid of exact precedents or exact parallels. They are always in part unpredictable." [44]

A plausible argument may be made to the effect that many American policies reflect an inadequate appreciation of the uniqueness of specific situations, an insufficient understanding of the background of events, and an unimpressive grasp of the grubby details of problems arising in distant areas. When these shortcomings are combined with a penchant for action, the result may be policy deduced from general principles derived in turn from municipal law, moral philosophy, or strategic theory. The tendency to attribute blame for revolutionary movements in non-Western areas to the manipulative genius of a malevolent international Communist movement directed from Moscow or Peking is illustrative of this tendency. A more subtle manifestation is that caution-induced habit of giving to potential adversaries "the benefit of every doubt in matters of strength and to credit him indiscriminately with *all* aggressive designs, even when some of them are mutually contradictory." [45] The tendency to project upon others the goals we would wish for them to have likewise betrays a lingering emotional and moral isolationism despite the massive engagement in world politics since 1940. This lingering neoisolationism is perceptible perhaps in what one observer has termed the American tendency to "mind other people's business without taking account of their views."

To sum up, the American style in foreign relations appears congruent with the political culture of a nation unified by a consensus on liberal procedures, managed by generally pragmatic leaders, and permitted, by virtue of its size and location, to indulge for most of its history an absorbing preoccupation with its domestic affairs.

[43] For a variety of illustrations, see Stillman and Pfaff, *op. cit.*, pp. 44–52.

[44] George F. Kennan, *The Realities of American Foreign Policy* (New York, N.Y.: Norton, 1966), p. 36.

[45] Kennan, *Memoirs* 1925–1950, p. 499.

5

Political institutions

In this chapter an attempt will be made to identify those features of the constitutional and political formula that shape the conduct and the content of American foreign policy. Special attention will be directed to a description of the pattern of authority and the distribution of power as it affects foreign-policy-making. Formal authority and effective influence do not, of course, invariably coincide. The former depends upon the Constitution, custom, and administrative fiat; the latter more upon personal style, role perception, the force of circumstances, and interpersonal and interagency relations.

Constitutional status of the government

The United States is ruled by a constitutional government; that is, a government limited in the idiom of the law. The Constitution itself and the most significant American contribution to political philosophy, *The Federalist Papers*, express a profound anxiety about the dangers of concentrated power. The essence of American constitutional theory is the attempt to hedge governmental power round with constraints. The utmost precautions were taken by the Founding Fathers not only to fragment governmental power both territorially and institutionally (through the system of federalism and the separation of powers) but to prevent the emergence of any governing class that might impose its will upon the society.[1]

This constitutional formula is designed to avert tyranny and guarantee the dignity and the natural rights of the individual. The ramifications of this conception—of the state as a utilitarian instrument of a free society of individuals—in the realm of foreign affairs are at once simple and profound. Nothing could be more alien to this conception of the state than the continental principle of the *"Primat der Aussenpolitik."* The life of the American political community is not to be sacrificed to the allegedly transcendent interests of an organic state. Foreign policy, on the contrary, is to be conducted, if necessary, in order that higher and more comprehensive purposes might be achieved at home. "A political society does not live," as George F. Kennan once commented, "to conduct foreign policy; it ... conducts foreign policy in order to live." [2]

One of the world's oldest democracies, the American government is aptly defined as *polyarchic.* Virtually all adults may exercise the franchise, with each vote weighted equally. Administrative officials are subordinate to elective officers of the national government; the latter thus enjoy the final word on public policy. Political leaders may, to be sure, enjoy some discretion between elections, but the electorate retains periodic opportunities to "toss the rascals out"— congressmen every two years, Presidents every four, and senators every six. The profusion of intermediate groups, the established rights of the opposition political parties, and the freedom of the press all insure that alternative policy choices will receive ample discussion, that voters will be exposed to nonofficial sources of information, and that official policies may be subjected to critical scrutiny.

Although there is unquestionably a tendency to exercise a more relaxed day-to-day accountability in the realm of foreign policy, the prerequisites of democratic control are clearly present. Policy emerges from negotiations among competing sets of leaders, whose actions are consistently monitored by an informed and assertive "attentive public" and who may be removed at regular intervals by the mass electorate. Between elections, moreover, the separation of powers, the composition and procedures of the Senate, bicameralism, the system of checks and balances, the constitutional restraints on legislative authority, the decentralized party system, and the devolution of power to committee chairmen in Congress all "provide a variety of narrow defiles where a skillful and aggressive group may fatally mine the path of any group of threatening leaders." [3]

---

[1] The church was disestablished, a professional standing army eschewed in favor of the militia system, a free market economy encouraged, prohibitions erected against a titled nobility, the freedom of scientific investigation guaranteed. the spoils system adopted, and efforts to sanctify property qualifications for the voting privilege vigorously resisted. All such measures revealed an "impatience with privilege" and a desire to disperse power widely.

[2] Kennan. *The Realities of American Foreign Policy*, p. 4.

[3] Robert Dahl and Charles E. Lindblom, *Politics, Economics, and Welfare* (New York, N.Y.: Harper Torchbooks, 1963), p. 336.

The loci of power in foreign-policy-making

Executive leadership in foreign policy was expressly implied by the framers of the Constitution.[4] But the terse provisions of that document constitute, in E. S. Corwin's pregnant obiter dicta, "a standing invitation to struggle for the privilege of directing American foreign policy." [5] Those provisions that presume to fix responsibilities and locate authority for foreign policy are aptly described as "brief, insufficient, and ambiguous." Power was fragmented, responsibilities shared. The consequence has been incipient struggle between the President and Congress as well as within both branches over the substance of policy and the right to make it.

The absence of hierarchy in foreign-policy-making is not merely a function of the Constitution's vagueness. The very nature of foreign policy makes it difficult to identify with any precision the loci of power for making specific decisions. The insistent demands for immediate action and the compelling pressure of events often permit little time for orderly deliberation, systematic reflection, and the careful processing of alternatives up through the chain of command. These difficulties are compounded by the complexity of the American government and its burgeoning size. The persistent element of conflict in presidential-congressional relations as well as the proliferation of executive agencies has resulted in a diffusion of bureaucratic power. In the process, many agencies that are theoretically subordinate to presidential control obtain a substantial autonomy from hierarchical direction.

Nor is it sufficient merely to identify the relationships among officials and offices. The distribution of influence frequently depends upon the control of votes, the mastery of a technical discipline, access to strategic positions in Congress and in the executive bureaucracies, manipulation of the mass media, or the possession of other political resources. In America the resources of power are various, and they are widely distributed. One can simply assert that the focus of policy-making is to be found in the bargaining relationships among presidential politicians,[6] congressional leaders, the executive bureaucracies, and other powerful lobbying interests. Beyond this it is impossible to generalize with confidence. As one former high official commented,

---

[4] So, too, was the federal government's supremacy over the states. Treaty-making and war-making powers and diplomatic responsibilities are lodged exclusively with the federal government, and treaties supersede even congressional statutes as the "law of the land."

[5] Quoted by Paul Seabury, *Power, Freedom and Diplomacy* (New York, N.Y.: Random, 1963), p. 195.

[6] These would include members of the White House staff preoccupied with foreign policy, leaders of the presidential bureaucracy, for example, Director of the Office of Science and Technology, Director of the Bureau of the Budget, the President's Special Assistant for National Security Affairs, the Chairman of the Council of Economic Advisers, and those presidential appointees in foreign policy departments and agencies whose task it is to reflect the Chief Executive's perspectives and priorities down into the executive bureaucracy.

"In action after action, responsibility for decision is as fluid and as restless as quicksilver, and there seems to be neither a person nor an organization on whom it can be fixed." [7]

A more modest claim may be proposed. In America the arrangement of power in foreign-policy-making appears less as a chain of command than a series of concentric circles.[8] The President stands at the center, assisted there by a presidential bureaucracy and executive appointees responsible directly to him. Around them one finds the chief officials of the permanent agencies with day-to-day responsibility for the management of American foreign policy—the State Department, the Department of Defense (DoD), and the Central Intelligence Agency (CIA). Then there are the other subordinate, operational agencies, such as the Agency for International Development (AID), the United States Information Agency (USIA), the Arms Control and Disarmament Agency (ACDA), and the Peace Corps; those executive departments whose participation in foreign policy is less regular and narrower in scope and intensity, such as the departments of the Treasury, Commerce, Agriculture, and Labor, the Atomic Energy Commission (AEC), the National Aeronautics and Space Administration (NASA), the Tariff Commission, and others; as well as a number of quasi-public, nonprofit research corporations under contract with one or several government bureaus. Finally, there is the wider arena of public involvement, where congressional committees, party leaders, nongovernmental groups, newspaper columnists, and members of the "attentive public" exert some influence.

It is the purpose of this section to identify the most significant participants, specify the nature of their responsibilities, and illuminate the sources of their power.

The President

"I make American foreign policy," Harry Truman once flatly declared.[9] "More than anyone in the government," one of John F. Kennedy's biographers wrote of the late President, "he was the source of ideas, initiative, and imagination in foreign policy." [10] Whatever the truth of these expansive claims, the President is surely the final source of authority for foreign policy, and in recent decades the presidential role has been enhanced at the expense of both the Congress and the executive bureaucracies. The President's primacy in the making of foreign policy is enshrined in the constitution, buttressed by his political resources, and reinforced by the stakes of international rivalries in the thermonuclear age. Presidents may extend varying degrees of priority to foreign policy and will certainly exhibit differential skill

[7] Roger Hilsman, *To Move a Nation* (New York, N.Y.: Doubleday, 1967), p. 7.

[8] *Ibid.*, Chap. 35.

[9] Quoted by Louis E. Koenig, *The Chief Executive* (New York, N.Y.: Harcourt, Brace and World, 1964), p. 211.

[10] Schlesinger, *A Thousand Days*, p. 426.

in the craft of diplomacy. Few can escape the obligations of leadership.

The formal authority of the Chief Executive in foreign policy is vast. The *powers of the Presidency* have been justly celebrated by political scientists. In the still fresh words of Chief Justice John Marshall, the President is "the sole organ of the nation in its external relations, and its sole representative with foreign nations." The President appoints the formal emissaries of the United States, and receives the representatives of foreign sovereigns. His is the power to recognize governments, or to deny them that recognition upon which formal diplomatic relations depend. He may negotiate treaties or transact business with other nations through executive agreements that need not have the acquiescence of the Senate. He selects the personnel for the executive establishment and may, within limits, reorganize the executive branch to redefine interagency relationships and recast the procedures of policy-making. As Commander in Chief he directs the nation's armed might in both war and peace. He is responsible for raising, maintaining, training, and deploying those forces that Congress is prepared to support. Finally, as Chief Legislator, he is expected to provide the initiative in formulating the massive and continuous programs that constitute the sinews of American efforts in foreign affairs; that is, military budgets, foreign aid programs, technical assistance projects, and cultural exchanges.

Beyond the formal authority of the Presidency, there are the political resources inherent in the office and available to an incumbent eager to fortify a personal role commensurate with his formal responsibilities. Above all, the President possesses the vital capacity to act. Congressional politicians may display an unkind disposition toward a President's proposals, but the initiative for concrete acts is his. He defines the issues demanding a response. He chooses the terrain for political struggles with congressmen. He may commit acts that leave them with little room to maneuver without repudiating the American Head of State and thereby diminishing American prestige. Ratification of his treaties has occasionally been withheld; such occasions are, however, rare. Confirmation for his appointments may be refused, but such acts of denial are infrequent. The President may order the development of a new weapon system that alters the strategic equation. He may order the deployment of troops to deter hostile actions, or transform a challenge into a crisis. He may issue important policy declarations that commit the reputation of the United States. The pattern of his official behavior will reinforce or weaken the credibility of formal pledges of assistance to others.

Beyond this, no other official enjoys his national electoral mandate, and any President derives prestige from the fact that he is the custodian of "national interests." His influence is enhanced by divisions among his subordinates and the general diffusion of power in the American system. His is the central will in an executive branch marked by the proliferation of agencies. His is the capacity for synthesis and coordination in an age when the specialized skills of soldiers, economists, diplomats, intelligence officers, and propagandists must be marshaled and synchronized in response to exceedingly complex foreign policy issues.

Although this proliferation of agencies and experts reflects an expansion in the scope of America's relations with the world and the growing complexity of those relationships, it is also the product of administrative cunning. President Roosevelt encouraged institutionalized conflict within the executive branch by defining jurisdictional boundaries casually, promoting competition among his assistants, and supplementing the formal chain of command with personal lines of communication down into the bureaucracies. Other Presidents have employed similar methods to enhance the *power of the President* in exercising the *powers of the Presidency*. By fragmenting power among a number of competing advisers and staffs, the President is able to preserve the drastic choices for himself. Conflicts among agencies and staffs are generally forced upward for resolution. Once they begin to climb the chain of authority, it is difficult to achieve a satisfactory resolution short of the Presidency, for, as Richard Neustadt has observed, "In logic and in law only the Presidency stands somewhat above all agencies, all personnel systems, all staffs." [11]

In his relations with legislators, the President's potential influence is ironically reinforced by the conspicuous absence of party discipline. In the British system of party government, in return for disciplined support on formal votes, the parliamentary leadership of the majority party yields substantial influence to factions within the party. The American government moves, however, through the mobilization of *ad hoc* majorities on particular proposals. Such a system tends to enhance the role of those who can galvanize a consensus for specific initiatives.[12] The President enjoys incomparable resources for such a role. Since he is not likely to obtain perfect support from members of his own party in Congress, he is not enjoined from searching more widely for support.

As the stakes of world politics have become more total, so, too, has the President's personal preoccupation with foreign policy. The basis of presidential priorities was implied by President Kennedy, who remarked, "Domestic policy can merely defeat us. Foreign policy can kill us." [13] The President is consequently more likely to devote his time to foreign issues, to expend his political resources securing assent for vital foreign policy programs, and to risk defeat on domestic measures in order to assure the passage of vital foreign policy legislation or gain the acquiescence of crucial congressional allies. Some elements of the Great Society program have thus been victims of the Vietnamese war, just as earlier federal aid to education

[11] See the testimony of Richard E. Neustadt in U.S. Senate Committee on Government Operations, *Administration of National Security, Hearings* (Washington, D.C.: U.S. Government Printing Office, 1965), p. 79.

[12] See Waltz, *Foreign Policy and Democratic Politics*, Chap. 5.

[13] Schlesinger, *op. cit.*, p. 426.

was foregone in 1961 in order to guarantee the passage of the Trade Expansion Act.

Indeed, technology, as Richard Neustadt has observed, has virtually amended the Constitution to permit—indeed require—the President to exercise virtually sole direction in matters relating to the vital issues of war and peace.[14] Military force has become so destructive that it must be constantly disciplined by political objectives and subject at all times to the control of the only nationally elected official. If the fragmentation of power among a number of foreign policy agencies preserves a margin of choice for the President on many issues, the growing unification of the Defense Department permits him to exert a more direct control over the military establishment. Given the risks of escalation intrinsic in even the most limited applications of force, Presidents have obvious incentives to circumscribe the autonomy formerly enjoyed by military theater commanders and field operatives of the Central Intelligence Agency. Needless to add, their capacity to exercise a detailed control depends upon circumstances as well as the skill and style of the incumbent Chief Executive.

Crisis management has become an integral element in foreign policy, and crises are the preeminent occasions for real displays of presidential power. During the 1962 Cuban missile crisis, the President decided who would be consulted, whose advice would be accepted, who would say what, how public communications would be handled, which ships would be stopped, and so forth. A comparable centralization of policy-making was apparent in the management of the Berlin crisis of 1961–62, and has been evident in President Johnson's handling of the Vietnamese war. President Kennedy also established a precedent likely to be continued by his successors when he opened direct and personal lines of communication with the highest leadership of the Soviet Union. In addition to the Hot Line established in 1963, he developed an extensive correspondence with Premier Khruschev, which possessed the advantages of informality and intimacy, enabled him to "by-pass the foreign policy bureaucracies in both countries," and permitted him to "omit the usual propaganda for public consumption and state positions without a backward glance at the press." [15]

Such enumerations of the formal authority of the Presidency and the political resources available to Presidents are more likely to impress outside observers than occupants of the White House. The latter have spoken more frequently, and often poignantly, of the "limits of presidential power." The President's responsibilities are enormous; his time is in short supply. Occasionally issues or problems may be lifted out of the foreign policy bureaucracies for his personal attention. President Kennedy was referred to as "Desk Officer for Laos" and the "day-to-day director of foreign policy . . . dealing personally with al-

[14] U.S. Senate Committee on Government Operations, *Administration of National Security*, p. 76.

[15] Sorenson, *Kennedy*, p. 552.

most every aspect of policy around the globe." [16] Doubtless there is a degree of exaggeration in this description. What is clear is that time does not permit the Chief Executive the luxury of detailed day-to-day surveillance and control on very many issues or problems. The President's personal influence will very likely be greatest during moments of supreme national danger. No President can now evade the responsibilities for crisis management. Yet even on such occasions, the President's margin for choice may be rather narrow, for it will be circumscribed by the options developed by lower echelon officials, actions previously taken, and the need to devise policies that can be executed with dispatch.

More generally, then, the President will exert influence over foreign policy indirectly and by delegation. In the appointment of men to staff the foreign and defense policy establishments he may designate assistants sharing his priorities and his perspectives. He may thus inform the content of policy by managing the personnel of the executive branch. Loyal appointees may bend established departments to his sense of priorities. Where the work of those departments is considered unsatisfactory, he may create special task forces directly accountable to him to oversee the development of policy on specific problems. Extraordinary authority may be delegated to special emissaries, personal advisers, or presidential troubleshooters. All represent a President's attempts to "gather around himself a group of men whose instinctive 'personality' reaction in tight spots [will] be in the same direction as his own." [17]

A President may further shape the substance of policies through his capacity to alter the procedures of policy-making. Some Presidents may choose to carefully staff decisions through the formal machinery of an elaborately designed National Security Council. Others may prefer to disestablish such formal channels in favor of highly personalized methods of decision-making. Operating methods reflect the personal style of incumbents as well as their own disposition toward the Presidency. Under President Eisenhower, the formality of procedures and the clarity of grants of delegated authority tended to promote consolidation and reduce the scope of the President's personal intervention in policy-making. Manifesting a more activist conception of the President's responsibilities, President Kennedy viewed the formalized procedures of the Security Council (as they had developed during the 1950s) as posing unwarranted delays, encouraging the "papering over" of policy disagreements among officials eager to avert the appearance of disharmony within the "official family," and erecting excessive barriers to initiative and innovation. He consequently dismantled them in order to permit more direct forms of presidential participation in policy-making.

Ultimately, of course, however impressive the President's formal authority, political resources, and opportunities for influencing

[16] Schlesinger, *op. cit.*, p. 425.

[17] Hilsman, *op. cit.*, p. 40.

policy formulation, his *power* consists of his ability to persuade other men that by accepting his directions they will be simultaneously acquitting their own responsibilities, serving their own constituencies, and advancing their own interests.[18]

The Executive Office of the President

The Executive Office of the President exists to assist the Chief Executive in providing policy leadership and control over a growing number of departments and agencies. The President has acquired his own staff resources to accumulate information, engage in policy analysis, and permit him a means of monitoring the vast number of programs undertaken by officials nominally subordinate to his direction. Through their efforts, some coordination of those programs may be achieved. Within the Executive Office one finds the White House staff, the Bureau of the Budget, the Council of Economic Advisers, the Office of Emergency Planning, the Office of Science and Technology, and the National Security Council. The Council of Economic Advisers and the Office of Emergency Planning are more indirectly involved in the making of foreign policy and hence will be omitted from this discussion.

The White House staff. The link between the increasingly personal role of the President in foreign policy on the one hand and the vast-sprawling scale of the executive foreign policy establishment on the other has been the emergence of the White House staff as an important adjunct to the President in foreign-policy-making. The specific role of the staff and the power of its various members obviously vary from President to President, adjusting to his personal style and his sense of his own requirements. Their power is largely a function of their proximity to the President, and a product of his need for substantial assistance. The staff may serve as the eyes and ears of the President, anticipating problems for him in hopes of extending his opportunities for reflection and improving his chances of shaping his options before the moment of drastic choice. The White House staff may also serve as a "midwife of policy," clarifying the alternatives before the President, providing an independent source of criticism for departmental proposals, and riding herd over those in the executive departments responsible for implementing his will. It may also provide "buffers of relief" for the President, protecting him from pressures, filtering for him the essential from the superficial, accomplishing staff work necessary for orderly executive decision, and occasionally assuming responsibility for routine tasks while the President is absorbed by the management of acute crises. In recent years, also, those in "Bundy's shop" or "Moyer's sphere of influence" have both serviced and monitored the influentials working for the

[18] Senate Committee on Government Operations, *The Administration of National Security*, p. 77. For a detailed discussion of this point see Richard E. Neustadt, *Presidential Power: The Politics of Leadership* (New York, N.Y.: Wiley, 1960).

President.[19] By obtaining access to the raw flow of intelligence information coming in through the State Department, the Defense Department, and the Central Intelligence Agency, they have been sufficiently informed to raise the "pregnant" questions of these respective departments, and thus render them more responsive to presidential direction and control. Finally, the White House staff, by working for the President, may come to share his transcendent perspective. They bear important responsibilities for identifying the interconnections among policy problems. Insofar as they provide good staff work, they must attempt to reflect intelligently upon the future implications of present decisions, the ramifications for American defense policy of foreign aid developments, the effect of presidential efforts at the summit upon the coherence of alliance policies, and so forth. In this realm they may contribute importantly to the integration of policy and to the coordination among executive agencies.

To be sure, a President may prefer to grant principal authority for many of these tasks to his Secretary of State. John Foster Dulles, for example, jealously guarded his personal relations with the President, interpreting the appointment of prestigious political figures to the President's staff as blatant threats to his preeminence. The position of Harold Stassen, who for a time was President Eisenhower's disarmament adviser with cabinet status, was never a happy one. During President Kennedy's tenure in office, on the other hand, "the presidential establishment . . . seem[ed] to cap the executive branch in a new sort of way, as a kind of fourth branch of government exercising authority not only through, but to some extent against, the echelons below." [20]

The Bureau of the Budget. Oldest of the staff units in the Executive Office, the Budget Bureau is also among the most significant. A "presidential servant with a cutting bias," the Budget Bureau exercises a number of responsibilities whose relevance for the formulation of foreign and defense policy is obvious. It provides leadership in preparing the budget, reviews departmental legislative proposals and assesses their financial implications before they are sent to Congress, and attempts to improve organizational and managerial practices within the executive branch. The International Division and the Military Division are of particular significance, since they assume the roles of persistent critic, skeptical auditor, perennial catalyst of program reevaluations, and vigorous challenger of departmental priorities on the foreign aid and defense budgets. Since proposals are legion and resources scarce, participation in the formulation of the budget assures Bureau personnel substantial potential influence in a number of important decisions.

The actual role the Bureau plays at any particular time is a

[19] See Richard E. Neustadt, "White House and Whitehall," *The Public Interest* (Winter 1966), p. 66.

[20] Marshall, *The Exercise of Sovereignty*, p. 79.

product of the policy orientation and operating methods of the President, the skills and perspectives of Budget Bureau personnel, and the character of the President-Bureau relationship. Under a President eager to present a balanced budget and to protect a reputation for fiscal integrity, the Bureau's role may be rather negative. Under a more activist Chief Executive, Bureau officials may promote executive reorganization and a rethinking of program priorities. They may even identify notable gaps as well as superfluous expenditures in departmental budget requests.

The National Security Council. Recognizing the need to integrate the requirements of foreign policy with the resources of the domestic economy, the National Security Act of 1947 provided for the creation of a National Security Council. The President, Vice President, Secretary of State, Secretary of Defense, and Director of the Office of Emergency Planning are statutory members of the Council. The Director of the Central Intelligence Agency and the Chairman of the Joint Chiefs of Staff are statutory advisers. Many officials—the Secretary of the Treasury, the Director of the Bureau of the Budget, the Director of the Agency for International Development, and others —may be invited to attend particular meetings where they may offer relevant advice or important perspectives.

The *modus operandi* and the influence of the Council have varied under different Presidents. The views and recommendations of the Council are merely advisory to the President. As a Cabinet committee to resolve national security problems, it meets at the President's discretion. Under President Eisenhower, the Council developed elaborate formal procedures for policy planning and implementation. President Kennedy preferred to dismantle the formal machinery and work through *ad hoc* task forces responsible for specific problem areas. The position of Special Assistant to the President for National Security Affairs was retained by the Kennedy and Johnson Administrations. But whereas Dillon Anderson, Robert Cutler, and Gordon Gray served President Eisenhower through their formal role as coordinators of a complicated cluster of committees, staffs, and secretariats, McGeorge Bundy and Walt W. Rostow have provided for Presidents Kennedy and Johnson a more personal liaison with the foreign policy establishment.

The Office of Science and Technology. Established in the aftermath of Russia's first space triumph, Sputnik I, this office initially devoted its attention to providing the President with a technical evaluation of weapon programs and searching reappraisals of the efficacy of military strategy in the light of the ongoing revolution in military technology. In addition, it played a significant role in mounting a space program, analyzing the technical basis for a test ban treaty, and promoting governmental reorganization measures designed to enhance the representation of scientific and technical considerations in foreign policy discussions within the executive branch.

More recently, the Office of Science and Technology has assumed leadership in designing science programs to be included in the foreign aid effort, offered extensive advice to the State Department on a host of contemporary issues, and continued to monitor national security programs with a view to their technical feasibility and their arms control implications.

The foreign policy bureaucracies

The State Department. Next to the President, the Secretary of State is generally the most significant spokesman of America's foreign policy. Enjoined by law to manage the business of the State Department "in such manner as the President of the United States shall from time to time order and/or instruct," he is the President's principal foreign policy adviser and the general manager of America's day-to-day relations with the world. The State Department is primarily engaged in making and evaluating detailed political and economic reports on every country with which the United States maintains official or unofficial relations. It handles the representation of the United States abroad. Its officials negotiate a variety of formal agreements with other sovereign states and perform a multitude of consular functions. Its claim to preeminence among the executive departments depends upon the importance of foreign policy issues and the alleged competence of members of the foreign service in the diplomatic art. The actual degree to which the Department shapes the substance and style of American foreign policy depends upon the personal qualities of its principal spokesmen, the relationship of the Secretary and some of his chief assistants to the President, and the Secretary's conception of his office. It is not a foreign office in the European sense, for it shares functions with more numerous rivals and enjoys no special deference from them.

The Secretary of State is the only official in the government aside from the President who is charged with looking at America's relations with the world as a whole. His location in the executive establishment permits him to acquire some of the presidential perspective. Occasionally he has become the prime architect of American foreign policy, as during the tenures of Charles Evans Hughes, Dean Acheson, and John Foster Dulles. His personal ascendancy in the making of foreign policy is, however, far from a natural condition. It is an achievement based upon political leadership no less than diplomatic skills. In recent years, moreover, the Secretary of State has had to attempt to regain a primacy neither automatically acknowledged nor easy to reclaim.

The power of the Secretary of State depends upon his relation with the President, that of his Department upon the Chief Executive's confidence in it. Where that relationship is marked by distrust and a lack of candor, trouble is unavoidable. Where mutual confidence and trust prevail, as in the relationship between President Truman and Secretary Acheson or President Eisenhower and Secretary Dulles, a Secretary may become the dominant foreign policy leader. An astute

Secretary will guard his access to the President carefully and assert himself across the entire contemporary front of foreign policy; an intelligent President will back an able Secretary consistently and refuse to compromise his position by parceling out tasks that properly fall in the Secretary's jurisdiction to other officers of his Administration.

The influence of the Secretary of State also depends upon his ability to perform a multiplicity of tasks in such a way as to render them mutually reinforcing. The Secretary is personal adviser to the President, ranking diplomat in negotiations with foreign nations, and chief coordinator of the various foreign programs of the American government. As a recent report of the Senate Government Operations Committee concluded:

> At the White House his advice and counsel gain weight because he speaks for his Department, bringing its knowledge, experience, and expertise to bear on questions of concern to the President. His public statements and guidance to the Department and other agencies carry force because he is so often with the President.
>
> The Secretary's roles can also be antagonistic. If he becomes too much a spokesman for the Department and the President comes to feel that he has been "captured" by the bureaucrats, the Secretary's credit as a Presidential adviser may be strained. But if the Secretary spends too much time at the White House or on the road as negotiator for the President—his direction of the Department may be impaired.[21]

Such dilemmas cannot be avoided. To master them requires a high order of political skill. To find a man possessing political acumen, competence in foreign affairs, and executive tact is no small order. The choice of the President is generally limited to a handful of men, and the results of the selection process appropriately have been described as an "uncertain tradition." [22]

In terms of their own perceptions of the role, Secretaries of State fall into several far-from-exclusive categories. Dean Acheson was clearly a *policy leader*. He considered his prime responsibility that of designing America's relations with the postwar world. He willingly assumed the correlative responsibility of vigorous advocacy of his point of view within the government. Since the State Department is but one among several competing sources of foreign policy advice, Acheson was forced to determine a course of action promptly in response to the changing tide of events and to assert himself forcefully in his quest for support. His assiduous wooing of the President was the basis for his power in policy formulation and for his capacity to discipline the various instruments of foreign policy to a single

[21] U.S. Senate Committee on Government Operations, *Administration of National Security*, pp. 34–35.

[22] See Norman Graebner, *An Uncertain Tradition* (New York, N.Y.: McGraw-Hill, 1961), for an evaluation of incumbents of the Secretary's office in the twentieth century.

conception of policy. His successor, Mr. Dulles, possessed a comparable conception of his role, and proved equally shrewd in securing presidential support.

Dean Rusk for the most part shunned the role of policy advocate, preferring that of *personal adviser* to Presidents Kennedy and Johnson.[23] He has eschewed expositing a Departmental point of view as distinct from those of the Pentagon and the CIA, in order to quietly assist the President in the selection of alternatives from among those thrust forward by others more prone to advocacy.

An earlier incumbent, Cordell Hull, President Franklin Roosevelt's Secretary of State for twelve years, lent strength to the President primarily as a *mobilizer of congressional and public support.* On the periphery of many important policy deliberations throughout Roosevelt's tenure, Hull enjoyed a notable rapport with former congressional colleagues and proved himself adept at insulating some programs from partisan in-fighting.

The significance of the Secretary's personal qualities, his relations with the President and his conception of his responsibilities is the more important in that the political resources of the State Department are insubstantial in comparison to those of the Defense Department or the CIA. The size of its budget is dwarfed by those of its competitors. Nor is its primacy automatically acknowledged. Historically the expansion of the world interests of the United States coincided with the tenure of President Roosevelt, who scarcely veiled his disenchantment with the State Department, practiced an administrative style encouraging the diffusion of responsibilities, and found it exceedingly difficult to fire ineffectual subordinates.[24] FDR undercut his Secretary, Cordell Hull, rather than replace him. He created separate agencies to handle lend-lease, to direct economic warfare, to disseminate propaganda, to undertake secret operations, and to organize relief and rehabilitation of war-torn areas. The new agencies operated with considerable freedom from any coordination short of the White House, where Harry Hopkins, "Wild Bill" Donovan, Donald Nelson, Robert Sherwood, and Laughlin Currie possessed greater influence than the Secretary of State.[25] When the cold war replaced the brief interlude of peace after World War II, the whole apparatus reappeared beyond the effective control of State. As John Paton Davies remarked, with evident regret, "By now the conduct of foreign relations is well established as everyone's business. With the Peace Corps in the act, butchers, bakers, and candlestick makers are eligible." [26]

Kept free of operational responsibilities, the State Department is supposed to provide policy guidance for the various instrumentali-

---

[23] Hilsman, *op. cit.,* p. 59 and *passim.*

[24] He would merely hire another and set him to work under an only slightly different mandate.

[25] John Paton Davies, *Foreign and Other Affairs* (New York, N.Y.: Norton, 1963), p. 184.

[26] *Ibid.,* p. 185.

ties of America's foreign relations, for example, AID, USIA, ACDA, CIA, and the Treasury Department. Since those agencies control the resources essential to the accomplishment of State's purposes, and since they possess their own unique perspectives, their own "distinctive competences," and their own constituencies, their bargaining assets are impressive. Actual control ranges from considerable, as in the case of USIA and AID, to slight, as in the case of the Defense Department and the CIA.

Nor does the State Department possess ardent public support. The news its diplomats purvey is frequently unpleasant. American diplomats arouse a native suspicion as a consequence of their association with foreigners, their slightly alien accents, and the equivocal character of much of their rather wooden prose. Nor does the Department dispense billions of dollars to suppliers (constituencies) across the land, or possess a string of domestic installations from whence public-relations staffs may build grass roots political support. Diplomats endure the unpleasant task of "boring the hard boards," while the Air Force puts up another satellite, the CIA engages in romantic undercover activities, and the other services act as guardians of American security. There is little question as to which performance is the least arresting to the average citizen.

Despite the tendency to employ the professional diplomats as all-too-available scapegoats, one must not underrate the influence exerted by the Foreign Service. Above all, they constitute the elite group within the American government whose expertise is highly valued, whose *esprit de corps* must be sustained, and whose advice cannot be consistently disregarded. As one observer noted, "The White House could always win any battle it chose over the [Foreign] Service; but the prestige and proficiency of the Service limited the number of battles any White House would find it profitable to fight." [27]

The Defense Department. Military force is an instrument of foreign policy. Since 1945 it has become for the United States more than simply one instrument among others. The objective of American security policy has been transformed to include the deterrence of war and the stabilization of deterrence relationships as well as the achievement of what remains of the concept of "victory" should war occur. The efficacy of much of America's foreign policy clearly depends upon the maintenance of sufficient and suitable types of force to sustain these objectives. It is clear that soldiers and civilian leaders of the Defense Department will continue to participate significantly and continuously in the formulation of foreign policy.

The tasks of Defense Department officials are fourfold.[28] In the first place, they are responsible for formulating a viable set of strategic concepts relating domestic resources to the accomplishment

[27] Schlesinger, *op. cit.*, p. 408.

[28] For an analysis of the Defense Department's management of these tasks during the 1950s and 1960s, see William W. Kaufmann, *The McNamara Strategy* (New York, N.Y.: Harper, 1964).

of central military and foreign policy objectives. Their counsel has been crucial to the weighing of the relative merits of strategies of "finite deterrence," "massive retaliation," "counterforce," and "flexible response." Second, theirs is the task of recommending the appropriate allocation of resources for the development and deployment of forces designed to implement the chosen strategy. Third, they bear substantial responsibility for the management of an extensive network of alliances or collective defense arrangements that link the United States with forty-two other nations. Consultation on strategy must be maintained, military assistance programs administered, weapon sales transacted, and the use of overseas base facilities negotiated. Finally, there are the day-to-day tasks of presiding over a military establishment with an inventory in excess of $135 billion, controlling more than 15,000 square miles of land, maintaining operations on a global scale, employing millions of civilians and soldiers, and spending sums regularly accounting for more than 50 percent of the federal budget and approximately 10 percent of the national income. Little wonder that the Defense Department exerts a substantial influence over American foreign policy.

A mere recitation of the problems confronted in recent years by American diplomacy reveals the extent to which the specialization of the Defense Department has become a central preoccupation. Among them one would surely find the promotion of cohesion within NATO, the negotiation of tacit or explicit arms control accords with the Soviet Union, the forging of satisfactory military instruments for purposes of countering insurgency in the non-West, and the relationship between overseas commitments and the balance-of-payments problem. Military considerations are given a generous hearing in foreign policy deliberations not only because of the costliness of such instruments but also because of the central concern with deterrence and a general realization that inept management of strategic forces may lead to "irretrievable" and possibly "irremediable" disasters.

It is this latter consideration that has contributed to consistent efforts to impose a measure of centralization and unification over the military establishment in order to make of it an instrument more directly responsive to presidential direction. Progress in achieving the functional unification of the Defense Department has been especially impressive since 1961. The power of the Secretary has been derived from (1) increased statutory powers; (2) the continued divisions among the services; (3) the skill displayed by former Secretary Robert McNamara and his staff in employing the analytic techniques of "cost-effectiveness," systems analysis, and operations research to control service programs; (4) the shrewd use of bargaining advantages inherent in the Secretary's ability to dispense budgetary allotments and weapon contracts in return for reforms in the procedures of policy-making that have enhanced the role of the civilian Secretary and his assistants in the Office of the Secretary of Defense. As he has provided vigorous executive leadership in a formerly diffuse defense establishment, the voice of the Secretary of Defense has taken on additional weight in those circles where high policy is determined.

The nature of the international situation in a loose bipolar, nuclear world occasionally permits strategy to overwhelm foreign policy. For example, the decision to rearm Germany was based upon hasty deductions regarding Soviet aims and Western military requirements at the time of the Korean war. Abortive attempts to deploy IRBMs on the territory of European allies as an interim missile capability in the face of Soviet missile developments in 1957 was another such case. The scale and justifications of the American involvement in Vietnam represent a third.

On the other side of the coin, the Defense Department, if well managed, can contribute immeasurably to the efficacy of foreign policy by providing a rational and coherent strategy, by proposing defensible weapon policies, and by promoting effective cooperation among the services. Faulty or inadequate preparedness may condemn American interventions to failure.[28a] The substantial investments in airpower over the past two decades surely contributed to the failure to give sufficient emphasis to conventional forces or to devise tactics more appropriate for counterinsurgency.

In short, the normal performance of their major responsibilities gives to civilian and military officials in the Defense Department a significant influence over the substance of policy. In addition, they are spokesmen for a particular set of interests that always demands a hearing in moments of trouble. A President needn't always accommodate his military advisers. Nor is he generally confronted by a unanimous set of views from those advisers. Yet pressure from the Joint Chiefs, for example, to resort to an airstrike or an invasion during the Cuban missile crisis in 1962, to give carte blanche for the use of all necessary types of force had the United States intervened in Laos in 1961–1962, for the expansion of targeting lists in the air war over North Vietnam from 1965–1968, or for the immediate deployment of a massive antiballistic missile defense system poses restraints upon the President and requires him to treat their views with respect, if not deference, for no President wishes to be charged with overruling the military spokesmen on "military" issues.

The Central Intelligence Agency. The ascendancy of the State Department in foreign-policy-making is challenged not only by the influence of the Defense Department but by that of the Central Intelligence Agency. Created by the National Security Act in 1947 as the successor to the wartime Office of Strategic Services, the CIA's statutory base and the prestige that it subsequently acquired give

---

[28a] The very mobilization of certain forces may pose temptations to use them. General Ridgway expressed reservations about America's capacity to support an intervention in Indochina in 1954. His doubts reinforced the judicious sense of restraint urged on the President by congressional leaders and British allies. In the 1960s a considerable conventional rearmament may have eroded such restraints somewhat.

to the Agency what one former Director has termed "a more influential position in our government than intelligence enjoys in any other government in the world." [29] Its duties include the collection and verification of information through both overt and covert intelligence operations on every country in the world; the analysis, evaluation, and interpretation of this information, as well as its distribution to appropriate government agencies; the formulation of national estimates regarding the intentions and capabilities of friends and enemies; the formulation of proposals for policy, and the implementation of occasional assignments of such a character that the government wishes to avoid the appearance of formal sponsorship, for example, espionage, the clandestine violation of frontiers, and the financing of coups.

The CIA possesses all the resources necessary for prodigious influence in Washington. Its budget is sizable (reportedly more than $.5 billion annually), and its leaders possess extraordinary flexibility in the use of funds, due to their freedom from normal auditing procedures. Information is power, and the CIA collects and interprets much of the information upon which policy is based. Its personnel are numerous and highly qualified, 50 percent of its analysts having advanced degrees. Unlike the Defense Department, the CIA has not been rent by internal divisions that permit outsiders to obtain a bit of leverage and a means of control. Until recently the Agency has been free of public and congressional suspicions, which have so frequently hampered the effectiveness of the State Department. It still enjoys powerful defenders on the Senate Armed Services and Appropriations Committees, which provide a measure of surveillance over its activities.

With more than 2000 men in the field, the CIA's resources for political and strategic intelligence are unsurpassed. Its station chiefs often enjoy longer tenure in foreign assignments than their counterparts in the State Department. At times CIA agents dominate the political sections of foreign embassies. Nor are they under comparable restraints from striking up contacts with unofficial and nongovernmental representatives in foreign societies. This occasionally gives them a stronger "feel" for the local situation than that of American diplomats. The secrecy of CIA activities not only provides a measure of immunity from congressional investigation but also enables it to undertake limited operations abroad without incurring the appearance of a major government commitment difficult to disavow later. The promise of action accords its spokesmen a favorable hearing from those disturbed by the equivocation of State Department officials.

The existence of formidable and diversified capabilities often encourages their use. The CIA has its agents abroad, the facilities for transmitting information and propaganda, and centers for the training of guerrillas. It has airplanes, ships (even a trained brigade

[29] Hilsman, *op. cit.*, p. 65.

of regular troops for the abortive Bay of Pigs invasion), and the necessary logistic capabilities to support them. As recent revelations attest, moreover, the CIA has developed a variety of techniques for using the considerable pluralism of American society to acquire a measure of direct access to foreign societies. Thus the overseas activities of labor unions, student associations, and cultural enterprises have been clandestinely subsidized by the CIA through a variety of "front" organizations.

Legends of CIA derring-do have perhaps outrun the facts. That the Agency has become a convenient whipping boy and scapegoat in many quarters is well illustrated by the *New Yorker* cartoon portraying two African natives observing the eruption of a volcano in the background and remarking, "The CIA did it. Pass it on!" Nevertheless, the diversity of CIA activities does inspire awe among some, fear among others. They have trained foreign armies (for example, Meo tribesmen in Vietnam), organized foreign parties ("Committee for the Defense of the National Interests" in Laos), brought down foreign governments (Arbenz's regime in Guatemala in 1954), and maintained impressive programs of technical surveillance over the Soviet Union (for example, U-2 flights).[30]

Other executive agencies

In addition to the extensive and continuous involvement of the State Department, Defense Department, and CIA in virtually all aspects of foreign policy, other executive departments and agencies participate in foreign policy formulation. Their involvement, however, is less weighty, less regular, and more restricted in scope. Above all, there are those wholly foreign-affairs agencies engaged in the execution of operational programs.

The United States Information Agency is principally involved in the administration of cultural exchange programs and the dissemination overseas of information about the United States and its policies. It may exert a marginal influence over policy formulation through its reports on foreign reactions to American initiatives. The opportunity for such influence has been assured by regularly inviting its director to meetings of the National Security Council and by giving USIA representation upon the Senior Inter-Departmental Groups that attempt to coordinate the programs of the State Department, Defense Department, Agency for International Development, USIA, and Central Intelligence Agency. Subject to policy guidance from the Department of State, USIA has gone through several stages of varying dependence on and autonomy from that Department.

The Agency for International Development is but the latest organization responsible for the administration of the bulk of America's foreign aid programs. An instrumentality of policy, its expertise

---

[30] For perhaps the most comprehensive public account of CIA activities, see the series of articles published in *The New York Times* (April 25–29, 1966).

and experience insure it a measure of influence in determining the magnitude and the allocation of foreign aid money as well as in the establishment of criteria by which it is dispensed and on the basis of which its utility is subsequently measured. Like USIA, it is a semi-autonomous agency operating under the guidance of the State Department.

The Arms Control and Disarmament Agency is a more recent creation, having been established in 1961 to serve as a source of ideas and an instrument of negotiation in the arms control and disarmament field. Matters of primary concern to this agency are so intimately related to the chief preoccupations of the Defense Department and the State Department that it has not achieved impressive independent stature thus far. Indeed, its representatives were not even invited to testify in the Senate Foreign Relations hearings on the Test Ban Treaty in 1963. Housed currently in the State Department's building, ACDA's influence is most likely to be effective when exerted jointly with the International Security Affairs Bureau within the Defense Department and the Office of Politico-Military Affairs of the State Department, or in cooperation with nonprofit research institutes like the RAND Corporation, the Hudson Institute, or the Institute for Defense Analysis.

Other agencies participate on an even more peripheral basis in foreign policy matters, though their influence may be substantial on an occasional specific issue. The Director of the Peace Corps may exercise a marginal influence over foreign aid policy, as may the Director of the Food for Peace program, located in the Executive Office of the President. The Atomic Energy Commission and National Aeronautics and Space Administration engage in activities that frequently require diplomatic efforts to obtain rights to create tracking stations, negotiate agreements to supply uranium, or make arrangements to exchange information, and participate in international conferences.

Specialized commissions also exist to advise the President on specific foreign policy issues. A Trade Policy Committee under the chairmanship of the Secretary of Commerce advises the Chief Executive on tariff commission cases, and a Special Representative for Trade Negotiations within the Executive Office of the President was responsible for managing negotiations for trade liberalization with other industrial states. The Director of the Office of Emergency Planning advises the President on import restrictions deemed necessary for national security, and the Agricultural Secretary provides comparable advice when imports threaten the system of price supports for domestic production. A National Advisory Council on International Monetary and Financial Problems with leadership provided by the Treasury Secretary concerns itself with matters suggested by its title, and offers advice and counsel to American representatives to the International Bank for Reconstruction and Development, the International Monetary Fund, and the International Finance Corporation.

Other departments and agencies may be preoccupied only

intermittently with foreign issues. The departments of Labor, Agriculture, Commerce, and Treasury are principally absorbed in domestic programs, but maintain substantial representation abroad and undertake a significant number of foreign programs. The latter is perhaps the most important of these as a result of the fact that the dollar is both the domestic currency and an international reserve currency.

Finally, one might mention those nonprofit corporations that have sprung up in recent decades to provide a regular source of ideas and advice to various government agencies. There are now more than 350 "think factories" involved in contractual research for the government. Three hundred university-located institutes also make contributions, as do well over a thousand corporations maintaining research establishments. Many of these do research essentially upon weapon possibilities and hardware projects. Others, however, contribute quite sophisticated studies and recommendations on strategic and political issues. There are also the scientific advisory boards maintained in such abundance by the military services, as well as the supervisory committees and the individual consultants. These provide talent, a source of recruitment to official positions, a constant stream of ideas, and an occasional individual capable of employing freewheeling techniques to mobilize support for an important change in official policy. For example, Albert Wohlstetter's exertions on behalf of a new conception of the United States overseas basing system in the early 1950s from his position as a RAND Corporation analyst, or Herman Kahn's forays into defense policy issues from his position as Director of the Hudson Institute. The independence enjoyed by such corporations and institutes lends prestige to their conclusions; their access to governmental intelligence information may lend realism to their recommendations.

The public arena

Congress. If executive ascendancy is generally assured in the formulation and execution of foreign policy, Congress is not without resources of its own to secure vital information about those policies, and occasionally to intervene with decisive results. The President may possess the initiative; occasionally he can act with secrecy and dispatch. He controls the levers of information. He makes the appointments, drafts the laws, negotiates the agreements, and deploys the troops. He must, however, rely upon an independent, proud, and powerful legislature for succor and support. He must be constantly alert lest his appointments be repudiated, his budgets cut, his laws refused, his programs vitiated by damaging amendments, his declarations compromised by the expression of contrary sentiments by important senators or representatives, or his treaties "ambushed" in committee. Occasionally, congressional prerogatives in foreign-policy-making are compared to the classic powers of Bagehot's Queen; that is, "the right to be consulted, to encourage, and to warn." This is to underestimate the very real influence that remains with Congress even when it yields the initiative and accords considerable deference to the executive branch. While secondary, its influence is far from insignificant. Indeed, far from witnessing the eclipse of Congress, the growing cost of foreign aid and military security programs as well as the "collapse of categories" between foreign and domestic issues (illustrated by the maintenance of costly foreign programs, the drain of the American gold supply this has caused, and the constraints such outflows of gold and the need to encourage foreigners to maintain dollar balances in American banks has worked on domestic monetary and fiscal policy) have projected Congress into an increasingly important role.

The formal prerogatives of Congress, although not equal to those of the President in foreign affairs, are nevertheless imposing. Congress has the power to regulate tariffs, duties, financial exchanges, and travel with other countries. It passes immigration acts and determines the conditions of naturalization and the rights of aliens. It fixes the size of the armed services and retains the power of the purse in the maintenance of those forces. By providing the money for foreign representation it may interfere in this aspect of diplomatic interchange. The Senate must confirm presidential ambassadorial appointments as well as the appointments to high office in the leading domestic agencies engaged in the formulation of foreign policy. Treaties must be approved by two-thirds of those present and voting in the Senate. Although the President may circumvent the Senate by negotiating executive agreements, those frequently require enabling legislation for their effective implementation. Others are based upon authority granted previously by the Congress, for example, presidential authority to negotiate reciprocal trade agreements, and such powers may presumably be revoked at a later date if they are unsatisfactorily exercised.

Through the powers of the purse, Congress may enfeeble or invigorate executive efforts. The repeated failure of the President to acquire the power of an item veto over congressional actions permits Congress, moreover, to attach riders to important pieces of legislation that may substantially compromise the intent of executive policies. The congressional power to create and fix the responsibilities of executive agencies through statute may render those agencies extensions of the committee system of Congress, and have the effect of compromising the loyalty of some executive branch officials to the President. The power to carry out investigations—increasingly without reference to particular legislation—permits Congress both to obtain a means of influencing the actual administration of foreign policy and to limit the flexibility of the Executive without setting rigid restraints in the law. Senators and representatives may indicate the limits of congressional tolerance through investigations, committee reports, close votes on important bills, amendments, debates, and occasional resolutions.

Actually, it is impossible to specify the range of congressional participation and potential influence in policy-making without distinguishing among various "issue-areas." With respect to those decisions reached under conditions of grave international crises, the importance of secrecy, the necessity for dispatch, and the imperatives of a deft diplomatic touch tend to increase congressional submissiveness to Presidential leadership. During the Cuban missile crisis, for example, powerful congressional leaders were informed of decisions; they were not consulted.

Congressional powers are most relevant to the administration of the executive bureaucracies. With respect to *program policies* such as the annual formulation of the foreign aid or military budgets, laws are required, appropriations are needed, and administrators may be kept under continuous scrutiny. Here the congressional powers of the purse, legislation, and investigation come importantly into play. Congressional influence on decisions will still depend upon the nature of the issue, the timing of congressional involvement, and the divisions within the executive branch over policy. In its handling of foreign aid budgets, for example, Congress is perceptibly more aggressive than in its participation in the formulation of the national defense budget. Where a multibillion dollar defense budget may be handled in a more or less perfunctory manner, with minimal cuts and few damaging amendments, foreign aid budgets are regularly assaulted with vengeance and apparent glee. Cuts are frequently deep, the debates normally cast some doubt upon the efficacy or even the need for such programs, and riders often severely limit the President's flexibility or lead foreigners to nourish honest doubts about American intentions. In recent years the multitude of riders to such bills have included the denial of aid to countries "engaging in or preparing for aggressive military efforts against any other nation receiving aid"; states appropriating American property without just, prompt, and adequate compensation; countries trading with Cuba or North Vietnam; countries "dominated by International Communism," and international organizations supplying aid to Cuba, among others. Normally, however, such specific restrictions may be waived if the President deems a potential recipient worthy and assistance to it vital to national security.

In relationship to *declaratory* or *anticipatory policy*, that is, the formulation of assertions regarding America's intentions under certain specified conditions, the President is in the driver's seat, but Congress is capable of sometimes annoying, sometimes helpful backseat driving. Congress participated in the formulation of the Truman Doctrine and the Eisenhower Doctrine only insofar as its "anticipated reactions" were taken into account by those drafting presidential statements. A somewhat more active role was played in the adoption of the Formosa Resolution in 1955 and the Tonkin Gulf Resolution in 1964. In both cases, however, Congress offered its assent rather than providing initiative. It is not to be expected, however, that Congress will automatically rubber-stamp such Presidential efforts to engage its prestige in his declaratory pronouncements. Rarely will the Chief Executive request a resolution conferring substantial additional powers in advance except in a grave crisis or in response to unequivocal dangers, for such a request may merely unleash a prolonged and divisive debate, embarrassing queries, close votes, a diminution of public confidence, and a consequent dilution of the desired authority.

The powers of Congress provide a counterpoint to those of the Executive. The latter can initiate a course of action, can attempt to impose a *fait accompli,* can informally commit the nation, can maneuver the country into a position from which it can only with difficulty retreat. Congress, on the other hand, plays the more passive game of deterrence. It has the power and the disposition to define within broad limits the range of permissible executive action. Like practitioners of deterrence, congressmen sometimes pose explicit threats against specific actions, for example, riders to foreign aid bills cutting off aid to states engaging in a variety of unpalatable actions; they sometimes articulate threats of a more ambiguous character by generating a climate of opinion that is hostile to impending Administration moves. Here the possibility of embarrassing rebuffs may achieve results. More frequently Congress trades off promises of cooperation for the foreclosure of unpalatable policies.

Another tendency is for Congress to assert itself more vigorously on the margins of important matters, especially those that have substantive implications for domestic policy or the constitutional relationships between the branches. Whenever its cherished powers are threatened, as, for example, in issues involving the powers of the purse (long-term financing of foreign aid), domestic propaganda (use of USIA films at home), immigration, internal security, or tariffs and quotas, the predictable response will be self-assertive.

Although Congress is most characteristically a source of delay, a poser of obstacles, and a definer of limits, it may at times attempt a more positive role. Since early 1966, Senator Fulbright has organized public hearings before the Senate Foreign Relations Committee designed to solicit the views of prestigious figures regarding the dimensions of an American policy for Asia. Clearly his objective has been to force a reevaluation of the wisdom of President Johnson's Vietnam policies. Yet coupled with this desire is an anxiety to pose constructive alternatives for mastering the tides of change in that area. Likewise, Senator Jackson has for some years used the resources of the Senate Government Operations Committee to counsel with an impressive list of witnesses regarding the effectiveness of the organization and procedures of the government for making national security policy. Occasionally, also, congressmen—Senator Keating during the Cuban missile crisis, for example—assist in galvanizing the government into action. More infrequently, the legislature may give rise to a genuine, new departure—for example, Senator Monroney's Resolution of 1961, which led to the establishment of the International Development Association. Earlier congressional insistence led to the use of certain Marshall Plan funds to encourage the creation of the European Payments Union. Such initiatives are comparatively rare, however, for congressmen are not privy to the detailed flow of information from overseas.

While the expertise of some congressmen is formidable, and that of the entire Congress comparable to any legislature in the world, the complexity of most international issues hampers their powers of initiative. In the distribution of experts, the Executive is still far more abundantly endowed. Nevertheless, even when exerting the powers to delay or obstruct, congressmen perform the useful function of forcing executive officials to justify programs with intelligence as well as zeal. It occasions public debates or dialogues that enhance public understanding of foreign policy issues. It provides an independent source of criticism and advice. And it helps to keep bureaucrats honest, as well as occasionally prodding them into activity or creativity. "The President proposes; Congress disposes," goes the maxim. But the congressional disposition toward presidential proposals may not be favorable or even tolerant. From the capacity to withhold consent is derived the power to shape the substance and the tone of policy.

Interest groups. America is a nation of joiners, and interest groups abound. Indeed, aside from voting, the most characteristic mode of political participation in the United States takes the form of lobbying activity. Lobby groups range from *ad hoc,* single-issue associations to highly bureaucratic organizations representing constituency interests on a wide variety of issues. The role of such groups in the formulation of domestic policy has long been acknowledged. The extent of their influence on foreign policy decisions is more difficult to assess.

There are surely plausible grounds for believing that the influence of associational interest groups may be substantial on matters of foreign policy. For one thing, in a truly national society the decisions of the federal government simultaneously affect all segments of the country, thus activating constituency interests eager to defend themselves against encroachments or anxious to exploit opportunities to gain special dispensations. The distinction, moreover, between foreign and domestic policy has become more and more obscure at a time when the maintenance of national security has become enormously expensive and hazardous, when the economy is geared to defense procurement, and when the society is constantly mobilized for the achievement of foreign policy objectives.

The more directly foreign policy decisions affect domestic interests, the more insistently will associational groups vie for influence over such decisions. Few groups express an interest in the recognition of a new government in Africa. Nor does the prospect of chillier relations with Afghanistan occasion much lobbying activity. Let the question of tariffs be raised, however, and a host of domestic groups will be galvanized into immediate action. Even then, trade policy is not determined by a mere mechanical aggregation of subnational interests. On the contrary, associational interest groups seem to exert in-

fluence only around the margins of important foreign policy deliberations. Several factors may account for this conclusion.

In the first place, those groups like the AFL-CIO, the National
Association of Manufacturers, the National Chamber of Commerce,
and the National Farm Bureau, which are well organized and well
financed, represent large and heterogeneous constituencies. On most
foreign policy issues, therefore, their members cannot be expected
to be of one mind. A low common denominator of agreement may be
expressed in the form of ambiguous formulas. But interests that are
not defined with precision and specificity are not apt to influence
policy decisively.

Second, the more substantial the impact of foreign policies on
American society, the more likely it is that lobbying groups will discern their particular interests with clarity and assert them with vigor.
Wide publicity is likely to attend the discussion of such questions.
Highly publicized issues are, however, precisely those on which the
room for partisan maneuver is most limited. As Bernard Cohen has
noted, "Particular groups are . . . most effective when the policy issue
in which they are interested is, for whatever reasons, not in the public
eye." [31]

Third, the limited influence of associational groups over foreign policy decisions is perhaps related to the executive locale of
policy-making on many such issues. The power of pressure groups is
enhanced in the congressional arena where a multitude of veto points
may be exploited to advantage. On foreign policy decisions, where
information is monopolized by executive agencies, where policies may
be framed in an atmosphere of some secrecy and under the compelling
pressures of time, the influence of *institutional interests*, for example,
the Foreign Service, the military bureaucracies, or the Central Intelligence Agency, tends to predominate over that of *associational interest
groups*.

Even on the issues over which Congress exerts substantial
influence, the power of lobbying groups is strictly limited. Producer
groups have at best been able to add "escape clauses" to trade legislation bearing a generally liberal stamp. Maritime interests have regularly obtained assurances that 50 percent of foreign aid commodity
shipments will be transported in American vessels, but the shipping
lobby has had little influence over the size or the distribution of foreign
aid funds. Peace groups critical of American policy in Vietnam may
have prompted the President to appoint a citizen's commission to
monitor the 1967 presidential elections in that Southeast Asian country. Prior to mid-1968, however, they seemed to have little perceptible
influence over the magnitude of America's political commitment or
the conduct of its military operations in Vietnam.

Fourth, few associational groups are consulted as a matter of
course on foreign policy questions. No administration would consider

[31] Bernard Cohen, "The Influence of Non-Governmental Groups on Foreign Policy-
Making," in *Readings in the Making of American Foreign Policy*, Andrew Scott
and Raymond Dawson (eds.) (New York, N.Y.: Macmillan, 1965), p. 106.

labor legislation without extensive negotiations with the unions. Access to foreign policy decision-making is more likely to be based upon knowledge than upon financial or organizational power. Nevertheless, it does not appear that the university or nonprofit research institutes that produce studies on strategic and foreign policy issues are regularly conceded the right to consultations on important decisions. Their advice may be sought, their wisdom tapped, and their services welcomed, but the purpose is to improve the quality of decisions rather than to assure their approval.

Of interest in this connection is the fact that many institutional interest groups within the government have created "backstop associations" or affiliates to lobby on their behalf from without the government. The Navy League, the Army Association, and the Air Force Association are, for example, barely disguised political instruments of the armed services. In the immediate postwar period they served the purpose of increasing public understanding of the need for preparedness even as they promoted the more parochial interests of their particular services. Many now see them as integral elements of a vast and ominous "military-industrial complex" that exaggerates America's security needs, conveys an excessively military bias to its foreign policy, and perpetuates a political atmosphere receptive to stale and outdated cold war clichés.

There can be little doubt that two decades of high-level defense spending have given certain communities, states, and even entire regions a stake in the maintenance of a large military establishment. Research and development have been closely geared to military requirements. New industries, producing specialized equipment for war and dependent almost entirely upon the Defense Department for contracts, have grown up. The dispersion of military installations and the widespread network of industrial suppliers insures grass roots support for generous defense budgets. As one high-ranking member of the House Subcommittee on Defense Appropriations observed, "Defense is only one of the factors that enter into our determinations for defense spending. The others are pump priming, spreading the immediate benefits of defense spending, taking care of all the services, giving all defense contractors a fair share, and spreading the military bases to include all sections." [32] Some have gone even further to imply that a high level of international tension is artificially contrived in order to justify the preservation of a "complex" that in reality exists to promote essentially domestic interests.[33]

This surely overstates the case. To acknowledge the influence of the military establishment and its industrial suppliers upon national security policy requires neither that one attribute to them the character of a sinister monolith nor that one concede that foreign and defense

[32] Cited in Douglass Cater, *Power in Washington* (New York, N.Y.: Vintage, 1965), p. 40.

[33] See, for example, Fred I. Cook, "Juggernaut: The Warfare State," *The Nation* (February 28, 1961); or *Report from Iron Mountain* with an introduction by Leonard Lewin (New York, N.Y.: Dial, 1967).

policies are hostages to the interests or demands of such a "complex." Rivalry among the military services and competition among their industrial suppliers is persistent and intense. The unity ascribed by some to the "military-industrial complex" is surely not very apparent on a host of issues related to strategy, weapon innovation, and defense budgeting.

The existence of powerful vested interests in a high level of defense preparedness does perhaps produce rather unequal competition in deliberations over defense expenditures. The power of such interests is suggested by the ease with which military budgets are rammed through the appropriations cycle, possibly by the unsympathetic treatment tendered most schemes envisaging disarmament, or conceivably by the facility with which, in a period of Russian-American détente, stereotypes of the Soviet Union, an impressive and formidable rival, have been transferred to the Chinese, whose weaknesses are overlooked and whose rationality in the conduct of foreign affairs is underrated.

On the other hand, professional military leaders have frequently complained at having their advice overruled by an assertive group of civilians in the Office of the Secretary of Defense. Efforts of the aerospace industry were unavailing in their campaigns to gain program approval for the B-70 manned bomber, to prevent cancellation of the Skybolt missile or the Dynosoar project, or to force the hand of the Secretary of Defense in placing an ABM system into production. On September 18, 1967 a decision to procure the Sentinel ABM system was announced, but the timing of this announcement suggests that it was triggered by prior Soviet decisions and accelerated progress in the Chinese nuclear program rather than by domestic pressures alone.

A *quantitative* view of power may encourage the belief that the very size of the defense establishment permits it to ride roughshod over other participants in defense and foreign-policy-making. The divisions within that establishment, however, offer the potential for its control. Still, firm conclusions are elusive. Rivalries among the services and competition among defense contractors permit civilian defense leaders to pick and choose among programs and weapon proposals. A measure of freedom to decide among alternative proposals does not, however, guarantee that major reductions in defense expenditures could be effected in the face of the determined resistance that military and industrial interests might muster.[34] Interest in arms control, implying the tacit coordination of military programs among potential military adversaries, has flourished, interestingly enough, simultaneously with the growth of America's preparedness economy. No equivalent interest in arms reduction has been evident. Greater civilian managerial control has been achieved over the military service departments during the past decade. The level of defense spending

[34] It is perhaps instructive to recall that the plateau of defense spending was reduced in the post-Korean war period. See Huntington, *The Common Defense,* Chaps. 14–21, for an analysis of the forces shaping the national security budget.

has, however, increased consistently throughout this period. A massive space effort has been undertaken that could absorb many of the products and employ much of the personnel of the aerospace and electronics industries, which currently devote a high percentage of their resources to military programs. The potential for industrial conversion has as yet not been put to the test.

Foreign and defense policy are not, then, determined by a mere aggregation of domestic group interests. The pattern of pressure group activity is shaped perhaps more by the development of official policy than policy is influenced by their lobbying. Certainly the relationships of influence between the foreign policy agencies and interest groups runs in both directions. And occasionally what superficially appears to be spontaneous lobbying activity by associational groups is revealed upon closer inspection to be the quasi-official maneuvering of the "backstop" associations of institutional interests within the government.

The mass media. An open society requires an atmosphere congenial to the free circulation of political information and a press independent of government control. Both conditions are met in the United States. Washington, as the British columnist Anthony Howard once commented, is a capital city in which "all hearts are open, all desires are known, and no secrets hidden (at least for long)." Neither politicians nor civil servants regularly manage to keep their own counsel on the great public policy questions. No press officers consistently succeed in concealing rather than revealing information to an inquisitive press corps. No official secrets act is interpreted generously by the government for its own protection. No public figures enjoy immunity either from congressional investigation or from the private speculations of "inside dopesters" in the press. Efforts made by Presidents to carefully monitor or rigorously discipline relations between their subordinates and newsmen (here one includes radio and television correspondents) predictably arouse the righteous indignation of officialdom and the eloquent rage of editorial writers.

In 1966 there were in the United States some 1754 daily newspapers with a circulation of 61,397,000. Some 578 Sunday newspapers achieved a circulation of 49,282,000. Ninety-three percent of all households in America possess at least one television set. The press, radio, and television industries employ about 600,000 persons, but perhaps no more than 60,000 actually write and edit the news. Fewer still enjoy such reputations for acerbity, wisdom, and wit that their columns are regularly read and studied by policymakers and the public alike. The comparatively small size of the American communication elite cannot, however, obscure the tremendous diversity of institutions and publications embraced by the mass media. The diversity of the media is complemented by their independence from governmental control. Private ownership and constitutional safeguards insure both independence and variety.

The roles played by the news media in the formulation of foreign policy are correspondingly various.[35] For one thing, the press links widely scattered officials and agencies by providing a common fund of information, by assisting in the establishment of standards for evaluating external developments, by generating a common framework of expectations regarding the policies of adversaries and friends, and by mediating the President's relations with the executive departments, Congress, and the "attentive" and mass publics. For another, the press constitutes an additional source of intelligence information on foreign developments. Newspapers of record, such as *The New York Times*, offer a medium for the lost art of diplomatic reporting. Whereas the official cables are full of specialized and detailed data on every foreign society, the best newspapers provide a useful supplemental record of the broad political, economic, and social developments in the world. Not only does the press provide an independent source of information; its reports are often transmitted more swiftly than those sent through diplomatic channels. Since an element of selectivity must always shape the presentation of the news, moreover, the way stories are played in the press and news magazines may help to clarify for officialdom the relative importance of various events, and thus influence the allocation of official energies and anxieties.

Of equal importance, so crucial is the role of the press—facilitating democratic control by describing the substance and speculating upon the motives of official acts—that it enjoys a quasi-constitutional mandate as a "fourth estate" of government. Press coverage of American foreign policy may influence the public's appreciation of current policies and future problems, deepen the public's awareness of available alternatives, and strengthen public support for those courses of action sanctioned by the government in foreign affairs. It assists decision-makers by providing "cues" as to the structure of public support for existing policies. It may even provide a surrogate for public opinion, since developments break with such dizzying speed that the mass public is often baffled, while the newspapers continue to provide the appearance of more or less coherent opinion. By publicizing the existence of fundamental disagreements within the government over impending choices, the press also enables perceptive outsiders to identify the moments for timely interventions in the policy-making process. In this latter respect, the press helps to broaden the arena of policy-making and to guarantee to members of the attentive public an occasion on which they may inject their own views into the "great debates."

The actual impact of the American press and mass media upon

[35] For appraisals of the American press and foreign policy, see James Reston, *The Artillery of the Press* (New York, N.Y.: Harper, 1967); Bernard Cohen, *The Press and Foreign Policy* (Princeton, N.J.: Princeton University Press, 1963); Douglass Cater, *The Fourth Estate* (New York, N.Y.: Houghton Mifflin, 1959), and Henry Fairlie, "The Press: Anglo-American Differences," *Encounter*, XXVI (June 1966), pp. 73–87.

the content of foreign policy—as opposed to the identification of their role in policy-making—is difficult to establish. The following hypotheses may be worthy of further analysis.

1. The very character of the American mass media makes them somewhat more effective in a supporting rather than a critical role vis-à-vis the President and the foreign policies for which he bears primary responsibility. As many critics have pointed out, the American press emphasizes *news* rather than elevating *opinion*. The local press tends to be notoriously provincial. The editorial policies of even many great metropolitan dailies are marked by what often appears to be a virtual lack of serious conviction. In the major newspapers of record, the effort to publish "all the news that's fit to print" generally results in a lack of selectivity. Consequently, genuine news may be obscured by the flow of events. The wire services like Associated Press and United Press International, moreover, were established originally as nonprofit cooperatives to serve a wide variety of different newspapers too small individually to support such ventures. One consequence is a tradition of impartial, neutral, and accurate reporting. Another is that controversial viewpoints are softened in the effort to please many audiences. Where news is emphasized at the expense of opinions, the President, as the prime generator of "news," is in a position to dominate the headlines and to impose his own definition of the meaning of events upon the public's understanding of them. Skillful Chief Executives have learned to turn presidential news conferences to particular advantage. Artful circumlocution, confusing syntax, and misleading statistics have all been employed upon occasion to convey impressions without clarifying presidential intentions. In any event, Presidents decide when to hold press conferences, whom to invite and recognize, and whether or not to answer or evade specific queries.

2. In the face of a vigorous and assertive free press, the American government can scarcely expect to shield its activities from the scrutiny of foreign and domestic critics. Expectations of publicity frequently affect the comparative advantage of one policy alternative over another. The risk of premature public disclosure threatens the efficacy of clandestine operations, posing obstacles to undercover paramilitary maneuvers and secret diplomacy alike.

The exception may perhaps suffice to illustrate the rule. The effort to foreclose public debate regarding the exile invasion of Cuba in 1961 contributed to the disaster, since the absence of discussion within the government resulted in a failure to scrutinize critically the CIA's plans. Despite extraordinary efforts to avert "leaks" to the press, enough of the story seeped out to provide Cubans and Americans alike with premonitions of the forthcoming expeditionary raid long before a single exile set forth for the Bay of Pigs. The attendant publicity thrust the issue into public debate in an atmosphere of rumor and suspicion. "Responsible" journalists, aware of the imminent invasion and dubious of its efficacy and its wisdom, were nonetheless reticent to reveal the full extent of American participation for fear of personally assuming responsibility for compromising further its low probability of success. Enough was known of the CIA's involvement to make the President alter the plans at the last moment in order to minimize the appearance of American participation. Once the project became a subject of public discussion and conjecture, it became a hostage to the ebb and flow of ephemeral moods and enduring foreign policy perspectives—impatience, fear of war, lack of sophistication in regarding the use of force in world politics, outrage at Cuban affronts to American property, sympathy for the Cuban exiles, anxieties prompted by analogies between the Russian's brutal suppression of the Hungarian revolt and the projected role of the United States in the Caribbean, and so forth.[36] The concatenation of these doubts, fears, and illusions was reflected in the manner in which the invasion was planned and executed. The result was a half-hearted attempt to execute an unpromising venture that officials were willing neither to fully abandon nor to fully support.

3. By emphasizing the spectacular or sensational at the expense of the intrinsically significant, the press perhaps tends to reinforce the tendency of the American government to attend to that which is urgent at the frequent expense of that which is important. The thrust and counterthrust of criticism toward American policies that is displayed daily in the press may prompt leading foreign policy officials, moreover, to spend as much time on the public-relations aspects of foreign policy as in dealing with the substantive problems associated with those policies.

Public opinion. In a democracy the outer limits of permissible governmental actions are determined by public opinion. In America, however, the *public* is no undifferentiated mass. There are, rather, many publics, and they are infinitely various in their knowledge about, and interest in, foreign policy issues. In his path-breaking study, *The American People and Foreign Policy,* Gabriel Almond distinguished between the *mass public* and the *attentive public.*[37] The former responds to foreign policy questions on the basis of emotion and mood. Its opinions have little intellectual content. Aroused, the mass public may pose rigid constraints upon policy-making elites. The attentive public, on the other hand, consists essentially of college-educated men and women who take a regular interest in foreign policy issues, attempt to inform themselves of the alternatives, and frequently upgrade the intragovernmental debates on foreign policy by providing a critical audience for them.

The constraints imposed upon American foreign policy by the "brooding omnipresence of public opinion" have been frequently overestimated by critics. Prior to World War II international commitments were shunned by Americans, possibly in order to avert a test of the

---

[36] Brzezinski and Huntington, *Political Power USA/USSR,* p. 387.

[37] Gabriel Almond, *The American People and Foreign Policy* (New York, N.Y.: Praeger, 1960).

compatibility of the processes of democratic control with the requirements of foreign policy. Since 1945, however, the demands of coherent policy have assumed an increased precedence, and attitudes
as well as institutions have been transformed to facilitate an active
engagement in international politics.

The attitudes of the mass public have been generally malleable. Their moods are far less ephemeral, their perspectives toward
foreign policy more stable and mature, and their deference to the
President's lead more consistent than many critics have been willing
to concede. The sacrifices required to sustain global commitments
have been accepted with remarkably good grace; no country has
spent so much in support of so many. Few countries have devoted
as large a portion of their national treasure to foreign policy endeavors in peacetime. Occasionally a President has explained his reluctance to undertake a specific course of action by implying that the
public would resist the assumption of additional burdens. Such limits of public tolerance often exist only, however, in the eye of the
beholder. Public opinion polls have consistently confirmed the public's willingness to support whatever level of sacrifice the President
deems essential to the preservation of vital national interests. Where
a firm course has been set by the Administration, "cues" on public
opinion are more likely to be taken as guides to adjustments in the
tactics of public-relations campaigns. Where the governmental consensus on policy becomes fragile, public opinion may play a more
crucial role.

Moreover, the proposition that in times of national danger
domestic divisions limit the government's ability to preserve a strong
military or diplomatic front is more persuasive as an abstract formulation than as a hypothesis that would explain the weaknesses of the
American political system for the conduct of foreign policy in recent
decades. The American people have repeatedly rallied behind the
President in moments of potential peril. An eminent newspaper columnist has aptly observed that in an age of continual crisis the public
instinctively follows and supports presidential initiatives. "In the old
days," James Reston noted, "the people tended to believe the government was wrong until war was actually declared; now, confronted
with torrents of confusing and often contradictory information about
questions that could lead to war, the tendency is to assume the government is right." [38]

Indeed the role of the public has been especially passive and
submissive during grave international crises. The potential for presidential leadership is greatest when the attention of the public is
captured by the drama of events. During the Suez crisis in 1956, the
intervention in Lebanon in 1958, and even the Bay of Pigs debacle in
1961, presidential popularity rose appreciably. The Chief Executive's
hand rarely has been forced or stayed by pressures of public opinion in the recurrent crises of the cold war. During the prolonged crisis

[38] Reston, *op. cit.*, p. 70.

over the Berlin access routes in 1961, President Kennedy was able to mobilize the reserves and substantially increase defense spending without losing public support. Nor did the resolution of the public falter in October, 1962 when the President solemnly declared that the possible consequences of the Cuban quarantine included thermonuclear war.

Nor have those shifts in public opinion that have transferred control of the White House back and forth from Democrats to Republicans disrupted the basic continuity of American foreign policy, even though foreign policy was a significant issue in several Presidential elections. In 1952 General Eisenhower capitalized upon a mood of frustration engendered by a costly and inconclusive war in Korea, and brought the Republicans their first presidential victory in twenty-four years. Far from eroding the American position in Korea, the effect of that election was to produce a new Administration possessing the popular standing to legitimate a settlement that the embattled Truman Administration would have found diplomatically acceptable but politically unmanageable at home.

To summarize, the "action" on foreign policy issues is generally most intense within the executive branch. To an increasing extent the bureaucratic character of American government exerts an influence over the content and style of foreign policy as decisive as that of its democratic features. The public arena remains important, for in the United States the voters retain their ultimate sanction: the right to select new leaders at periodic intervals. Polls provide an efficient means of ascertaining public attitudes on the most critical policy questions. What they most strikingly reveal, however, is the malleability of mass opinion. Lobbying groups have proliferated, but their influence on foreign policy is most apparent around the fringes of the important decisions. The press may have acquired the quasi-constitutional status of a "fourth estate," but its influence is still more impressive when it plays the role of active supporter than when it adopts the stance of hostile critic. Competition between the Republicans and Democrats is continuous and at times fierce, but the dynamics of bipolar competition between heterogeneous mass parties competing for the same groups of "swing" voters tends to narrow the range of disagreement among them, especially on foreign policy issues where the tactics of bipartisanship have been carefully cultivated. Elections occur at frequent intervals, but they are consistently accompanied by efforts to avoid mortgaging national commitments to partisan maneuvers. In the next chapter, consequently, the analysis focuses primarily upon the interactions among discrete executive agencies, the processes of planning, budgeting, and consensus-building, and the implications of these activities upon America's foreign policy.

6

Political processes

The constitutional and political formulas in America have obvious consequences for the substance and style of American foreign policy. So, too, do the procedures and techniques adopted by political leaders to mitigate the effects of the extreme fragmentation of power and authority for foreign policy decisions. In this chapter an attempt will be made to (1) identify the principal effects of widely diffused power and (2) examine the techniques of planning, budgeting, and consensus-building that are available to a President in his efforts to develop coherent and efficacious policies.

At the outset it is well to remember that all modern states must deal with the diffusion of governmental power. Even totalitarian states must cope with a measure of institutional diversity and bargaining among specialists. Still, the United States is unusual in the degree to which the diffusion of power possesses a constitutional sanction, in the extent to which a system of "separated institutions sharing powers" produces a pattern of more or less *public* bargaining, and in the relative weakness of centripetal institutions. The Presidency is clearly the most impressive centripetal force in the American government. The formulation of a coherent set of policies by the President and his advisers, however, is but the beginning of a generally protracted and enervating effort to persuade and cajole executive and congressional politicians, civil and military bureaucrats, news columnists, and societal leaders to either enthusiastically endorse or quietly accept his plans. The stakes at issue in most important foreign policy decisions, as well as the plethora of departments, agencies, and men whose interests must be accommodated, guarantee that policy-making will always involve a struggle over the aims of policy and over the means by which they are to be achieved.

In this chapter, attention is principally directed at the intra-executive branch politics of policy-making. Secondarily the focus is upon Washington politics, that is, the struggles among the White House, the executive departments and agencies, and Capitol Hill. Yet while much of the emphasis is upon the executive *locale of foreign-policy-making,* this should not obscure the fact that the *process of policy-making* resembles legislative bargaining quite as much as executive decision-making. That process is consequently characterized by conflict as well as cooperation, by "erratic zigs and zags" rather than an unfolding progression of mutually reinforcing decisions, by arm's-length bargaining as well as painstaking analysis, by bluff and bluster as often as precise declarations, and by confusion and turmoil rather than order and clarity.[1]

If the diffusion of power describes one feature of the foreign-policy-making environment in Washington, the growth of the foreign policy bureaucracies suggests another. Old departments have expanded; new agencies have been created. In 1939 the State Department had but 971 employees and possessed the smallest budget of all ten executive departments. By 1953 its personnel had increased tenfold, its expenditures fifteenfold. By 1965 the Department was employing more than 24,000 persons; its expenditures had mounted by 1967 to more than $420 million.

Meanwhile the Pentagon has grown like Topsy. The Secretary of Defense now directs the activities of millions of civilian and military employees (their number approximates the population of Sweden), spends more money each year than would be accounted for by the total national incomes of perhaps one-third of the members of the United Nations, and manages real estate at home and abroad equivalent in size to the states of Tennessee, Rhode Island, and Delaware combined.

The growth of the foreign policy bureaucracies is not attributable to the diffusion of power in Washington. It has been prompted by the changing requirements of the international situation, above all by the demands of World War II and the cold war; by the expansion in the number of America's foreign allies, clients, and adversaries; by the development of new instrumentalities of foreign policy such as the aid-giving and propaganda-disseminating agencies; by the dynamics of Parkinson's law; by the strenuous efforts made by several agencies to provide all the amenities of home to their employees on overseas assignments; by the tendency displayed by several Presidents to consign ineffective officials to a purgatory of routine and perhaps unnecessary assignments rather than relieve them of their jobs.

These two phenomena—the diffusion of power and bureau-

[1] Hilsman, *To Move a Nation,* p. 8.

cratic growth—are not however, unrelated. A government as large and as divided as America's possesses built-in inducements to further expansion. The need to maintain liaison with a multiplicity of departments and agencies, to free individuals for participation in a seemingly endless series of committee meetings at which decisions are reached (or evaded), the temptations of empire-building, and the realities of bureaucratic in-fighting all promote an expansion of staffs.

To safeguard representative institutions and personal liberties from encroachments at the hands of an arrogant officialdom, moreover, Americans continue to divide the bureaucracy in order to control it. Thus the "unification" of the military services in 1947 actually provided for the independence of the Air Force and a loose coordination of three and a half more or less autonomous military bureaucracies. When new tasks must be shouldered, new agencies are generally created rather than yielding additional prerogatives and powers to old ones. The diffusion of power implies a need for consensus-building in the search for policy. The mobilization of support for preferred policies may encourage an expansion of staffs. The resultant increase in the size of government will then further complicate the task of gaining consent for policy initiatives.

Related as they may be, it would appear that these two features of the environment of policy-making ought to be treated as separate variables exerting an influence over both the *procedures of policy-making* and the *content of policy*.[2] The process characteristics and the policy consequences of diffuse power in a milieu of big government must now be examined, in order to discover the virtues and the shortcomings of the policy-making system.

The policy-making consequences of diffused power

Caution and conservatism

The process of defining foreign policies that presidential, congressional, and bureaucratic politicians will support is exhausting, enervating, and time consuming.[3] One British scholar, well acquainted with the committee mode of decision-making employed by the Prime Minister and his Cabinet, has asserted that "the process of evolving decisions in high policy is probably more difficult [in the American government] than in that of any other government in the world.[4]

[2] This distinction is suggested in Warner R. Schilling's "The Politics of National Defense: Fiscal 1950," in Schilling, Hammond, and Snyder, *Strategy, Politics and Defense Budgets*, pp. 15–27.

[3] The term "bureaucrat-politician" refers to those executive department and agency officials who, however responsive they may ultimately be to presidential or congressional direction, represent the bureaucratic interests, the "distinctive competence," the peculiar policy perspectives, and specific intragovernmental and extragovernmental constituencies of a specific department or agency as well.

[4] Alastair Buchan, *Crisis Management* (Boulogne-Sur-Seine: The Atlantic Papers, 1966), p. 47.

The sources of initiative in policy-making are abundant and dispersed. Timely proposals may come from obscure officials, eminent politicians, well-known columnists, experienced diplomatists, or sundry "grey eminences" in Washington. In policy-making, however, "ease of proposal is counterbalanced by ease of veto." [5] Consequently, although the options proposed may be numerous, those actually implemented are surprisingly few. Successful policy innovations require the negotiation of a multitude of obstacles and the circumvention of a variety of ingenious schemes designed to either veto the proposal or compromise its effect.

It is, then, hardly surprising that the American foreign policy establishment makes haste slowly. Monumental efforts are frequently expended in delivering mice. The pace of external developments often outruns the mobilization of governmental support for decisive action or reaction. A Pentagon official once wryly commented that "by the time a message to the field has been composed in Washington, it had ceased to be an operational order and had become a philosophical essay." [6] Important opportunities may be lost between the moment expert opinion crystallizes on the wisdom of a new departure and the moment its efficacy is accepted by all whose veto must be avoided. However enthusiastic Administration officials may be about a policy of peaceful engagement in Eastern Europe, until the Chairman of the House Ways and Means Committee can be persuaded of the advantages of such "bridge-building," East-West trade legislation is not likely to be substantially revised.

The requirements of consensus-building may produce excessive caution as well as prolonged delays. Policy innovations often entail such costs in administrative time that harried officials, anticipating another exhausting round of negotiation if the existing policy consensus is destroyed, are sorely tempted to take the path of least resistance, namely, the perpetuation of existing policies. Like stones tumbling down a steep embankment, policies once initiated acquire an enormous momentum and may prove difficult to arrest. Henry Kissinger has noted the "curious phenomenon that decisions taken with enormous doubt and perhaps a close division become practically sacrosanct once adopted. The whole administrative machinery swings behind their implementation as if activity could still all doubts." [7] Some leaders will prefer the perpetuation of even disastrous policies to the admission of error implied by a change of course. Others are so overwhelmed by operational duties they have little time to initiate policy analysis anew, reexamine the assumptions behind programs, or renegotiate a basis of agreement among agencies to support a change of policy. This perhaps suggests an explanation for the notable gap that frequently exists between a rhetorical emphasis upon innovation

[5] Brzezinski and Huntington, *Political Power USA/USSR*, p. 216.

[6] Schlesinger, *A Thousand Days*, p. 327.

[7] Kissinger, "Domestic Structure and Foreign Policy," *Daedalus* (Spring 1966), p. 509.

and "new departures" on the one hand and the reality of massive continuity in basic policies on the other.

The content of policy is obviously informed by the difficulties experienced in mobilizing political support for decisions. In an atmosphere pervaded by bargaining and marked by jurisdictional conflicts among competitive sets of foreign policy leaders, the substance of proposals may be eroded in the quest for agreement. Hopes for policies reflecting a long-range view are frequently deflated by momentary pressures, ephemeral moods, and imminent crises.

Critics of American foreign policy often complain about the "reactive" quality of many United States initiatives. Dramatic initiatives are indeed prompted generally by emergencies or crises. Only unequivocal dangers, it seems, can challenge effectively the inertia of existing policies. This is surely cause for concern inasmuch as the margins of choice are somewhat more limited during crises by the context of events themselves. Stanley Hoffmann argues plausibly that the American policy-making system works most efficiently when the policy alternatives are most sharply circumscribed by the necessities of the international situation.[8] This may explain why the United States has difficulty defining policies that are relevant in the intermediate-range future, between the press of immediate crises and the distant dreams of a new world order. Consensus-building becomes more difficult as the issues become more hypothetical. This system of decision-making—combined with a pragmatic political style—does encourage a waiting upon events. It places a premium upon deciding as little as possible. Incrementalism becomes a way of life, a "strategy of decision," and a "science of muddling through." Forward planning is often shunned in order to avoid expanding the circle of individuals or agencies preoccupied with a specific issue. The wider the arena of decision, the greater the difficulty of obtaining agreement. The more likely also are the "leaks" of information into the public domain that may expose policy choices to the eddies of partisan maneuver. Secretary of State Rusk reportedly sought to avoid requesting a decision on the possibility of introducing American troops into Laos in 1962 should the Pathet Lao continue their nibbling tactics, for fear that options might be foreclosed that might better be kept available even at the expense of keeping them unexamined.[9]

The rigors of consensus-building may also encourage what Theodore Lowi has termed the tendency to "oversell" the crisis and the remedy. The former may promote overreactions, the latter may possibly occasion public frustration with policies that are less than spectacularly successful.[10] Surely the tactics of mobilizing support left an

[8] See his "Restraints and Choices in American Foreign Policy," *Daedalus* (Fall 1962), pp. 668–704.

[9] Hilsman, *op. cit.*, p. 543.

[10] See Theodore Lowi, "Making Democracy Safe for the World: National Politics and Foreign Policy," in James N. Rosenau, *Domestic Sources of Foreign Policy* (New York, N.Y.: Free Press, 1967), pp. 295–332.

indelible mark upon the containment policy. State department officials conceived that policy as a limited response to the crisis in Greece and Turkey in 1947. They contemplated economic assistance and some limited military aid to these two countries, which the British were no longer able to support. President Truman's presentation of the decision to the Congress, however, wielded Manichean, ideological terminology that transformed a limited engagement into an imprecise commitment to "free peoples ... resisting subjugation by armed minorities or by outside pressures." The President's speech, interestingly enough, was drafted at the initiative of the State Department's public-relations office. Remonstrations against its grandiose and universal rhetoric were vain, according to George Kennan, for "no one wanted to repeat the agony of collective drafting that had been invested over the preceding days in the production of this historic piece of paper." [11]

Overselling of crises has been a persistent feature of the public-relations aspect of postwar foreign policy. Repeated emphasis upon the threat of communism, the malevolence and manipulative genius of a monolithic international Communist movement, or the prospects of "falling dominos" has served the purpose of officials anxious to heighten the public's perception of specific threats and to foster a public and congressional mood permissive of policies requiring more than "masterly inactivity." Likewise the tendency to justify actions in terms of "test cases" encourages the assumption that precedents are established once and for all, that favorable or unfavorable results are definitive for the future, and that "this effort may be the last required." This is not to imply that innocuous situations have been self-consciously and deviously transformed into crises to facilitate executive decisions or to clear the path for congressional assent. It does imply, however, that rationalizations of decisions have been framed with one eye on skeptical domestic audiences, and that the tactics of "brinksmanship," while possessing an obvious utility in creating support for new initiatives, may also give policies an unintentional and undesirable twist and produce stereotypes of adversaries and friends that themselves acquire a substantial influence on subsequent policies and that may even alienate the more sophisticated "attentive" public.

The requirements of consensus-building may explain three other features of contemporary American foreign policy. First, the expansiveness of the CIA's activities may be attributable to the relative ease with which that Agency may undertake operations without the normal widespread discussion and approval. Delegation of many political tasks to them may thus constitute a means of short-circuiting an otherwise time-consuming process of accumulating concurrences. Second, the frequency with which foreign aid is justified in terms that fail to elucidate with precision the rationale and expectations behind the programs is perhaps due to the desire to sustain widespread support from groups whose assent or enthusiasm is based upon mutually contradictory premises. Third, executive officials rely heavily

---

[11] Kennan, *Memoirs*, p. 315.

upon quantitative or otherwise graphic indicators of success as a means of insuring support. This can easily promote a preoccupation with programs promising short-term benefits or an exorbitant emphasis upon those that assure early results. A host of illustrations could be derived from any examination of the pacification programs in Vietnam.

Confusion

When officials from diverse groups daily advocate a variety of points of view, a measure of confusion is an inevitable by-product. On any particular day the public statements of the President, the Secretary of State, the Chairman of the Joint Chiefs of Staff, prominent senators and congressmen, prestigious ambassadors, respected public figures, knowledgeable experts, and widely read columnists may provide ample grounds for confusion as to what precisely the intentions of the American government are. At home, an informed and attentive public may monitor this cacophony of conflicting voices with a certain sophistication, discriminating among those who speak with authority, those who, like the King's mistress, enjoy influence without authority, and those who are merely kibitzing. Abroad, the foreign policy dialogue must resemble a tower of Babel. As one Laotian leader complained, "since so many voices are heard, it is impossible to tell which has an authoritative ring." [12]

Such confusion derives not alone from the number of voices raised in advocacy or explanation, but from the necessity to adjust remarks to specific audiences despite the possibility that others may be listening in.[13] In appraising the meaning of a presidential statement, it is necessary to determine whether it was intended to put down domestic critics, encourage sympathetic understanding by congressional leaders, suggest a basis for the settlement of conflicts with adversaries, reassure anxious allies about American resolve, reaffirm American devotion to United Nations Charter principles, or keep rebellious subordinates in line. The latter function of presidential statements is becoming more prominent. As Averell Harriman commented to the Senate Government Operations Committee, "The work of the Cabinet, the National Security Council, and other groups at which he is present, are but one mode of communication between the President and those who operate the machinery of government. His public statements are often as much directed to government employees as to the American people." [14]

It is no simple matter to distinguish between those messages

---

[12] Schlesinger, *op. cit.*, p. 326.

[13] In this respect, the generality and vagueness of many policy pronouncements are not a consequence merely of diffused power, but reflect as well the range of America's responsibilities and the variety of constituencies served by most participants in foreign-policy-making.

[14] Senate Committee on Government Operations, *Administration of National Security Hearings,* 88th Cong., 1st Sess., 1963, p. 51.

intended to foreclose debate within the government and those designed to communicate precisely with a foreign audience. Particular difficulties are encountered by the President and Secretary of Defense as they simultaneously attempt to formulate coherent weapon policies in the face of determined constituency interests in the services, defense industries, and many communities without either becoming vulnerable to the charge that they are compromising the nation's security posture or hopelessly confusing the strategic dialogue that is being constantly conducted with the Soviet Union.

The "leaderless" character of the foreign-policy-making process

In some ways the American policy-making system is analogous to the free market.[15] Initiative is widely dispersed. Most of the important foreign policy issues do not fit into neat categories, do not fall clearly within the jurisdiction of a single agency, and do not depend for their success upon the effective application of a single instrumentality such as military force or foreign aid. Most of the important foreign policy decisions activate many of the agencies in the foreign policy establishment, and the character of policy is shaped to a considerable degree by the initial definition given to a problem. This in turn depends frequently upon the vagaries of bureaucratic politics. It has been alleged that an excessively military approach to the Vietnam problem was the result of Secretary of State Rusk's reluctance to grasp the issue in the early 1960s and impose a definition on it that ran contrary to those offered by the Defense Department.[16] The validity of this contention is not at issue here. It illustrates, however, how significant issues are defined through a process of adjustment among relatively autonomous agencies. The process may yield violent struggles or a "radar approach" to policy-making, with officials watching and waiting upon events and upon one another.

The consequences may range from that "evasion of responsibility" that Secretary Rusk once identified as the essence of the "bureaucratic problem" to the utter neglect of problems for which no one bears specific responsibility. Responsibilities that are widely shared may be nowhere met. Interest in arms control languished during the 1950s in part because there was no agency specifically concerned with it. Another possibility, in the absence of any single point of leadership short of the lofty eminence of the Presidency, is that agencies may harmonize their conflicting perspectives and proprietary interests in such a way as to produce policies whose rationale is compelling to no one. Needless to add, initiative for criticizing various proposals may migrate from department to department, agency to agency, and individual to individual with the same rapidity and unpredictability as the initiative for generating proposals.

[15] Attention was called to this feature of the American policy-making system by Gabriel Almond, *The American People and Foreign Policy*, p. 145.

[16] Hilsman, *op. cit.*, Chap. 9.

Another consequence of such a policy-making system is the tendency for issues or "issue areas" to be somewhat artificially segmented. Apparently discrete political processes mark the formulation, for example, of tariff policy, military strategy, foreign aid policy, and governmental reorganization measures. In each area, policy is informed by a unique set of historical precedents and fashioned by a reasonably stable set of participants, operating within certain limits of anticipated budgetary or political support and working through recognized sets of procedures.

Professor Samuel Huntington has developed a useful distinction between "strategic decisions" and "structural decisions" that suggests where power and initiative are apt to be found with respect to different types of problems.[17] Strategic decisions represent attempts to adjust to the contingent circumstances of international politics. They are normally framed within the executive branch. They more nearly approximate "closed politics," in which Congress, pressure groups, and the public are informed of decisions after the fact rather than consulted before they have been taken. Proposals may "bubble up" from a variety of agencies and individuals (principally in the executive branch). The mobilization of political support may take a variety of patterns, depending on the issue and the protagonists. As counter-proposals appear, conflict over policy is the natural corollary. Such conflict is normally mitigated through bargaining. The budgetary process and meetings of the National Security Council, the Joint Chiefs of Staff, and Senior Inter-Departmental Groups provide the incentive and the focus for efforts to resolve such conflicts. When agreement among various agencies is achieved, decisions are ratified by the President and subsequently communicated to Congress and the public.

Structural decisions are made in the currency of domestic politics. They generally concern the budgetary support, the personnel policies, and the organizational basis for the implementation of strategic decisions. Proposals normally emanate from executive officials, are revised and amended by departments, agencies, the Budget Bureau, and the President before their submission to the Congress, where they wend their way slowly through the complex web of substantive and appropriations subcommittees in a manner similar to other domestic legislation. Since the ultimate decision on structural questions is rendered by Congress, pressure tactics, public relations campaigns, and bargaining strategies tend to be directed at the numerous foci of decision-making in the House and Senate even as those decisions are decisively shaped by the congressional structure of power and climate of opinion.[18] Indeed, a variety of policy-making subsystems exists on structural questions, since different executive

[17] The terms have been coined and defined by Samuel P. Huntington, *The Common Defense* (New York, N.Y.: Columbia University Press, 1961), pp. 3–7, 123–135, and *passim*.

[18] *Ibid.*, p. 125.

agencies and congressional committees concern themselves with the problems of the budget, personnel, and organization.

Naturally the line of demarcation between structural and strategic decisions is difficult to draw with any precision. Strategic decisions have obvious implications for structural decisions, just as budgetary and manpower ceilings have their own strategic implications. Thus whether a matter is handled through the one set of procedures and political relationships or the other often depends less on the subject matter than on the way the issue is defined.

In the realm of defense budgets, the "requirements-firsters" define the problem as strategic; the "budget-firsters" possess a structural orientation. In this dialectic between those primarily concerned with adjustments to the international milieu and those most sensitive to the domestic consequences of foreign and military policy, the methods and procedures of policy-making depend on which group can impose its definition upon the issues. Nor is there any necessarily "correct" definition of "the" problem. Rather, agencies and individuals vary in their perceptions of what the problems are, what issues they pose, and what decisions are thus required. The "budget-firsters," for example, are inclined to be most anxious about fiscal integrity, threats to a balanced budget, and increments to defense spending that might produce what, in their view, would be undesirable domestic economic consequences. The "requirements-firsters," on the other hand, are variously concerned with maintaining what they considered adequate capabilities in the light of their own appraisals of the external situation—which lends itself to a variety of interpretations.

In politics, as in games, the outcome generally depends substantially upon the rules honored. Yet in politics competition frequently focuses precisely on the matter of whose game is to be played. Prior to 1962, tariff legislation was handled as though it were a matter of domestic legislation. As the foreign policy implications of American foreign trade policy have become more evident and significant, logrolling for interest-group advantages has been disciplined by presidential efforts to employ trade as an instrument for foreign policy purposes.

Since more or less discrete policy-making systems exist to reach decisions on different issues, the problems of coordination become immensely more complicated. Crisis policy is a form of strategic decision-making par excellence. The participants are fewer, the role of the President sharply enhanced, the deliberations relatively "closed." As one moves into other areas of strategic policy the number of participants increases, the conflict among executive departments becomes more and more pronounced and colored by "institutionally grounded" biases,[19] and the bargaining becomes both more pervasive

[19] That is, biases reflecting the peculiar responsibilities of particular governmental institutions or organizations. The phrase is Warner Schilling's.

and more public. Finally, on the structural issues, the arena of policy-making has become equivalent to that of domestic legislation. Naturally the dispatch with which innovations may be adopted varies with the issue, becoming more difficult to arrange as one moves away from crisis situations and strategic decisions, toward the management of large ongoing programs with which institutional vested interests are associated. This naturally suggests that the American government can alter its declaratory policy or attitude toward specific countries, regions, or situations more rapidly than it can refashion strategies, force structures, or foreign aid programs to implement such changes.

This also may explain the frequent lack of integration among the instrumentalities or even the objectives of various policies. Mutually contradictory policies may at times appear when different issues intersect, as they frequently do in efforts to fashion policy for a wide region. With respect to Europe, for example, the Defense Department adopted in 1962 a revised strategic policy framed with reference to the difficult problems of command and control over the nuclear weapons of the alliance, the prospects of nuclear proliferations, and the apparent preference for an integrated alliance with a clear-cut division of labor among its participants. The concept of an integrated alliance did not, however, mesh perfectly with a trade policy, formulated largely in the State Department, that was adapted to the reality of a united European trading entity and that anticipated an Atlantic community resting upon twin pillars. Where military considerations seemed to counsel an organic integration of defense capabilities, trade policy was based upon an image of European-American relations reflecting loose partnership between equals. There is, of course, nothing wrong with allowing the nature of the issues to shape the terms of interstate collaboration. These two policies, however, were based upon rival assessments of what Europe would become.

At times agencies may adopt policies that work more directly at cross purposes with one another. In 1960 precisely this seemed to occur when the Central Intelligence Agency, the State Department, and the Defense Department found themselves supporting different factions in the civil conflict in the Asian kingdom of Laos. In the Vietnamese war one hears frequent references to the "air war," the "ground war," and the "other war"—meaning the central task of pacification. In truth, responsibility for these various "wars" has at times been separately exercised by the Commander of the Pacific Fleet, the Commanding General of American Forces in Vietnam, and the Ambassador in Saigon. By factoring issues or problems into separable parts and farming them out to specialized bureaucracies, the dilemmas of consensus-building may be eased. The integration of policy will in all probability suffer. As someone once observed, "What a nation would do if it were one person with a single will and a single intellect is often quite at variance with what it actually can and does do when those in charge must seek to resolve the multiplicity of thrusts into a single direction."

The consequences of "bureaucratic sprawl"

Above all, the implications of the vast and growing size of the foreign policy establishment are to be found in the claims that such bigness imposes upon the time and energy of the leading political executives. So much time is spent reconciling jurisdictional squabbles, placating staffs, keeping the machinery of policy-making oiled, and obtaining the innumerable but necessary concurrences that little may be left for defining purposes, deciding where one ought to be going rather than where the present is taking one, asserting priorities, and digesting the information so assiduously amassed by underlings.[20] As one disenchanted civil servant once commented about the Agency for International Development data books, "Seldom has so much been written by so many for so few." [21]

As the amount of intelligence information available grows, its digestion can absorb more and more of the time that top officials find in such short supply. The Central Foreign Policy file in the State Department grows at a rate of 400 file drawers a year. It takes an intelligence staff of 200 professionals reading and analyzing 100,000 documents each month to keep the file up to date. Most of this is filed for a single bureau. Its existence is not always known to others in need of such information. In an emergency its contents may be ignored as new experts are called in from the outside for advice.

The House Defense Appropriations Subcommittee reported in July, 1968 that the intelligence services were collecting information so rapidly that those responsible for processing and evaluating it scarcely had time to read it. Unprocessed reports on Southeast Asia alone reportedly filled 517 linear feet of file drawer space at the headquarters of the Defense Intelligence Agency. Testimony before the subcommittee showed that the failure to provide timely analysis of incoming materials probably contributed to the seizure of the intelligence ship, the *Pueblo*, by North Korea in January, 1968, the absence of warning of the Israeli attack on another such ship, the *Liberty*, in June, 1967, and the lack of advance information about the Tet Lunar Holiday offensive staged by the Vietcong and North Vietnamese in the spring of 1968.[22]

The style of communication that often accompanies this truly monumental accumulation and dissemination of information within the bureaucracies is not particularly felicitous. Consequently, govern-

---

[20] Richard Neustadt has written poignantly of the dilemma posed by the new dimension of risk introduced into policy-making by typewriters, mimeograph machines, radio, telegraph, and telephones. "Choking people to death with information is one of the oldest bureaucratic techniques known to man. Never have there been such opportunities as now." Senate Government Operations Committee, *Hearings, Administration of National Security*, 88th Cong., 2nd Sess., 1964, p. 99.

[21] Thomas Hovey, *United States Military Assistance* (New York, N.Y.: Praeger, 1965), p. 204.

[22] *The New York Times* (July 10, 1968), p. 33.

ment civil servants are constantly in danger of losing their audience (the President or the Secretary of State, for example) to individuals outside the government who may express their views more lucidly— though by no means necessarily more accurately or relevantly. An alternative possibility is that political leaders confronted daily by a welter of conflicting advice may take refuge in the seeming security of simple homilies enjoying the currency of conventional wisdom, for example, the "Munich analogy." Certainly the size of the foreign policy establishment influences its receptivity to advice and counsel from without as well as within. George Kennan has referred to Washington's receptivity to advice as being "determined by subjective emotional currents as intricately imbedded in the subconscious as those of the most complicated of Sigmund Freud's erstwhile patients." His perplexity over this is tinged with apprehension as to the capability of a government to cope with a rapidly changing world when "the subjective state of readiness on the part of Washington officialdom to recognize this or that feature" of the world is more salient for American policy than the "observable nature of external reality." [23]

The very inertia that seems the natural accompaniment of large size may tempt activist Presidents to seek to operate outside the foreign policy bureaucracies. President Kennedy is said to have entertained particularly vivid dreams of "establishing a secret office of thirty people or so to run foreign policy while maintaining the State Department as a facade in which people might contentedly carry papers from bureau to bureau." [24] This was obviously an idle dream; such a centralization is neither feasible nor desirable in view of the complexities of international politics. It does dramatize one of the President's problems, and it explains in part the attractiveness to the Chief Executive of summit diplomacy, visits with foreign heads of state, presidential trips, personal correspondence with the world's statesmen, and an active White House staff for foreign policy issues. All constitute means by which he may obtain a personal feel for the vital issues and an independent source of advice and counsel, free of the institutional interests and the bureaucratic inertia of established departments.

Sustaining the integrity of foreign policy designs

Pervasive intragovernmental bargaining may so erode the substance of policy that it becomes a reflection of the relative power of rival bureaucracies rather than a response to external challenges; thus the need for methods of disciplining adversary relations to the requirements of the international situation. Where agreement upon policy may be facilitated by segmenting issues and devising a number of discrete policy-making processes, procedures must also be discovered

[23] Kennan, *op. cit.*, pp. 294–295.

[24] Schlesinger, *op. cit.*, p. 413.

for coordinating policies. This is the more difficult in the American government, moreover, since the very institutions that might link issues, provide perspective, and force policy integration display a similar tendency to become fragmented. Congressional committees have devolved responsibilities upon their specialized subcommittees. The Joint Chiefs of Staff and the National Security Council are collegial bodies that engage in considerable logrolling. Ambassadors are often only nominal directors of "country teams."

From the vantage point of the President and his chief appointees, the test of leadership is in their capacity to enforce their priorities within a context of conflict and bargaining. Their choices concerning policy objectives, operating methods, and formal rules of procedure may discipline the bargaining and shape its results.

Foreign policy *doctrines* may be serviceable to some degree as a means of disciplining the centrifugal forces participating in foreign-policy-making. They may provide a standard for the integration of diverse day-to-day decisions, a means for narrowing the range of foreign policy debate, a tool with which to determine the gross priorities, slogans with which to mobilize and sustain public support, and shibboleths with which to cloak decisions or rebuff criticisms. Since 1947 the containment doctrine has indeed offered a rough criterion for identifying America's adversaries, a simplified framework for analyzing developments in world politics, and a reasonably specific strategic objective.

Nevertheless, while a doctrine such as containment may confine the arena of policy conflict, it cannot eliminate bargaining. On the contrary, it is the product of extensive and continuing intra-governmental negotiations. Indeed, containment may be termed a doctrine only in the very loosest sense, since it scarcely rests on a systematic body of ideas. George Kennan, to whom much credit has rightly been given for articulating the assumptions behind the original containment thesis, assumes no pride of authorship for its subsequent manifestations. The containment of Communist influence in world politics has been the objective of many American policies. But one can scarcely deduce from that goal an optimal level of defense spending, the extensiveness of mutual security commitments, the magnitude or allocation of foreign aid budgets, or appropriate reactions to non-Western national liberation movements. Nor is such ambiguity unique to containment. Its successor—the "Atlantic Community"—has been compared to a mirage whose exact dimensions become more difficult to fathom the more carefully it is examined.[25]

The need for leadership in sustaining an adequate set of

[25] Seyom Brown has noted the utility of the Grand Design of the Kennedy Administration in serving as "an orienting goal and legitimating ideology for policies which, in the face of a decline in enthusiasm for anti-Communism as an orienting principle, were becoming increasingly difficult to defend." The Grand Design—which emphasized Atlantic Interdependence—enabled the United States to cling to integrated military planning within the Alliance, unified command and control over nuclear weapons, a common Western economic policy toward the Communist world, and the maintenance of American leadership in new advances toward the East. See his *The Faces of Power*, p. 301.

priorities has thus encouraged Presidents to persistently seek a greater centralization of authority over foreign policy decisions, particularly when the Secretary of State was unwilling or unable to achieve mastery over the foreign policy establishment. During President Eisenhower's tenure in the White House, the National Security Council served as the President's cabinet for foreign relations. Secretary of State Dulles played the role of "legislative leader." When policies could not be coordinated voluntarily, the President could theoretically impose a solution. During President Kennedy's brief term in office, the White House staff played a crucial role in disciplining consensus-building efforts to the presidential policy perspective. An activist President was served by a staff of generalists anxiously preserving his options, pondering the interconnections among issues, offering perspective to offset the "partial view of the national interest" represented by various agencies, and seeking to prod the permanent government into activity. Apart from such general services, McGeorge Bundy, Richard Goodwin, Michael Forrestal, Bromley Smith, Ralph Dungan, Jerome Wiesner, Myer Feldman, Karl Kaysen, Arthur Schlesinger, Jr., Robert Komer, and Theodore Sorensen maintained specific oversight over particular "issue areas."

President Johnson preferred to encourage the State Department to accept its proferred role as general manager of America's foreign relations. Because of his identification with one particular service, the Foreign Service, the Secretary of State has always found it difficult to preside over a number of other relatively autonomous civilian services and operations. In March, 1966 the Senior Inter-Departmental Group was established to bring together the Deputy Secretary of Defense, the Directors of AID, CIA, and USIA, the Chairman of the Joint Chiefs of Staff, White House representatives, and others whose interests are affected by specific decisions at the convenience of and under the chairmanship of the Undersecretary of State. By granting power of decision to the State Department Undersecretary, while allowing other participants to retain their right of appeal to the President, an element of hierarchy was injected into the policy-making process, which, it was hoped, might facilitate clear-cut choices rather than the low-common-denominator compromises that are not infrequently the products of the committee mode of decision-making. Heretofore, little evidence exists to suggest that such organizational reforms can suffice to insure that individual rivulets of policy can be channeled into a single stream. Presidents rarely have the time, Secretaries of State the budgetary or personnel powers, to exercise a detailed surveillance and control over the other foreign policy agencies.

The distinction between the making of policy and its administration has never been very clear. Those who execute policy may be able to significantly amend, obstruct, or modify it. As President Truman once noted, "In the world of the Presidency, giving an order does not end the matter. You can pound your fist on the table, or you can get mad or you can blow it all and go out to the golf course. But nothing gets done except by endless follow-up, endless kissing and coaxing, endless threatening and compelling." Policies resting upon a firm consensus at home may yet undergo important transmutations when applied abroad, for their execution will be in the hands of a different set of officials. The best laid plans, moreover, must be adapted to the peculiarities of local circumstances. Distance from Washington also conveys an extra measure of discretion to diplomats and soldiers, despite the persistent erosion of the autonomy granted formerly to ambassadors and theater military commanders.

The postdecision struggle over policy may be less visible than the effort to arrange a consensus to support it, but it can be equally intense and no less significant. Of paramount importance are the decisions designating one or another agency jurisdiction over the implementation of policy. A decision to place executive responsibility over a new program in an established agency with myriad claims upon its administrative competence may seriously dilute the novel features of the program. Alternatively, should a new agency be created, for example, the Peace Corps or the Arms Control and Disarmament Agency, it is more likely that it will represent the priorities and interests of the more vigorous advocates of policy innovations. The Agency for International Development, United States Information Agency, Central Intelligence Agency, National Aeronautics and Space Administration, Arms Control and Disarmament Agency, and many others stand as evidence of congressional reluctance to lodge executive control over most overseas activities in the State Department. To be sure, all may come under a measure of policy guidance by that Department, but none can be easily subordinated to the executive authority of the Secretary of State, because he possesses little influence over their budgets or their personnel. The State Department has not the "professional talents, the internal organization, [or] the executive experience to lord it over these other agencies." [26]

The coordination of agency activities in the field has proved no less difficult. The execution of policy is complicated by the need to mesh various functional instrumentalities, for example, military force, economic aid, and propaganda, in the support of policies related to a given country or region. Ideally, the disciplining of various instruments to a coherent set of objectives might be undertaken by the ambassador in his capacity as chief of mission and head of the country team. The primacy of the ambassador, however, tends frequently to be more a "polite fiction" than an established fact. Despite serious efforts to upgrade the authority and prestige of American emissaries, their positions are invariably precarious. Ambassadors continue to conduct many negotiations with foreign governments, but generally with more detailed instructions than formerly, and often as part of a team, top-heavy with Washington officials. Representative duties have not diminished; competition in their performance has

[26] Thomas Schelling, "PPBS and Foreign Affairs," *The Public Interest* (Spring 1968), p. 32.

increased. The scope of reporting duties have also been expanded, even as ambassadors have had heavy executive responsibilities thrust upon them due to the need to coordinate the overseas activities of many federal agencies.

The "Ambassador's dilemma," as it has been termed by the Senate Government Operations Committee, has been well described in one of their staff reports:

> One: He is expected to perform his traditional diplomatic functions in a most untraditional setting, with less independence and less policy authority than Ambassadors once exercised—and with far more people underfoot;
>
> Two: He is expected to contribute to the policy process from the perspective of a single-country mission, while those at home who have to make the policies treat almost nothing as a single-country problem;
>
> Three: He is expected to serve as leader and coordinator of his "country team" while lacking power or even much influence over the budgets, the personnel systems, the reporting requirements, and the operating policies of many of the field staffs theoretically subordinate to him.[27]

The corollary to the Secretary of State's problem in coordinating the policy initiatives of numerous agencies in Washington is the Ambassador's difficulty in integrating the activities of those agencies in the field. Occasionally, exceptional individuals succeed in asserting their authority over the official personnel stationed in their country. The ingredients of success include professional competence, personal integrity, and the confidence and support of the President and Secretary of State. Even those Ambassadors who have been the undisputed masters of their "country team," however, have been known to complain at times of obstacles to their access to the files of other agencies in Washington; limited influence over the forward planning of the aid mission, the military assistance program, or the CIA programs in their country; slight discretion in budgetary and fiscal matters; or the rigidities of policy imposed on them by congressional statutes.

Thus the divisions among foreign policy agencies in Washington have a way of reappearing in the field. The obstacles to centralized programming at home are matched by obstacles to synchronized execution abroad. The Ambassador is charged with the responsibility for overseeing the totality of programs which affect America's relations with a particular country. Political prowess as well as diplomatic skill is required if oversight is to be transformed into effective control.

In the Department of Defense the growing centralization of

---

[27] Senate Government Operations Committee, *Administration of National Security*, Staff Reports and Hearings, 88th Cong., 1st Sess., 1965, p. 57.

power in the Office of the Secretary has been accompanied and facilitated by the application of various analytic techniques. Above all, the budgetary process has been reformed through the systematic use of systems analysis and cost-benefit analysis. During the 1950s defense budgets were fashioned after Stan's law, according to which money was divided in such a manner as to produce a rather "uniform distribution of dissatisfaction." [28] A tacit separation of powers developed between the Secretary of Defense and the service departments. The Secretary was permitted to set (in conjunction with the President, the Secretary of the Treasury, and the Director of the Budget Bureau) the "ceiling" for defense expenditures and to allocate rough shares among the services, largely on the basis of past precedents. In return the service departments obtained a substantial autonomy in deciding how to spend their portions of the overall budget. Little wonder that their programs often conflicted or failed in mutual support. Little wonder that each service could promulgate a strategic doctrine anticipating different kinds of war even as the services sought control over weapons performing nearly identical missions!

The planning-programming-budgeting system (PPBS) instituted by Secretary McNamara has served both as a means of enhancing the Secretary's managerial control over the Department through his central role in the budgetary process and as a means of rationalizing the defense program by forcing a more explicit assertion of objectives, description of methods designed to achieve them, measurement of the relative costs and benefits of alternative program packages, and identification of the decisions that can be safely postponed and those that require immediate attention (as well as the relationships between the two). In truth a revolution in the formal procedures of policy-making has been effected by linking planning to budgeting via programming. As a system, PPBS links within the budgetary process resources to purposes, inputs to outputs, and budgetary decisions to long-term planning. This contributes to presumably better estimates by decision-makers of the costs and consequences of alternative choices.

PPBS does not automatically produce more rational decisions or policies. As Thomas Schelling has pointed out, the planning-programming-budgeting system may be "a splendid tool to help top management make decisions" if the political executives in the Pentagon wish to make decisions. It may also be "a seductive comfort, and in the end an embarrassment, to a lazy executive who wants his decisions to come out of a process in which his own intellect does not participate." [29] Such techniques are less helpful in foreign affairs, as opposed to defense policy, insofar as they are more difficult to apply to the budgetary process in which individual agencies make separate requests, and inasmuch as foreign affairs, as emphasized above, is a more disorderly business, fraught with surprises, placing a premium

[28] Maurice Stans was Director of the Bureau of the Budget from 1958 to 1961.

[29] Schelling, "PPBS and Foreign Affairs," *op. cit.*, p. 27.

upon judgment and intuition, and defying the best laid plans. In addition, foreign policy objectives are less easily quantified, and the budgetary process less useful for asserting the gross priorities.

If intra-executive branch bargaining has been constrained somewhat by doctrine, hierarchy, and analysis, determined efforts have also been made by political executives to safeguard unstable policy equilibria from the intrusions of outside pressures. Cold war Presidents have generally attempted to shroud deliberations over new strategic policies in secrecy. They have encouraged congressional and public deference to themselves in adapting policy to the changing exigencies of the international situation. They have liberally invoked executive privilege on sensitive matters when confronted by inquisitive legislators, discouraged dissent by subordinate officials on vital matters, and generously publicized successful policies and impressive capabilities while discounting the importance of apparent policy failures or marked deficiencies in capabilities.

In recent years the President has also on more than one occasion taken disquieting liberties with the truth in shielding official plans from public scrutiny or in going beyond artful circumlocution in obscuring their intentions. In searching the record of American policy during the U-2 crisis of 1960, the Bay of Pigs fiasco of 1961, the Dominican intervention of 1965, or the Vietnamese war throughout the 1960s, evidences of a lack of candor by high officials in their relations with the press and the public are easily discovered. The occasional resort to deception in the management of information about American policy may help a President keep his options open, keep his opponents guessing, and prevent inadvertent or intentional "leaks" from destroying a precarious consensus on an agreed course of action. It can also promote a cynical skepticism by the public toward the official pronouncements of their leaders. This cannot but weaken the force of such statements to foreign audiences as well.[30]

Manipulating the domestic political costs of foreign policy

While one set of procedures has emerged from concern over preserving rational policy in an environment in which interagency and interdepartmental bargaining could easily focus upon largely internal bureaucratic stakes, another has evolved out of the desire to preserve flexibility in handling foreign issues at a time when the costs of foreign involvements have grown enormously. Notable in this regard are the tactics of bipartisanship and the allocation of the burdens of foreign policy to domestic groups perceiving acute threats.

The utility of bipartisan or nonpartisan techniques seems obvious in a governmental system in which the alternation of parties or the possibility of divided government (that is, different parties controlling the White House and Congress, respectively, as occurred

---

[30] For an analysis of Presidential attempts at "news management," see William McGaffin and Erwin Knoll, *Anything But the Truth: The Credibility Gap—How the News Is Managed in Washington* (New York, N.Y.: Putnam's, 1968), esp. Chap. 3.

from 1946 to 1948 and through six of President Eisenhower's years in office) poses the prospect of either significant discontinuities of policy or immobilism and stalemate. Presidents have thus understood the prudence of adopting elementary defensive tactics to mobilize broad congressional and public support for their policies as insurance against these possibilities. Actually the tactics of bipartisanship merely describe the efforts made by those bearing responsibility for foreign policy to associate with their policies all those partisan politicians whose endorsement is essential for an enduring consensus or whose opposition might be sufficient to derail an Administration's carefully made plans. Most notably, bipartisanship has involved a generous sharing of credit and blame for foreign policy. Democratic Presidents have been especially assiduous in appointing Republicans to high foreign-policy-making posts. President Roosevelt created a "national government" of sorts in the face of war by appointing Frank Knox and Henry Stimson to lead the Navy and War Departments, respectively, in 1940. President Truman neutralized partisan opposition to his postwar policies by assigning important duties to such Republicans as John J. McCloy, Paul Hoffman, Robert Lovett, and John Foster Dulles. President Kennedy even more self-consciously practiced this stratagem by calling upon Robert McNamara, McGeorge Bundy, Douglas Dillon, Henry Cabot Lodge, and William Foster, among others, to participate in the fashioning of high foreign and defense policy. Nor have the views of old politicians and soldiers been disregarded. Presidents are predictably photographed with their predecessors or with other prestigious public figures during moments of national danger or when national unity appears more than usually fragile.[31]

Consultations with congressional leaders are part and parcel of bipartisan foreign policy. Whether a President will "consult" or merely "inform" leaders on Capitol Hill will, of course, depend upon the strength of their potential opposition. Powerful figures like the former Chairman of the Senate Foreign Relations Committee, Arthur Vandenberg, may successfully insist on an active role in policy formulation and substantive concessions on specific policies. Others, like one former Chairman of the House Foreign Affairs Committee, may be less demanding, settling for prompt notification of important decisions in order to sustain the appearance of participation before inquisitive newsmen and gullible constituents. The concessions extended in order to secure or preserve support may range from sham consultations (frequent) to joint policy-making procedures (rare). This depends upon the stature and disposition of congressional leaders, the extent of a President's plurality and public standing, the character of the specific issue in question, and the importance attributed to the maintenance of national unity or the necessity of securing congressional assent.

[31] President Kennedy and President Johnson displayed such a studious regard for the views of former President Eisenhower that the latter's aide, General Goodpaster, was permitted a weekly briefing by the President's Special Assistant for National Security Affairs.

If the tests of bipartisan procedures are the continuity of policy, the maintenance of national unity in the face of repeated crises, and the general acceptance by foreigners that international commitments undertaken by one Administration will be honored and fulfilled by its successors, whatever their party, then bipartisanship has proved notably successful. That the tactics of consultation and appointment or the habit of restraining the Secretaries of State and Defense from electioneering are responsible for this success seems more dubious. In truth, the potential for discontinuities as a consequence of alternations in party control of the government is offset by the fact that bipolar party competition tends to diminish differences between them on the significant policy issues. This is a result of their tendency to compete for the allegiance of the same groups of swing voters. Such differences as are revealed between the parties on foreign policy issues during frequent election campaigns are in fact more likely to reflect their positions as "ins" or "outs" than they are to be the products of ideological positions or partisan conceptions.

Immobilism, moreover, can threaten even a government in which both the White House and Congress are securely in the hands of a single party, for powerful and independent sources of potential opposition must still be appeased. Most policies that are adopted must win the support of a significant number of political groups. Such policies naturally possess impressive durability, whatever may be the shifting tides of party fortunes. Perceptible changes in foreign and defense policy may accompany changes in the composition of Congress or control of the White House, but such changes will normally be kept within the limits acceptable to most of the powerful factions within the two dominant parties.

In sustaining the acceptability of policies, successive postwar administrations also have demonstrated considerable ingenuity in manipulating the costs and benefits of overseas programs. The maintenance of public support and the continuance of congressional appropriations are most essential and most difficult to assure during ambiguous wars such as those fought in Korea from 1950 to 1953 and Vietnam from 1961 to the present. Alongside efforts to impose limits on the use of military power in the field and on the diplomatic consequences of unpopular wars in international forums, Presidents also attempted to limit their impact upon domestic groups. During neither conflict has war been formally declared, price controls invoked, or materials rationed. In both cases the avoidance of such measures was designed to avert arousing passions, expectations, or demands from the public that might have significantly reduced the President's margins for maneuver in settling for limited gains or accepting limited losses.[32]

[32] The widespread disenchantment with the Vietnamese war evident among college students and residents of the urban ghettoes reflects the fact that many of those who may be asked to pay the highest price of war—as a result of conscription and deferred programs of urban reconstruction—are least comfortable with and least persuaded by the stereotypes of the cold war on the basis of which the Vietnamese war has been customarily defended.

The tactics of redistributing the benefits and burdens of foreign policy operations have been most energetically applied in the annual battles over foreign aid. Such programs have been expensive. The aid-disbursing agencies are controlled to some extent by congressional statute. Public skepticism about the value of foreign aid makes it difficult for a President to control Congress by mobilizing its constituents. Thus congressional influence is profound and frequently negative.

Few efforts have been spared to render the program directly profitable to a variety of domestic groups. The enforcement of "Buy American" strings transforms much of the aid effort into an export subsidy program. Maritime interests have been appeased by providing that at least half of the commodities shipped abroad are transported in American vessels. The Public Law 480 agricultural surplus program has provided a means of maintaining a higher level of agricultural productivity than the domestic market might otherwise support. Commercial interests have been accommodated by recent legislation forbidding the use of aid funds to support projects likely to produce foreign-manufactured items that might compete with American exports. By engaging universities, corporations, banks, state governments, labor unions, private foundations, and agricultural cooperatives in the administration of programs, a wide variety of expertise and managerial talent has been tapped even as wider support for the aid effort may have been mobilized.

Unpopular programs have been financed by embedding them in others that enjoy greater support. For years a considerable amount of aid was authorized and appropriated by designating it for "defense support" and by combining the bills for economic and military assistance.[33] Strategies of "commitment" are not unknown. The Administration may gain the assent of a small and sympathetic subcommittee in Congress and subsequently use it to undertake a solemn international obligation, which other congressmen will feel obliged not to repudiate. In January, 1964 a bill was passed in Congress authorizing the Governor of the International Development Bank to vote an increase in the Bank's resources and to subscribe the American share. By March, when Otto Passman, the Chairman of the Foreign Operations Subcommittee of the House Appropriations Committee and a notorious opponent of the aid program, got his chance at the aid legislation, the United States appeared firmly committed internationally.

The terminology of the foreign aid debate is also revealing. Emphasis upon "soft loans" disguises to penurious congressmen the

---

[33] The package approach not only promised to increase congressional support, but enhanced the authority of the House Foreign Affairs Committee, whose chairman, Thomas Morgan, considered the foreign aid legislation his most significant item of business and had little enthusiasm for seeing a major portion of it handled by the Armed Services Committee. Possibly the congressional preference for bilateral grants and loans is partly explained by the desire of some of these same committee members not to lose business to the Banking and Currency Committee.

extent of the gift. References to sales in local currencies are rarely accompanied by acknowledgments that many such currencies are inconvertible. The growing tendency to make loans rather than grants suggests businesslike transactions rather than an international dole. Descriptions of programs as either temporary stopgaps or self-liquidating endeavors are designed to offset the impression of an endless burden. Administrators have also been eager to disclose the extent to which burdens are being shared, and "self-help" is both the complement to and the objective served by such exertions.

The results of these stratagems are interesting. Although the name and structure of the principal aid-dispensing agency has been altered almost as often as it has received a new director, the aid effort has been maintained for more than two decades without drastic changes in the general magnitude of the program or in the manner of its financing. It is equally clear that the program has been significantly shaped by the political context in which it is regularly considered.

The constant reorganization (a means of putting a new face on an essentially stable program) has been disruptive. The temptation to turn on the aid faucet in response to conjured images of Communist inroads gives undue bargaining advantages to countries prepared to create the appearance of imminent disaster. The preference for military assistance, defense supports, and activities related to civic action and counterinsurgency may have inadvertently distorted the pattern of political development in many a fledgling state. It has also alienated many a liberal supporter. The smuggling of one program through Congress on the back of another may have given rise to both false expectations and inappropriate "strings." Efforts to enhance the palatability of the aid program to the business community by setting up "blue ribbon panel[s] of bonded conservatives . . . to cast a presumably cold eye on the aid effort and then to recommend its continuance as essential to the national interest" [34] have occasionally backfired when verdicts were handed down that were detrimental to the President's hopes of unqualified endorsement. The Clay Report in 1963, for example, favored a reduction in the magnitude of foreign aid expenditures.[35]

Political structure and political leadership

Constitutional government, it is said, permits a people to be governed by laws rather than men. On the other hand, a prominent Senate Committee concluded after an exhaustive analysis of the procedures of policy-making that the quality of executive personnel was more

[34] This was Arthur Schlesinger's apt description of the intended function of the Clay Committee in *A Thousand Days*, p. 597.

[35] It was not, however, without its benefits—for example, the emphasis is placed upon concentrating aid in countries making substantial efforts of their own and capable of intelligently applying external capital. In FY 1969, for example, nearly 90 percent of AID funds will be concentrated in sixteen countries.

crucial for the determination of national policy than the methods they employed to reach decisions. Clearly the content of a state's foreign policy is shaped by the degree to which experience or aptitude in the management of external relations are taken into account in the selection of political leaders. Since elective officials in the White House and in Congress play such a substantial role in foreign-policy-making in the United States, it is essential to consider whether the process of office-seeking places a premium upon the same skills as that of policy-making. The frequency and depth of turnover in policy-making posts, moreover, affects the ease of innovation and the likelihood of continuity in the realm of foreign as well as domestic policy.

Regular turnover at the top is one of the characteristic features of American politics. Occupancy of the White House is limited by constitutional amendment to eight years. Congressmen and senators confront reelectoral contests at two- and six-year intervals, but in neither House is there a limit on the number of times an incumbent may be returned to Washington. The other important foreign policy positions are filled by political appointees. In contrast to the British parliamentary system, in which members of the administrative class in the civil service, for example, Permanent Undersecretaries of the ministries, provide a source of continuity by mediating continuously between Whitehall and the cabinet, presidential appointees control the commanding heights of the foreign policy establishment, seeking to insure its responsiveness to presidential direction and controlling the flow of departmental work to the White House for decision.

Although many of America's earliest Chief Executives served apprenticeships in important diplomatic assignments, a career in professional diplomacy is no longer so likely to provide the type of experience or the range of contacts that an electoral politician aspiring to the Presidency would find useful. While there is no single road to the White House, professional politicians predominate among its recent inhabitants. Six of the last nine incumbents had almost exclusively political careers.

Attaining the Presidency requires that one display an unerring sense of timing in running for the right office at the right time en route, demonstrate a capacity to manipulate the difficult issues in such a way as to avoid alienating important constituencies, and develop those qualities of personality and style on which success with the mass electorate increasingly depends.

In Congress, the seniority rule prevails; longevity in service is the prerequisite for substantial influence. Congressmen from "safe" districts and senators from "single-party" regions thus enjoy a differential advantage, as the number of Southern committee chairmen suggests. Midwestern Republicans enjoy comparable advantages when their party controls Congress.

There is, of course, no guarantee that an electoral politician who can persuade local party bosses that he is a plausible presidential candidate or who can even prevail in the presidential election contest will possess empathy for foreign societies, sound judgment in evaluating foreign leaders, or success in winning the confidence of foreign statesmen. The Presidency is such an important office, however, that Presidents are chosen with an eye on the problems with which they will be forced to grapple. Since foreign policy problems have posed the most critical challenges to presidential leadership during the past two decades, the anticipated ability of rival candidates to manage such challenges have regularly informed the judgment of the electorate. Vice Presidents are more likely to be selected on the basis of their capacity to bring balance to a party's ticket. Of the past five incumbents in that office, only one, Hubert Humphrey, brought substantial credentials in dealing with the problems of security policy to the exercise of his official responsibilities.

The most durable congressmen and senators tend to come from the Deep South or those interior regions of the continent where one might suspect provincial, rural, noncosmopolitan attitudes to prevail. Where long service rather than obvious merit assures power, there is little insurance that changes in the international environment will be adequately acknowledged by aged legislators. Since 1945, however, the most influential Senate spokesmen on foreign policy questions have rarely adopted a narrow outlook or posed unyielding obstacles to presidential leadership in foreign affairs. Moreover, there is a process of self-selection at work in relationship to committee assignments that allows those with substantial interest and aptitude for foreign relations to achieve eminence on the appropriate committees. Those interested merely in "pork" for their constituents have little incentive to seek assignments to the Senate Foreign Relations Committee or the House Foreign Affairs Committee. Under these circumstances, long service may permit the acquisition of valuable experience.[36]

To be sure, electoral politicians may inherit the Presidency or important power on Capitol Hill without the expertise of the foreign affairs specialist or the experience of the foreign policy executive. There is little reason to assume that the latter have any monopoly on wisdom, however, in making political judgments. Ultimately such judgments represent the most significant contribution that politicians may make. As Richard Neustadt has written of the President, it is his task to evaluate the "political "easibilities of contemplated action vis-à-vis our world antagonists: judgments on where history is tending, what opponents can stand, what friends will take, what officials

[36] The long tenure of congressional leaders equalizes somewhat the relationships between the President and Congress. Power is limited in time as well as scope. A President enjoys an expansive scope of influence; his tenure in office is strictly limited. At most he enjoys about six years to impose his own imprint on the office, for even if he is reelected, it takes time to learn the ropes, and during his last year, his influence is circumscribed by the prospect of his early departure. Whereas tenure is brief and turnover abrupt in the executive branch, in Congress tenure is much longer among the leaders, and turnover gradual. Congressmen can, thus, outwait a President if they cannot "outwit or outmaneuver him." Presidents come and go; committee chairmen in the House and Senate abide. This poses problems for the President and helps account for the prodigious amount of presidential time and energy channeled into eliciting congressional support for his initiatives.

will enforce, what 'men in the street' will tolerate; judgments on the balance of support, opposition, indifference at home and abroad." [37]

As control of the White House changes hands, changes in the leadership of the foreign policy bureaucracies are predictable. This is not to say that one may predict who will inherit particular posts, for America has no functional analogue to the British parliament or civil service or the Bolshevik *apparat* for regularly training its foreign policy executives. In January, 1960, for example, one could not anticipate who would be elected to the White House or who would soon become Secretary of State, Secretary of Defense, or directors of the various foreign affairs agencies. Nor was it clear who the prime candidates for the latter jobs might be.

When the regular turnovers in personnel reach deep into an Administration, discontinuities in policy may result. There were many causes of the Bay of Pigs disaster in April, 1961. One was the house-cleaning that had been recently effected throughout the executive branch. President Kennedy was new to his duties, though not without knowledge of foreign affairs. His chief advisers included a Secretary of State and a Secretary of Defense whom he had scarcely known before appointing them and who only a scant four months previously had been the presidents of the Rockefeller Foundation and the Ford Motor Company, respectively. His Special Assistant for National Security Affairs was appropriated from the Dean's Office at Harvard University. The competence each subsequently displayed in managing his various responsibilities does not entirely dispel the impression that one of the essential costs of this pattern of regular and abrupt turnover is the "period of adjustment" that each transition from one Administration to another brings. "On-the-job training" takes time, as does the adjustment of powerful and ambitious men to one another's strengths, weaknesses, and personal idiosyncrasies. As two astute observers have noted, "The new leaders have to spend a year or more simply establishing themselves in office, getting to know one another, learning the ropes of their individual offices, familiarizing themselves with the complexities of Washington politics if they are new to government, and developing a common outlook, a common set of policy priorities, and a common political style." [38]

All this may occasion the recurrence of delay, fitful starts and stops, and a diplomacy marked by vacillation, then bursts of energy, as incumbents seek to avoid committing their unknown successors, as newly elected or appointed officials attempt to fulfill promises perhaps imprudently or inadvertently issued in the heat of electoral battle, and as the more durable strata of career officials try to adjust to the convulsions in administrative method that are a regular feature of these transitions.

With innocent novitiates regularly replacing experienced

---

[37] Richard E. Neustadt, Senate Committee on Government Operations, *Administration of National Security, Hearings,* 88th Cong., 1st Sess., p. 77.

[38] Brzezinski and Huntington, *op. cit.,* p. 181.

political executives, professionalism may be difficult to sustain. At times, in fact, critics have contended, political appointees have moved in and out of Washington so rapidly that they scarcely had time to become familiar with their official duties. Statistics on the length of tenure by men of secretarial rank in the Pentagon in the 1950s provoked such complaints. During the Eisenhower Administration, Deputy and Assistant Secretaries of Defense served for only slightly more than eighteen months on the average. The record in the State Department was no better. The principal foreign-aid-dispensing agency has been led by no less than ten executives, assisted by eight separate directors of personnel. Each, according to one report, brought with him "his own ideas as to how the agency should be organized, who his top assistants should be, and what kind of personnel program was needed." [39] In 1963 not a single United States ambassador had been at his post for as much as five years, with the average tenure of the fifty-six professional ambassadors standing at just over seventeen months. Such evidence has generally prompted the conclusion that American foreign policy must be hopelessly amateurish, that co-ordination among men of such disparate backgrounds and brief experience must be impossible,[40] and that both democratic control and diplomatic prowess must be compromised in the process.

Such charges are at best incomplete; at worst they are seriously misleading. Rapid turnover in the executive branch is deplorable only if it is unceasing, only if occasional discontinuities are not offset by a greater capacity for innovation, and only if the lack of experience frequently brought to the conduct of foreign policy is not to some extent compensated for by a reinvigoration of the bureaucracy permitted by the regular influx of new men at the top. The record is not as bad as the previously cited charges imply.

In the first place, rather than unceasing turnover, one finds periods of stability and periods of rapid change, in irregular sequence. During the Truman Administration when the broad guidelines of American foreign policy were being set, the leading foreign policy posts were occupied by four men: James Forrestal, Dean Acheson, George C. Marshall, and Robert Lovett. During the entire period one of these men administered the Defense Department for all but eighteen months, the State Department for five of the seven years.

[39] Report of the Committee on Foreign Affairs Personnel, *Personnel for the New Diplomacy* (Washington, D.C.: Carnegie Endowment for International Peace, 1962), p. 24.

[40] One former diplomat decried, only half facetiously, the likelihood of fruitful exchange between "a time-motion engineer from Detroit, temporarily with the Defense Department; a city hall reporter from the Northwest trying out Federal employment in the Voice of America; a Wall Street lawyer on leave to the Treasury and worrying about conflicts of interest; a union organizer on a training tour in the Department of Labor; a 4-H graduate from the Peace Corps; a politician unable to contain the fact that he is from the White House; and two middle-aged, inarticulate career officials, one a little chief from the Pentagon, the other an uprooted ambassador versed in Arabic affairs whose job had been given by the articulate politician from the White House to someone in the White House." John Paton Davies, *Foreign and Other Affairs*, p. 173.

Nor could they fairly be described as amateurs. Before assuming their respective executive duties as Department Secretaries, each served fruitful apprenticeships: Forrestal as Secretary of the Navy, Acheson as Assistant Secretary of State, Lovett in high posts in both the State and Defense departments, and Marshall as Chief of Staff of the Army.

While the rate of executive turnover was rather more marked during President Eisenhower's two terms in office, Secretary of State Dulles headed his Department for six years. His successor, Christian Herter, was promoted from his post as Deputy Secretary, and possessed vast and varied political experience as a diplomat, a congressman, and a governor. In the Defense Department, Charles Wilson was Secretary for more than five years. Although he was unembarrassed by any familiarity with the intricacies of strategy, this merely reflected the President's preference for Secretaries who would serve as expeditors of production and industrial mobilization rather than innovators of strategic policy.

Admiral Arthur Radford, meanwhile, served for four years as Chairman of the Joint Chiefs of Staff, providing military support for the New Look doctrine implemented by the Administration. Wilfred McNeil continued throughout this period as Controller of the Department of Defense, a position that proved equally crucial in the fashioning of the new strategy. Secretary McElroy, who succeeded Wilson, and his own successor, Thomas Gates, served for only two years each. The first served without notable distinction, and his continuance in office was no more desirable than his qualifications were relevant. Gates, on the other hand, proved a capable Secretary whose accomplishments were impressive despite his short tenure. His previous experience in the Department of the Navy clearly served him well. In the White House, General Robert Cutler served the President for nearly four years as Special Assistant for National Security Affairs and Executive Secretary of the National Security Council. Gordon Gray, who succeeded him in 1958, had a briefer term of service, but was also not without experience, having previously worked as Assistant Secretary of Defense for International Security Affairs and Director of the Office of Defense Mobilization.

Continuity in office has likewise been rather pronounced in the Kennedy and Johnson Administrations. Secretary of State Rusk and Secretary of Defense McNamara each amassed more than seven years in office. Douglas Dillon, who served as Secretary of the Treasury for four years, was favored for that post as a consequence of his previous experience as Ambassador to France and as Assistant Secretary of State in a Republican Administration. Averell Harriman, Paul Nitze, Harold Brown, William Bundy, Richard Helms, and Walt W. Rostow are among other high-ranking foreign policy and defense officials whose service extends through the Kennedy and Johnson Administrations.

The charge of amateurism is softened not only by a look at the long tenure of many of the most influential officials but also by a recognition of the growing "depoliticization" of the important foreign policy positions, which permits men of either political party to serve an Administration. Democratic Administrations have been most assiduous in seeking bipartisan support for their foreign policies through the appointment of prominent Republicans. Robert McNamara, McGeorge Bundy, William Foster, John McCloy, Douglas Dillon, Henry Cabot Lodge, and Allen Dulles were among those initially appointed by President Kennedy. Most had gained experience under a previous Administration. Moreover, among the Democrats appointed by Kennedy, almost 40 percent had held responsible positions during the Truman Administration. President Eisenhower was under fewer compulsions to resort to the appointment tactic to sustain his policies, for Democrats were unlikely to demand that he undo the fruits of their labors. Still, experience was not lacking among his appointees. Secretary of State Dulles had long experience in diplomacy, including service as chief negotiator of the American-Japanese Security Treaty. John McCone and Lewis Strauss were other Republicans whose previous foreign policy experience had been acquired under Democratic Administrations. They were complemented by the appointment of an occasional Democrat, such as David E. K. Bruce, Walter Robertson, James F. Byrnes, and Gordon Gray, to high diplomatic or governmental posts.

The movement of men from one agency or department to another also serves to promote coordination among the "quasi-sovereign" entities of the executive branch by insuring the presence in each department of at least a few key men who sympathetically understand the procedures, personnel, problems, and perspectives of their counterparts in other agencies. Illustrative of this are the cases of Paul Nitze, Deputy Secretary of Defense, whose previous experiences include a stint as Director of the State Department Policy Planning Staff as well as a variety of important posts in the Defense Department; William Bundy, who worked for ten years in the Central Intelligence Agency and four more in the International Security Affairs division of the Department of Defense before becoming Assistant Secretary of State for South Asia and the Pacific; John Leddy, whose experiences in the State Department and the Treasury prepared him for reassignment to the State Department, and Averell Harriman, the prototype of the man who contributes to a broader conception of policy and facilitates interdepartmental coordination as a result of wide and varied previous experience in government.

That frequent turnover in personnel does not automatically produce discontinuous policies is evidenced by the regularity with which policies survive the policy-makers. The basic policy of containment has been sustained through two decades and has survived to witness those transformations in Soviet political behavior vaguely anticipated in George Kennan's initial statement of the policy's assumptions. The stability of foreign aid expenditures has been markedly greater than the survival of its directors in Washington. The trends toward functional unification of the Defense Department and a rationalization of weapon policies reveal a constancy that is impressive through four Administrations.

Continuity in the broad framework of policy, however, is not symptomatic of the stagnation of a tradition, the inertia of an establishment, or the immobilism of a bureaucracy shielded from critical scrutiny. Frequent turnover does not compel innovation, but it surely permits it. And there have indeed been marked shifts in priorities and emphases with each change of Administration. The diversity of the recruitment of political executives encourages a rather continuous infusion of fresh energy into the Washington bureaucracies, permits a periodic reevaluation of assumptions behind the major lines of policy, and assures broader access to talented men and interesting ideas than is possible in any of those countries possesing the alleged virtue of an entrenched political bureaucracy. What is desired in the pattern of recruitment of political leaders for duty in the foreign policy establishment is what Kenneth Waltz has termed the right balance between "turnover for the sake of refreshment, shuffling of personnel from one agency to another to aid in the coordination of policy, and retention of some persons in a single office for a number of years in order to foster continuity of policy and procedure." [41] The American system, whatever its shortcomings, seems hardly deficient in comparison to other great powers in these respects. On the contrary, it has permitted defensible adjustments to the exigencies of the world situation. Neither innovation nor continuity are rendered impossible or unlikely by the system. Political accountability is not sacrificed to the demands of "rationality," since the President must at periodic intervals confront the electorate for a renewal of his mandate.

The virtues of a pluralistic policy-making system

Now that some of the apparent deficiencies of the foreign-policy-making system have been highlighted, it is well for one to recognize that it also possesses the virtues of its vices. First, it ought to be acknowledged that obstacles to timely innovation, to the integration of diverse policies, and to the clarification of American intentions are not insurmountable.

Policy innovations are doubtless most likely to be approved in emergency situations. Nothing, however, prevents diplomatic incidents from being interpreted as challenges or challenges as grave international crises. As Kenneth Waltz has observed, nothing intrinsic in the situations in Western Europe in 1947, Korea in 1950, the Formosa Straits in 1958, Cuba in 1962, or Vietnam in 1965 com-

[41] Waltz, *Foreign Policy and Democratic Politics*, p. 132.

pelled American Presidents to respond as though the gauntlet had been thrown down.[42] Once such situations were defined as crises, the problems of galvanizing political energies, resolving jurisdictional struggles, and surmounting political obstruction became manageable.

Nor have the policies generated during such periods of crisis invariably born the stamp of *ad hoc* palliatives. Out of the hastily arranged discussions about Western Europe conducted in the State Department in the spring of 1947 emerged plans for the Marshall Plan, the germ of a multilateral collective defense system for the Atlantic community, and an attitude congenial to the reincorporation of West Germany (and Japan) into the comity of Western nations. The North Korean attack across the 38th parallel in June, 1950 prompted not only American military intervention in Asia but a reformulation of American strategic doctrine and the development of a preparedness posture adjusted to a "long-haul" perspective. The Cuban missile crisis was treated by President Kennedy not merely as another incident or episode in the cold war but as the possible starting point for the process of gradual reconciliation with the Soviet Union.

The dispersion of power does pose obstacles to dramatic policy innovations. Policies, once adopted, tend at times to be more durable than the conditions that produced them. Still, criticisms directed at the "massive continuity" of American policy presuppose that the containment policy—which describes with reasonable accuracy the general policy design for the postwar period—either did not represent a defensible conception of the national interest or was too rigidly framed to permit gradual adjustments to an evolving situation abroad. Neither claim is unassailable. American security interests have surely been sustained through two decades. Nor has American policy been as inflexible as some suggest. The focus on containment did not inhibit encouragement for the aspirations of many anticolonial independence movements, prevent adjustment to the more moderate Soviet foreign policy posture of recent years, or proscribe changing priorities in the emphases and regional efforts in American foreign aid and mutual security programs. "Building bridges" surely implies a quite different emphasis than "building strength."

While durable public support for basic policies has been sustained by invoking the now-familiar terminology of cold war stereotypes, public opinion displays a generally permissive character. Not only is public opinion malleable, but the mass public displays a substantial deference to the President in the management of grave foreign policy problems.

As a variety of discordant voices compete in explicating American aims and proclaiming American intentions, considerable confusion may result. The system is not, however, without some built-in correctives for the careful foreign spectator of American politics. Indeed it is precisely this confusion that regularly prompts Presidents

[42] Waltz, *op. cit.*, pp. 104–109.

to attempt to clarify and refine American overseas commitments. Publicly expressed doubts about the efficacy of American policies by senators, opposition leaders, prominent generals, diplomats, civil rights leaders, businessmen, labor leaders, academicians, and others repeatedly force Administration officials to explicate their objectives and the rationale for policies. Badgered by inquisitive congressmen and newsmen, Presidents and Secretaries of State may take refuge in ambiguous or evasive statements. They may be harassed into careless indiscretions. Such public discourse, however, provides numerous occasions for ambiguities to be reduced, evasions to be challenged, and declaratory policies to be rendered more precise. One recalls, for example, significant and felicitous modifications introduced by Secretary of State Dulles in his doctrine of "massive retaliation" in the wake of the public furor arising from the initial public exposition of the new strategic policy. In general, the costs of an "open-mouth" policy-making process are well recognized, the benefits too little appreciated.

If the American policy-making system occasionally exhibits a "leaderless" character, the existence of multiple sources of ideas and initiative has its rewards as well. In the early 1960s, for example, many critics accused the State Department of unimaginativeness in formulating new courses of action in the Western Hemisphere. Yet the existence of a Presidential Task Force led by Adolf Berle, the interest in Latin America sustained by Douglas Dillon, the new Secretary of the Treasury, and the anxiety of AID officials to develop a new program for the Latin republics insured that there was no dearth of ideas and proposals.

The diffusion of power among a variety of competing agencies produces notable problems of coordination. It may also guarantee that the purposes of new programs are not lost or diluted beyond recognition by being absorbed into the activities of established agencies. The occasional coordination problems posed by the autonomy of the Peace Corps appears to be a price well worth paying for the maintenance of the integrity of an endeavor that might otherwise have been jeopardized through its merger with other aid efforts. Moreover, in coping with the baffling problems of political and economic development, there are distinct advantages in developing the multiple approaches represented by the Agency for International Development, the Food for Peace Program, the Export-Import Bank Credit Extension Program, and the various multilateral agencies through which American funds are channeled. Different programs may be based upon contradictory premises regarding the dynamics of development. Confusion may accompany American efforts. But if the shot is scattered, the possibilities of a direct hit—or even a glancing blow on the problem—may be enhanced. Competition and rivalry among three proud and autonomous military services may yield some wasteful duplication of effort. It also serves as insurance against gross oversights in America's preparedness policies.

Recalling the distinctions among crisis policy, anticipatory policy, and program policy, it is possible to discern additional advantages in the American policy-making system. With respect to crisis management, it is difficult to demonstrate irremediable deficiencies in the American system. During crises the Presidency becomes the "vital center" of the policy-making process, and *ad hoc* arrangements have been regularly devised that permit the Chief Executive to exercise authority commensurate with his responsibilities. During the Cuban missile crisis, the Executive Committee of the National Security Council provided a forum for careful and responsible high-level policy analysis subject to the control of the President.

One of the essential requirements of American foreign policy is the capacity to prudently shoulder commitments. In framing declaratory policy, the government seeks to articulate with precision American intentions with respect to specific contingencies. It is surely reasonable to suppose that vigorous debate is likely to yield more sensible and carefully expressed commitments. In 1954, for example, when Secretary of State Dulles and Admiral Radford, Chairman of the Joint Chiefs of Staff, proposed to commit American prestige and power in the Indochinese crisis, congressional leaders presented conditions for their acquiescence in such an undertaking. The French, they demanded, must accelerate their decolonization of that area and agree not to withdraw their military forces from the region should America intervene. Moreover, support for France was made contingent on the policies adopted by America's European allies. In the light of subsequent events, these conditions appear to have been intelligent preconditions for action, and the fact that they could not be met served to postpone for a time what, in retrospect, appears would have been an unfortunate involvement. Not only, however, may some imprudent engagements be avoided, but those undertaken are invested with greater credibility for having weathered partisan discussion and public debate. When obligations are carefully and earnestly assumed, rivals are less likely to doubt the seriousness of American intent, the extent to which the national prestige has been committed, or the degree to which a failure to honor external obligations would entail domestic political consequences.[43]

With respect finally to program policy, there are other advantages. Many critics complain of the way in which foreign aid programs are compromised by the meddling of congressional committees or the bargaining among executive agencies. The case is more easily stated than sustained. Thomas Schelling has persuasively argued that, in bargaining, "weakness is strength." That is to say, notable bargaining advantages accrue from an inflexible negotiating posture. To AID officials, eager to define the conditions of American grants and loans, skeptical or hostile congressional appropriation subcommittees contribute obvious services. The threat to Country X, "Reform your tax collection system or face the prospect of congressional cuts in this or that portion of the aid program," can scarcely be dismissed as an empty bluff. Administrative interference may have contributed to

[43] For a discussion of this point see Waltz, *op. cit.*, Chap. 4.

excessive caution and helped to produce occasional shoddy results. It is equally probable that the prospect of congressional oversight encourages a measure of administrative efficiency. Nor has the persistent criticism of the aid program at home and especially in Congress jeopardized the continuity of major programs. The level of economic assistance has remained remarkably stable throughout the entire postwar period, and in the yearly trials of the budgetary cycle, the proponents of the program have a perfect opportunity to marshall those arguments that may shore up public belief in and governmental support for the aid effort.

The incessant bargaining among partisans that marks the relations among policy-makers creates the appearance of confusion and turmoil in Washington. It also produces an adversary system in which political executives representing a variety of perspectives and institutional interests engage in a sustained and generally animated debate on the major foreign policy issues. Through such debate, relevant information is accumulated, assumptions may be refined, and serious intellectual efforts are encouraged as officials seek to produce defensible proposals that can withstand partisan discussion. The virtues of such a system may be demonstrated by citing the exceptional policy that was framed within the narrower confines of "closed politics." The disastrous Bay of Pigs debacle was planned and executed in what, for the American government, amounted to extraordinary secrecy. So secret were the details of the abortive invasion that, within the government, the analysts of neither the State Department Bureau of Intelligence and Research nor the National Estimates Office of the Central Intelligence Agency were asked to make their own independent assessment of the operational feasibility of the plan. The Secretary of State—and possibly even the Joint Chiefs of Staff—were unable to appraise its merits on the basis of information supplied by any officials except those who had staked their reputations on its efficacy. It seems likely in retrospect that the procedures of debate and discussion that generally accompany important policy decisions would have exposed the futility of the endeavor, the unrealistic premises upon which it was based, and the unfortunate consequences that its failure would bring.[44]

One illuminates but one side of the American policy-making system by emphasizing the potential for stalemate and paralysis; by noting the possibly disproportionate influence of strategically located minorities, such as congressional committee chairmen; by dwelling upon the tendencies toward bargaining and logrolling; by

[44] To be sure, if a state is to engage in secret political operations, organize subversive undertakings, and seek to bring down foreign governments, precautions will naturally be taken to shield such planning from the "normal" process of open, partisan discussion. The comparative ease with which the CIA engineered the demise of the Mossadegh government in Iran in 1951 and the Arbenz government in Guatemala in 1954 encouraged misplaced optimism among leading intelligence officials, even as it apparently prompted Cuban leaders to protect themselves against any repetition of those events, to the point of arming a people's militia and soliciting external protection from the Soviet Union.

citing the frequency with which policies represent compromises among bureaucratic interests rather than clear responses to external dangers or opportunities. It is far too casually assumed that more hierarchical forms of decision-making would alleviate these shortcomings. The gravest liability of the most perfectly conceived hierarchy, of course, is the possibility that significant values, interests, or policy considerations may be neglected. In the American system, if sins of omission are relatively frequent, the disasters emanating from imprudent blunders (sins of commission) are happily rare. Continuity is at a premium; adaptability at a discount. Persistence in the pursuit of a sensible objective may be matched by an inability to alter course in a timely fashion, even if a policy is palpably unsuccessful! Resembling a raft rather than a sailing sloop, the American policy-making system is slow, cumbersome, unresponsive to the deft touch of the helmsman, yet durable in a sudden squall. "It will not sink, but one's feet are always wet." [45]

[45] Fisher Ames's commentary on the strengths and weaknesses of American democracy, as paraphrased by Huntington, *The Common Defense*, p. 447.

7

Recent American foreign relations

Since 1945 America's foreign relations have been framed in response to the emergence and evolution of a system of Communist states, the demise of the former imperial system, and the continuous revolution in military technology. In the face of these interlocking problems, the United States has adhered to several basic objectives. Above all, the United States has attempted to contain Communist influence in world politics. It has also promoted the reconstruction of Europe's economic vitality and assisted the social, economic, and political development of many fledgling states in the former colonial areas. Cooperative schemes of a regional or functional character have been encouraged as building blocks to a wider system of international order. Finally, the United States has sought to play a conciliating role in the world by attempting to facilitate the amelioration of former enmities, the reconciliation of former foes, and the bridging of cold war schisms.

Maintaining the territorial and political balance between East and West

The general contours of the containment policy were described in Chapter 3. It remains to appraise the success of that policy and describe some of its contemporary expressions. On the record of the past twenty-three years, it appears that the policy has been remarkably successful. Reduced to its essentials, containment involved American resistance to unilateral changes in the frontiers between the Communist and Free World systems, where such changes were to be effected by force directly or indirectly applied.[1] With but minor exceptions, the demarcation lines between East and West established by the outcome of World War II have remained in force. Since old boundaries tend to be good boundaries, it is fair to say that a certain territorial stabilization has occurred. China, North Vietnam, and Cuba have, to be sure, been taken over by Communist movements since 1945. The fact that each of these movements selected its own leaders, pursued its own strategy for seizing power, and developed its own constituency by mobilizing national sentiments has meant that all have been able successfully to assert their independence of Soviet direction or defiance of Soviet policies.

Although each of these events prompted anxious soul searching among policy-makers at the time they occurred, the United States refrained from attempting any forceful restoration of the status quo in Eastern Europe and China in the 1940s or Southeast Asia in the mid-1950s, and it swiftly called off an abortive counterrevolutionary intervention in Cuba in 1961 when its futility was early revealed. In each case the costs of overt military intervention were deemed high, the benefits dubious. On other occasions, however, when the consequences of American inaction were considered significant, the United States intervened with force even though the risks and costs entailed were acknowledged as great and though the objectives could not always be formulated with precision; for example, Korea in 1950, Lebanon in 1958, and South Vietnam in 1965. Through the zigs and zags of American policy one central thread is discernible: whenever the global balance of power or the psychological balance of deterrence between the United States and expansionist Communist states was thought to be at stake, the United States has acted to preserve the balance, for no President has been prepared to risk an imbalance which might mortgage American security to the goodwill of a powerful adversary.[2]

Under what conditions, one may ask, has containment been most effectively achieved? What methods and techniques have been employed in the service of containment? What kinds of challenges to the international political or territorial status quo have inspired American resistance? How have the "lessons" of one crisis influenced subsequent American responses to challenges posed by Communist states or revolutionary movements? What effect has the priority attributed to containment had upon American perspectives on decolonization and upon American relations with its allies? What strategic premises and capabilities have undergirded the United States commitment to the containment policy? In attempting answers to these

---

[1] For a restatement of the principle, see Walt W. Rostow, "Another Round in the Great Debate," *United States Department of State Bulletin* (November 6, 1967), p. 606.

[2] Brown, *The Faces of Power*, p. 19.

questions it must be remembered that containment is a policy that requires that the adversary be met upon the territory of third parties. This explains why the focus of American diplomacy has been upon filling power vacuums in Europe and Asia, organizing collective defense arrangements in those and other regions, and promoting economic and social development throughout the non-Communist world.

The theaters of containment

Europe has provided a more favorable environment for the containment policy than have other regions. In Europe, America's policies have served the traditional objective of denying hegemony to any single continental state. American assistance has been extended to well-established communities, many of whom had enjoyed long-standing ties of friendship with the United States. The dangers, moreover, that confronted the Western Europeans—particularly in the first postwar decade—were unequivocal, and the identity of the potential disturber of the balance of power was scarcely in doubt.

In the Middle East, Asia, Latin America, and Africa, on the other hand, military threats to America's friends and allies have been more ambiguous. Habits of political cooperation among non-Communist states in those regions have frequently been conspicuous by their absence. Public authority in many non-Western states has been tentative and fragile. Consequently, governments often have been unable to make effective use of American assistance. More than once the urge to contain Communist influence in the new states has impelled the United States to link itself with regimes of a notably unprogressive character. This has complicated the mobilization of public enthusiasm and allied support for American objectives and policies in those areas.

The methods of containment

Varying combinations of means ranging from diplomatic support to military intervention have been employed in the service of containment. In Greece (1947–50) and in the Philippines (1948–55), counterinsurgency techniques sufficed. The United States provided economic assistance and military advice to both governments. Both recipients proved to be militarily competent and politically astute. In neither Greece nor the Philippines were Communist-backed guerrillas able to secure a broad national following. In Greece, American aid was instrumental in bolstering the confidence of an embattled government and permitted a dramatic expansion in that government's military effort. The display of American interest in the outcome also helped to provoke the split between Russia and Yugoslavia. Once Tito defected from the Soviet bloc, he introduced a note of caution into his foreign policy, abandoned the Greek insurgent cause, and denied the guerrillas sanctuaries on Yugoslav soil.[3] American economic and mil-

[3] See Herbert Dinerstein, *Intervention Against Communism* (Baltimore, Md.: Johns Hopkins University Press, 1967), pp. 7–13.

itary assistance to the Philippine government was kept to rather modest levels, but American influence was exerted skillfully on behalf of the political activities of a remarkable leader, Ramon Magsaysay, whose campaigns against corruption and whose grasp of the political aspects of counterinsurgency brought decisive results against the Huk insurgents.

In Korea (1950–53) and South Vietnam (1965–   ), America dispatched conventional troops to fight limited wars in defense of existing territorial and political arrangements in Asia. In Korea a conventional military response was appropriate to the challenge of regular armies crossing an internationally recognized frontier. In South Vietnam the United States has "conventionalized" an ambiguous guerrilla war, in order to enhance the relevance of American military power to the conflict. The efficacy of that effort remains in doubt.

In the Berlin crises of 1948–49 and 1958–62, as well as in the Cuban missile crisis of October, 1962, America's vital strategic interests were considered threatened by the Soviet Union. In each case the United States was anxious lest a gradual erosion of American rights or the violation of those rights in a swift and unexpected *fait accompli* sharply diminish American prestige, thus America's ability to control the global balance of power. In meeting those successive challenges, the United States relied upon a combination of demonstrative military gestures and the residual threat of escalation to induce caution in Soviet policy.

On each occasion, the United States invested a challenge to its rights or interests with symbolic significance far transcending the local issues involved. In each case, America sought to act before the Soviet Union could employ deterrent threats of its own to defend a forcefully altered status quo. In each case, the United States successfully "shifted the initiative" for drastic and dangerous actions to its adversary. When, for example, Stalin imposed the Berlin blockade in 1948, President Truman neither accepted a gross violation of America's access rights to the former German capital as legitimate nor authorized military action to reopen the overland routes through the Soviet occupation zone by force. Rather he initiated an airlift that supplied the beleaguered city of Berlin for more than a year, thus rendering the blockade ineffective and ultimately forcing its abandonment.

Similarly, when President Kennedy discovered that the Russians were clandestinely seeking to alter the strategic balance by installing intermediate-range ballistic missiles in Cuba in 1962, he refused the counsel of both those who argued against any action and those who were eager to either invade the island or authorize "surgical" airstrikes against the missile sites. By instituting a naval quarantine around Cuba, the President forced the impetuous Soviet Premier Khrushchev to decide whether to turn Russian missile-bearing ships around before a single shot was fired over the bow of a Soviet vessel or to challenge an American blockade in an area where the United

States obviously enjoyed the advantages of local military superiority.

On several occasions the urge to confine Communist influence in non-Western areas has led to prophylactic interventions of an international or unilateral character. In 1956 and 1960, the United States supported U.N.-sponsored "preventive diplomacy" measures in the Middle East and the Congo, respectively. The internationalization of those conflicts was deemed an expedient way of averting the extension of Soviet-American competition into Africa. The neutralizing presence of U.N. forces in the Sinai Peninsula and in the Congo Republic was largely subsidized by the United States, though no American troops were involved.

In 1958 American marines were landed in Lebanon at the invitation of the Chamoun government, which claimed that it was about to be engulfed by Arab nationalist movements based in Damascus and Cairo. United States forces were not committed in the civil strife, but their presence may have bolstered the self-assurance of authorities in Beirut.

More forceful measures were undertaken to crush revolutionary movements in the Western Hemisphere. Suspicions of increasing Communist-influence in revolutionary movements in Guatemala and the Dominican Republic prompted preventive interventions by the United States in 1964 and 1965, respectively. In each case, new governments acceptable to Washington were installed. In 1961, when the Castro revolution in Cuba openly avowed its Marxist-Leninist character and developed links with the Soviet bloc, the containment reflex resulted in an American-sponsored exile invasion whose purpose was remedial but whose fate was disastrous.

Beyond these responses to specific challenges or crises, the political influence of expansionist Communist states has been countered with a combination of deterrent threats, diplomatic isolation, and economic sanctions.

It is noteworthy that these American actions were fashioned with one eye on the containment of communism and the other on the avoidance of a general war. Thus the pattern of American responses to crises reveals a tacit acceptance of certain rules of restraint. Direct participation in guerrilla insurgencies was avoided where indirect support sufficed—Greece, the Philippines, and South Vietnam until the early 1960s. Though allied access rights to Berlin were upheld in 1948–49 and 1958–62, a military showdown was avoided. In Korea limitations on the geographic scope of hostilities and upon the aims of America's intervention were imposed to hold down the possibilities of escalation. In Eastern Europe in 1956 the United States made no attempt to "liberate" a Soviet satellite; it did, on the other hand, refuse to sanction a military campaign by its European allies against a leading neutralist state in the Middle East. American policy-makers planned and authorized the abortive Bay of Pigs invasion, but they also abandoned the project immediately when stern resistance was encountered and the exile force failed to establish a beachhead. The Soviet attempt to clandestinely introduce ballistic missiles into the

Western Hemisphere was sternly rebuffed, yet President Kennedy made no effort to humiliate the Russians. He sought rather to "make their setback in Cuba not the kind that would bring about an increase in hostility but perhaps provide for an easing of relations." [4]

Defining which gauntlets to pick up

The implementation of the containment policy has compelled the United States to redefine continuously the limits of American tolerance for various actions undertaken by Communist states and revolutionary movements. Naturally, American responses to challenges have been shaped by the circumstances of the moment. Still, several general guidelines emerge from a retrospective glance at the pattern of America's postwar policies.

America has reluctantly conceded the Soviet Union considerable freedom of action within Russia's zone of imperial interests, Eastern Europe. The Prague coup in 1948, the Russian intervention in Hungary in 1956, the construction of the Berlin wall in 1961, and the Soviet invasion of Czechoslovakia in 1968 occasioned official protests, public outcries, and occasional congressional resolutions, but no coercive sanctions. On the other hand, attempts to extend Soviet influence into contiguous areas have been consistently resisted. Thus President Truman issued blunt warnings to the Russians to abandon Iranian territory in 1946, helped the Greeks overcome a Communist-backed insurgency, fortified the resolution of the Turkish government to yield no concessions to Soviet intimidation, organized the Marshall Plan, guaranteed the security of Western Europe through the NATO Treaty, and intervened in Korea to thwart overt aggression.

The United States has been particularly sensitive to military challenges to the status quo. In Korea, American intervention was instinctive and immediate. In the Berlin crises and the Cuban missile crisis in 1962, American policy was animated by a determination to demonstrate the inadmissibility of nuclear pressures in areas of vital interest to the United States. More recently America has chosen to treat Vietnam as a test case of its ability to defeat a "national liberation" movement alleged to be controlled by Hanoi.

Revolutionary wars have posed the greatest confusion for American policy-makers. No very stable policy guidelines exist to inform American policy in situations where warfare is conducted *within* rather than *between* nations. The United States initially accepted the results of the Chinese civil war, though Chiang Kai-shek's Nationalist forces had been heavily supported. In Indochina, although the United States virtually subsidized the French war effort from 1950 until 1954, President Eisenhower refused to extend more than a "limited liability" commitment to the successor government to the French in South Vietnam. When a bloody coup d'état brought down the pro-Western government of Nuri El-Said in Iraq in 1958, the United States sought to encourage restraint on the part of the Leftist-oriented regime

[4] President Kennedy, quoted in Schlesinger, *A Thousand Days*, p. 841.

of General Kassem through its symbolic intervention in Lebanon. No attempt, however, was made to reverse the tide of events within Iraq itself. In the 1960s American policy in Vietnam has been based upon the conviction that the struggle there has been mounted from outside South Vietnam and, therefore, constitutes "as certain a form of aggression as the violation of the 38th parallel by the North Korean armies in June, 1950." [5]

Within the Western Hemisphere the limits of American patience with revolutionary movements have been even more marked. The basic United States attitude was well expressed in a declaration introduced by Secretary of State Dulles to the Tenth Inter-American Conference of the Organization of American States in the spring of 1954. "The domination ... of the political institutions of any American State by the International Communist movement," the Secretary proposed, constituted a "threat to the sovereignty and political independence of the American States, endangered the peace of America, and would call for appropriate action in accordance with existing treaties." [6] The willingness of the United States to intervene in Guatemala, Cuba, and the Dominican Republic suggests that those were more than mere idle expressions of sentiment. Indeed, they demonstrate that, within the Western Hemisphere, the United States has had little tolerance for revolutionary regimes or movements that *may become* Communist, and that it has been prepared to sponsor counterrevolutionary ventures in order to prevent the consolidation of Marxist-Leninist regimes in the Caribbean. [7]

The weight of precedents

Policy-makers are often inclined to apply principles and policies that have been successful under one set of conditions to situations that appear at least superficially similar. It is scarcely surprising that the interrelated elements of the containment policy that evolved in America's relations with Europe in the late 1940s should reappear in American policies in Asia and Latin America in response to challenges from revolutionary governments in China and Cuba. In a more specific sense, however, American experiences in one cold war crisis invariably leave their mark on subsequent assessments of the adversary's intentions and America's capabilities.

The Korean war, for example, convinced Secretary of State Dulles that the Soviet Union might encourage Communist aggression

[5] See the Address given by Walt W. Rostow, the President's Special Assistant for National Security Affairs, on June 28, 1961 to the U.S. Army Special Warfare School at Fort Bragg. Cited in Bernard Fall, *The Two Vietnams* (New York, N.Y.: Praeger, 1966), p. 243.

[6] Quoted in Eisenhower, *Mandate for Change*, p. 423.

[7] Having acknowledged the permanence of Castro's government in Cuba implicitly by abandoning the Bay of Pigs adventure, the United States reoriented its policies toward Cuba to accord with the more traditional elements in the containment policy. Thus the United States sought Cuba's diplomatic isolation within the hemisphere and launched its own movement for "peaceful revolution" through the Alliance for Progress.

wherever American intentions to resist were not unequivocally stated. The former Europe-first orientation subsequently was modified, and the containment policy was globalized. The costs and risks of American policies in Korea were considered acceptable, since a reputation for upholding commitments in forward positions throughout the world came to be viewed as a vital ingredient in America's ability to preserve the balance of deterrence. Secretary Dulles thus chose to render the American commitment to defend a host of Near Eastern and Asian states explicit and unambiguous, and to emphasize the strategic interdependence of those commitments.

At the same time, the Korean experience convinced many Americans—including most of those who voted for Eisenhower in the 1952 election—that fighting limited wars on the Asian mainland was a costly and foolhardy business. Since it also confirmed Republican suspicions of the malevolent and militarily aggressive character of the Soviet Union, the new Administration had somehow to reconcile its anticommunism with its determination to avoid future Koreas. The synthesis of these twin desires was accomplished in the New Look military strategy. According to this new declaratory policy of "massive retaliation," the United States threatened aggressive Communist opponents with dire retribution without specifying very precisely the circumstances in which such threats might be executed. By shouldering additional collective defense obligations, the United States sought to convey its determination to respond to aggression wherever it might occur. By expositing the New Look doctrine, it created a calculated uncertainty as to the character of future American reactions to attenuated provocations in non-European areas.

If the Korean war left its mark upon subsequent policies in Asia, the Guatemalan intervention of 1954 yielded its own "lessons," which proved later to be somewhat misleading. The appearance of Communists in influential positions in the government of Jacobo Arbenz in 1954 aroused vivid memories of the Sovietization of Eastern Europe. Preventive measures were immediately initiated. The "small-scale intervention by proxy" that the CIA masterminded produced swift and decisive results. Arbenz was replaced by a government whose composition was heavily influenced by the American Ambassador, John Peurifoy. When, six years later, Fidel Castro revealed the full depth of his commitment to social revolution and displayed a public affinity for Communist rhetoric and a voracious appetite for Soviet military assistance, recollections of the ease with which the Arbenz government had been dispatched without even the appearance of overt American involvement undoubtedly colored official estimates regarding the efficacy of an exile invasion of Cuba.

It seems clear that the gradual transformation of Castro's revolution from one proclaiming liberal principles to one employing totalitarian methods shaped American reflexes toward events in the Dominican Republic in 1965. The Cuban experience certainly made President Johnson immensely sensitive to the political costs of allowing the establishment of another Communist regime in the Caribbean.

This presumably increased his disposition to authorize a preemptive intervention against a revolutionary movement in which Communists enjoyed even a very low probability of gaining ascendancy.

The United States between its allies and its anticolonialism

The containment policy has left its mark on North-South as well as East-West issues. As a result of the priority attributed to containment, the traditional American opposition to colonialism has been modified and confused by the very intimacy of its involvement with many of the colonial powers. For two decades, American foreign-policy-makers have wrestled with the dilemma of maintaining the solidarity of the NATO alliance without unduly compromising their support for anticolonial movements. How, in other words, was the United States to remain true to its own heritage and its deep commitment to the principle of self-determination without jeopardizing the cohesion of its principal alliance?

In the earliest postwar period no such tension existed in American policy. President Truman supported Britain's withdrawal from India. He chided the French for their policies in Indochina. He employed financial pressure to encourage Dutch withdrawal from Indonesia, and provided his good offices to facilitate a resolution of that conflict.

As the United States became more preoccupied with the cold war in the 1950s, America's stance on colonial issues was rendered somewhat equivocal. After 1950 the French war effort in Indochina was heavily subsidized. American denunciations of European colonial practices became more restrained. Secretary of State Dulles insisted that the new states choose sides in the East-West struggle. Even then, however, the United States continued to remind non-Western peoples of its own revolutionary past. It sought to dissociate itself from the colonial policies of its allies. It mediated disputes between the British and French and their colonial dependencies in Cyprus and Algeria. It sought to insulate the former colonial areas from cold war competition. And it attempted to moderate the demands of neutralist leaders for an immediate end to colonialism even as it encouraged an acceleration of the pace of decolonization through pressure upon its allies.

In the 1960s the tone of American policy changed anew. President Kennedy displayed a notable sympathy for regimes practicing neutralism or nonalignment. His Administration went to considerable lengths to demonstrate its lively concern for the aspirations of peoples in the Third World. The United States expressed its aversion to colonialism more publicly in U.N. voting and in presidential advocacy of "Africa for the Africans."

The role of the middleman has not been entirely eschewed. After the Congo episode, especially, many Americans entertained second thoughts regarding the prudence of precipitate European liquidation of their imperial responsibilities. A continuing desire to retain base rights in the Portuguese-controlled Azores Islands induced American restraint with respect to U.N.-sponsored measures directed against Premier Salazar's colonial policies. Sensitivity to Britain's balance-of-payments difficulties has been responsible for an equivalent reserve toward Afro-Asian sanctions against South Africa. Nevertheless, pressure upon Portugal to withdraw from Central Africa has been constantly applied. Private investments in Angola and Mozambique have been officially discouraged, Export-Import Bank loans to those areas have been refused, and sales of arms to Portugal have been accompanied by demands for assurances that they will not be employed outside the NATO area. With respect to South Africa, the United States has condemned the apartheid practices of the Verwoerd and Voerster governments, but has resisted efforts to impose coercive sanctions to force a change in South Africa's domestic policies. It has also ceased providing arms to the South African government on grounds that they might be employed for repressive purposes internally, and has refused Export-Import Bank credits for sales to South Africa.

One might note, finally, that the tension between Europe and America over colonial issues has taken an ironic twist during the past few years. As the Europeans withdrew, the United States assumed the principal burdens of providing for the defense and prosperity of Europe's former dependencies. Of late the United States has vainly implored its allies to demonstrate a livelier concern for the fate of their former wards, while the Europeans have chided the United States over its lack of foresight in becoming embroiled in a colonial war in Southeast Asia!

Containment policy and deterrence strategy

It must be emphasized that the containment policy has been predicated upon the maintenance of a deterrence posture adequate to dissuade opponents from attacking America directly and from engaging in provocative actions against America's allies. The American military posture and the strategic concepts that guide its use have undergone a continuous evolution in response to the innovation of novel weapons, the transformation of political relationships in the world, and periodic redefinitions of American interests.

Mention has already been made of the New Look doctrine. That strategy, formulated by the Eisenhower Administration, was designed to deter a wide range of Soviet moves through ambiguous threats of nuclear reprisals "at times and in places of America's choosing." American military policy during the 1950s thus relied heavily upon the Strategic Air Command (SAC), tactical nuclear forces for the local defense of Europe, and the maintenance of the United States lead in the development of new military technology. The New Look was progressively modified during the late 1950s to accommodate the development of a more reciprocal balance of terror.

Only after 1961, however, was the strategy of "massive retaliation" replaced by a strategy of "flexible response" or "graduated deterrence." Almost exclusive reliance upon SAC gave way to the development of a balanced arsenal and a force structure providing "multiple options" for meeting military challenges. Emphasis upon nuclear deterrence was complemented by an enhanced desire to limit the damage that would be inflicted upon the continental United States in the event that deterrence inexplicably should fail. Concern over the prospect of "national liberation wars" in non-Western areas sparked an evident fascination with the techniques of counterinsurgency. The desire to retain American superiority in the field of military technology was moderated by a growing concern with arms control issues. In short, as the balance of terror has stabilized somewhat, the United States has sought to provide itself with a wide array of capabilities for conventional and irregular war. Some contend that the very existence of vastly improved capabilities has tempted America to make interventions that have proved unwise. This is to suggest that the American tolerance for changes in the territorial or political status quo narrows as its capacity to resist them increases.

The promotion of economic and social development

Other governments have employed grants and loans to buttress their alliance commitments or to secure commercial concessions. But Americans have been particularly inventive in the development of public programs of economic assistance for other states. By distributing economic aid for the purpose of encouraging the more rapid industrialization of many new states, the United States experimented with an instrument of diplomacy that was genuinely "something new under the sun." The evolution of American programs of economic assistance has been continuous since 1940. The objectives of programs, the identity of the recipients, and the criteria governing the allocation of aid have changed frequently, along with the names of the aid-disbursing agencies.

During World War II, foreign aid was linked clearly to American security interests. Some $48.5 billion in commodities and war materiel was shipped to beleaguered Britain and to a host of other wartime allies. Repayment was not demanded, for the United States was anxious that there be no repetition of the troublesome war-debts problems that plagued relations among the Western democracies during the 1920s. When the Second World War ended, the United States, which had become the world's leading creditor nation, provided more than $3 billion in food, clothing, and shelter to peoples threatened by famine, disease, and economic chaos. Those funds were distributed primarily by American military authorities acting under the aegis of the United Nations Relief and Rehabilitation Administration. The purpose of the relief was merely the short-range amelioration of suffering.

By 1947, when it became apparent that more substantial measures had to be taken if the severe dislocation of the European economy was to be overcome, the Marshall Plan was conceived and reconstruction replaced relief as the central aim of American economic assistance. The proposal, enunciated first by Secretary of State Marshall in June, 1947, invited the Europeans to provide the initiative in planning the restoration of their war-torn economies. Marshall intimated that if the Europeans could cooperatively assess their common needs and were prepared to distribute such aid as was provided, the United States would heavily subsidize a massive reconstruction program. The response of Europe's statesmen was immediate and positive. As a result, the United States shipped more than $13 billion in commodities to the members of the newly formed Organization of European Economic Cooperation between 1948 and 1952.

The Marshall Plan was an extraordinary success. By 1952 industrial and agricultural production in the recipient countries exceeded the prewar levels by 35 percent and 10 percent, respectively. Inflation had been checked, living standards increased, a high level of employment had been achieved, budgets had been brought into balance, intraregional trade barriers were being progressively dismantled, currencies were becoming convertible, and a start had been made toward the reincorporation of Germany—at least the Western portions of it—into the European economy. Above all, Western Europe had recovered sufficiently to be independent of any need for further extraordinary foreign economic assistance. By removal of the ominous prospect of economic stagnation, the threat of internal subversion had been successfully overcome.

The purposes and priorities of the American foreign aid program were drastically changed with the outbreak of war in Korea. The Marshall Plan was essentially a financial and economic effort, designed to restore the political confidence of the European states. Suddenly the aid program acquired mutual security emphasis—a label with evident military overtones. The aid program was reoriented toward the mobilization of local defense forces in states located along the periphery of the Soviet bloc. Prior to 1949 military assistance had been a neglible feature of the aid effort. By 1952 more than $5 billion in military assistance was flowing to overseas friends and allies.[8] The focus of American efforts also shifted away from Europe to the Near East, South Asia, and the Far East. Furthermore, the countries that accepted American military assistance were also high on the list to receive economic aid. Thus a willingness on the part of others to enter collective defense pacts with the United States and to share the burdens of the common defense was to provide the central criterion for the distribution of economic as well as military assistance.

In the mid- and late 1950s the cold war battleground had shifted again. By this time Europe was economically prosperous and well defended. The Korean war had ended with the restoration of the status quo ante. The pace of decolonization was being accelerated, and

[8] By 1955 that figure had declined to slightly more than $1 billion, and it has fluctuated between $1 and $2 billion since that time.

the states emerging from decades or centuries of colonial rule became the object of uncommon interest by both cold war protagonists. Aid to the underdeveloped nations was not unprecedented. In 1949 President Truman had initiated a modest program of technical assistance, popularly known as Point Four. Nevertheless, between 1948 and 1952 Europe received 69 percent of all American aid. During the same period Far Eastern countries received 16 percent, Near Eastern and South Asian states 9 percent, and Latin American nations 3 percent.

As the territorial balance in Europe showed signs of stabilization in the 1950s and as the colonial empires of Atlantic allies began to crumble, American foreign policy leaders displayed a growing awareness of the potential importance of the less developed countries in the Third World. Secretary of State Dulles' tendency to equate neutralism with immorality gradually gave way to policies designed to avoid alienating irrevocably proud, nationalistic, neutralist regimes to the Soviet bloc. In 1956 Dulles' anxieties on this score counseled abstinence from the effort of two of America's most trusted allies to coerce Egypt's Nasser. The development of a set of concepts that might inform American attempts to strengthen the sociopolitical character of the developing countries in order to fortify their ability to sustain their independence and preserve a genuine neutrality took somewhat longer.

By the late 1950s, foreign aid came to be seen as an instrument to be employed for the alleviation of conditions of poverty and despair in which Communist movements were alleged to thrive in the non-West. The promotion of economic development for its own sake thus took its place alongside earlier objectives of the economic assistance program: the provision of relief, the support of European reconstruction efforts, the buttressing of America's global system of alliances and the subsidization of allies' rearmament programs. The establishment of the Development Loan Fund in 1957, the substantial increase in the lending authority of the Export-Import Bank authorized in 1958, and the capitalization of the Inter-American Development Bank in 1959 revealed the new emphasis.

The Kennedy Administration sought to rationalize these developments with a new set of premises regarding the relationships between economic assistance, social reform, industrial productivity, political democracy, and pacific foreign policies. The value of aid came to be appraised within the context of a general theory of modernization in which the operational objectives became the promotion of conditions in the developing countries that would permit self-sustaining economic growth. Special efforts were undertaken to promote the development of states in the Western Hemisphere. Whatever one's appraisal of the success or failure of the Alliance for Progress, initiated in 1961, it provided evidence of the Administration's acceptance of the need for social reform in Latin America, its understanding of the role of central planning in the industrialization of states with meager resource bases, and its enthusiasm for Latin America's Democratic Left as the vanguard of "peaceful revolution." Needless to add, it was scarcely coincidental that American attentiveness to the Latin American republics perceptibly increased with the accession of Fidel Castro to power in Havana!

In the course of three decades' experience with foreign economic assistance, a number of discrete types of aid have evolved. More than half of the contemporary nonmilitary aid program consists of *development loans*. Such loans support the development of both social overhead capital, such as transportation facilities and electric power installations, and directly productive enterprises like mines, textile manufacturing plants, and fertilizer factories. Repayment terms on development loans have been quite generous. *Technical assistance and development grants* finance the acquisition of specialist skills and modern facilities in the fields of agronomy, public health, public administration, and education. Development grants provide for the modest capital expenditures occasionally required in such programs. *Military assistance* covers the transfer of military equipment and the providing of military training and other services to nations threatened by external aggression or internal subversion. Turkey, Iran, Pakistan, India, Laos, South Vietnam, Thailand, the Philippines, South Korea, and Taiwan have been the prime recipients of such aid in recent years. Most such assistance is given in the form of outright grants. *Supporting assistance* is given to permit nations to maintain larger armed forces than their own resources would allow, to safeguard the economic stability of friendly states during emergencies, to reinforce the determination and capacity of states located in sensitive areas to sustain their independence in the face of intimidation or blatant pressure, and to assure the United States access to strategic bases overseas. South Vietnam, South Korea, Laos, Jordan, Thailand, and the Congo have been among the major beneficiaries of such assistance in recent years.

In addition to its bilateral programs of economic assistance, the United States subscribes to a number of international aid-disbursing agencies. America makes the largest capital contributions received by the International Bank, the International Development Association, the International Monetary Fund, the International Finance Corporation, various regional development banks, the United Nations Expanded Program of Technical Assistance, and several consortia arrangements providing multilateral support for specific country or regional development projects.

In the 1960s public support for foreign aid has become increasingly difficult to mobilize. This has led to various changes in the economic assistance program designed to increase its appeal and improve its effectiveness. Notable in this regard is the growing emphasis upon self-help. On more than one occasion American aid has served as a *substitute for* rather than a *supplement to* indigenous efforts at economic reform. In recent years, the United States has displayed an increasing tendency to help those who have demonstrated the capacity to help themselves. It is now generally acknowledged that economic development is contingent upon those antecedent qualities of government and administration that permit the effective utilization of foreign aid funds. External capital can do relatively little to erode the "miasma of apathy and fatalism, superstition and distrust that vitiates every attempt to improve hopelessly inefficient modes of work and patterns of resource use" in Asia. It has scarcely greater utility for overcoming the "crippling inhibitions of obsolete social institutions and reactionary social classes" in Latin America, or for "establishing the very underpinnings of nationhood itself" in Africa.[9]

A more modest view of the leverage that aid programs may secure for the United States over the political and social situations in most developing countries has fortified the conviction that America should not dissipate its meager resources of influence promiscuously. Thus the United States has begun to concentrate its aid programs in countries in which the existing political and social framework permit the possibility of significant progress in the short-run future. This concentration of the American effort has benefited such countries as Chile, Mexico, Peru, Brazil, Turkey, Greece, Iran, India, Pakistan, and Taiwan.

Self-help criteria have been applied with special rigor in connection with the Food for Peace program, through which agricultural surpluses have been made available to developing nations that cannot provide for their own food needs. Since 1965 American surplus foodstocks have been declining, and it has been all too apparent that many countries have postponed an assault on their own food production problems in the expectation that American aid would always be available. In 1967 President Johnson withheld promises of additional grain shipments to India and Egypt until their own governments had undertaken steps that promised improved grain-production yields in the future. The construction of chemical fertilizer plants and the improvement of local food-distribution systems enjoy a special priority for governments hoping to assure themselves access to continued American assistance.

Related to this renewed emphasis upon self-help, the United States has increasingly directed its development assistance toward the promotion of regional economic cooperation. Convinced that many of the newest states are not large enough to support efficient industries, the United States has encouraged the development of continental markets in Latin America, Africa, and Asia in order to permit the required economies of scale, the development of factories of an economic size, the saving of scarce foreign exchange through the development of import-substitution industries, and the development of communication and commercial ties among states on the same continents. By multilateralizing the distribution and the receipt of foreign aid, moreover, pressures on the donor may be diminished even as habits of political cooperation are induced among the recipients.

In contrast with an earlier emphasis upon investments in social overhead capital or directly productive enterprises, the most

[9] Robert Heilbroner, "Counterrevolutionary America," *Commentary* (April 1967), pp. 31–38.

recent foreign aid programs have emphasized investments in social capital *per se*. Major expenditures are now devoted to public health programs, including family planning; to the improvement of agricultural techniques, and to the education of the young. Since the food production and population control problems have consistently plagued the developments of many non-Western states, this redirection of American investment appears welcome and long overdue.

A final development worthy of note concerns the assumed relationship among aid, trade, and economic growth. Developing countries earn approximately three times the amount of foreign exchange through trade that they regularly obtain in loans and grants from creditor nations. Consequently, their prospects for development depend heavily upon their capacity to stabilize and expand their export earnings. The stabilization of export earnings has often been sought through the negotiation of commodity agreements regulating the production and sale of certain primary products, such as tin, rubber, coffee, cocoa, and wheat. Despite its adherence to the International Coffee Agreement, for example, the United States has had little enthusiasm for such agreements, fearing that they would perpetuate patterns of inefficient production rather than encourage the diversification of the economies of commodity-producing countries. On the other hand, while tariffs on a number of tropical agricultural products have been entirely eliminated by the United States, preferential tariffs for the developing states on manufactured items have been resisted heretofore. America has participated in the United Nations Conferences on Trade and Development; thus far, however, little deference has been displayed toward the demands of the Third World majority at such conferences. At the moment, defining new patterns of relations among the industrially advanced nations seems to take priority in the eyes of Washington policy-makers over the development of a new pattern of North-South relationships.[10]

What, finally, may be said about the success or failure of the American aid program? First, the program has contributed clearly to the success of the containment policy, particularly in Europe. Second, it is evident that helping Europe recover from the devastation of war was a more manageable problem than the industrialization of other regions. Outside Europe, the economic infrastructures of many recipients have been underdeveloped, their governmental institutions weak, and the potential for intraregional cooperation less impressive. Only gradually has the United States overcome the tendency to mechanically apply the "lessons" of the Marshall Plan in areas where those lessons scarcely apply. Third, American aid efforts have not always been guided by an adequate appreciation of the relationship between economic and political development. Assumptions regarding the relationships of external capital to internal growth prospects, economic development to political stability, internal stability to the establishment of liberal political institutions, and liberal institutions to pacific foreign policies have generally reflected blind faith rather

---

[10] See, for example, George Ball, *The Discipline of Power*.

than systematic analysis.[11] Fourth, the American experience with foreign aid demonstrates anew that gratitude is not easily purchased. France, Indonesia, and Pakistan have all been prime recipients of American aid. Each has managed to assert its independence in ways that have been more than slightly annoying to American policy-makers. Fifth, America's experience in distributing foreign aid has not given its policy-makers any particular time-tested formulas for manipulating the political processes within developing countries in ways which insure rapid industrialization or social justice or political stability. The conjunction of this absence of demonstrably dramatic results of the aid effort and the gradual waning of the cold war has made it increasingly difficult to extract foreign economic assistance monies from penurious congressmen.

Institutionalizing cooperation among states

In addition to promoting social and economic progress abroad, the United States consistently has encouraged what Walt W. Rostow has termed "organized interdependence in the world community." [12] During World War II, President Roosevelt conceived of the United Nations as an interlocking directorate of the great powers—the United States, the Soviet Union, Great Britain, France, and China—each of which would continue to exercise policing powers in its zone of special responsibility. Later, when that vision of world community was shattered, the United States developed various regional collective defense systems, promoted customs unions for Europe and Latin America, and devised a host of other institutional schemes for the organization of cooperation among non-Communist states.

Initially, Europe enjoyed the highest priority among America's postwar concerns. America enthusiastically supported the establishment of institutions that would strengthen the unity of Western Europe and link those states to the United States and Canada in a broader Atlantic community. The offer of Marshall Plan assistance was linked to the establishment of the Organization for European Economic Cooperation. Congress expressly provided that some of the Marshall Plan funds were to be used as inducements to the Europeans to dismantle intraregional trade barriers and to create a multilateral payments-clearance mechanism, the European Payments Union. Proposals to

[11] See Hans J. Morgenthau, "The American Theory and Practice of Foreign Aid," *American Political Science Review*, LVI (June 1962), pp. 301–10. It is well to note, however, that production in those Third World states that have been among the principal beneficiaries of American developmental aid since the late 1950s has increased by about 4 percent a year, on the average. Since population growth has been nearly as rapid, improvements in *per capita* income have come slowly, and the gap between rich and poor continues to grow.

[12] See his important statement of many of the premises underlying the Johnson Administration's approach to foreign policy, "The Great Transition: Tasks of the First and Second Postwar Generations," *United States Department of State Bulletin* (January 30, 1967), p. 158.

establish a European Coal and Steel Community, a European Defense Community, a European Atomic Energy Commission, and a European Economic Community were all warmly endorsed by Washington policy-makers. Indeed, when parliamentary resistance in the French National Assembly threatened ratification of the European Defense Community Treaty in 1954, Secretary of State Dulles vaguely hinted at an "agonizing reappraisal" of Franco-American relations. The ambiguous threat proved unavailing and the treaty was rejected, but the episode revealed the depth of America's commitment to supranational solutions to problems relating to Europe's military security as well as its economic organization.

The development of a supranational aggregation of power on the continent served a variety of American interests and appealed to a number of latent American prejudices. Many Americans assumed that federal governmental institutions would provide an obvious solvent to those national rivalries that had so often thrust the continent into war. Others doubted that Europe's economic vitality could be restored unless the quest for autarchy was overcome and separate national economies were combined into a "single market within which goods, money, and people could freely move and within which all barriers to trade and payments had been permanently swept away." [13] In the late 1940s, moreover, neither Europeans nor Americans expected the latter to be willing to provide indefinitely for the former's security. Nor was it anticipated that individual continental states possessed sufficient resources to provide for their own self-defense. A unified Europe, on the other hand, was expected to be more stable, more democratic, more peacefully inclined, more capable of self-defense, and more willing to share the burdens of the cold war than the individual states that were to become its constituent members. More specifically, it was assumed that European unification provided the most promising method of channeling German nationalism into constructive paths. Needless to add, American enthusiasm for a unified Europe rested upon the implicit and largely unexamined assumption that a revived and united European political entity would invariably pursue foreign policy aims compatible with the interests of the United States. Thus no conflict appeared initially between the promotion of unity within Europe, on the one hand, and the creation of a broader Atlantic community, on the other.

Doubts began to appear on this latter score in the 1960s as French President de Gaulle assumed a more active leadership in European politics. His actions rendered the early transformation of the European Economic Community into a political federation improbable. He made the limitation of American influence on the continent one of the cardinal principles of French foreign policy, and articulated positions on most international questions that diverged from the policies of the United States.

---

[13] Paul G. Hoffman, cited by Harold van B. Cleveland in *The Atlantic Idea and Its European Rivals* (New York, N.Y.: McGraw-Hill, 1966), p. 129.

These developments prompted several discernible shifts in American policy. The earlier enthusiasm for a tight-knit community of the Six gave way to a growing concern about the emergence of an "inward-looking" Europe. The United States became an ardent champion of Britain's application for membership in the Common Market. It seems unlikely that President Kennedy's widely publicized support enhanced Great Britain's welcome in Paris. One can only speculate as to whether a European Economic Community including Britain would be more "outward-looking" or more deferential to American leadership. What is obvious is that official Washington thought that it would. The episode likewise illustrates the degree to which American policy began to be framed in terms of countermoves designed to offset Gaullist initiatives.

Second, the United States began reasserting the importance of the Atlantic community as a framework for the organization of cooperative policies in the realms of defense and commerce. This involved merely a shift of emphasis. The strategic interdependence of Europe and America had since 1949 been embodied in the NATO alliance. Nor was that alliance considered simply another politico-military arrangement between states of disparate traditions and converging interests. On the contrary, it had been invested generously with the symbols of community. Signatories of the Treaty committed themselves not only to assume reciprocal obligations for the collective defense of a specific geographic region, but to settle their own disputes with one another peacefully and to develop larger possibilities of cooperation on commercial and foreign policy matters.

The alliance seemed the natural vehicle for handling the formulation of strategy and controlling nuclear weapons. Throughout the 1950s such matters had been unilaterally managed by the United States. To be sure, the French and British were represented in the NATO Standing Group, but this failed to secure them access to American decision-making. When the French bid for nuclear weapons through the development of their *force de frappe* threatened to inspire emulation by the Germans and Italians (or so it was assumed it would by many influentials in Washington), multilateral nuclear forces under the control of NATO assumed a sudden attractiveness. Various proposals for a multilaterally owned, financed, controlled, and manned nuclear force were discussed in the early 1960s. A plan for a multilateral force (MLF) consisting of a mixed-manned fleet of missile-bearing surface ships was promoted with especial zeal following de Gaulle's veto of the British application for membership in the Common Market in January, 1963.[14] Despite the ardor of its pro-

---

[14] The MLF was to be composed of 25 surface ships, each bearing eight A-3 Polaris missiles. The ships were to be manned by crews representing at least three nationalities. No NATO member was to contribute more than 40 percent of the total. The extent of a nation's financial contribution was to determine its share in the command of the force. The control system was always somewhat obscure. For details of the scheme and a thorough analysis of its merits and its fate, see Henry A. Kissinger, *The Troubled Partnership* (New York, N.Y.: McGraw-Hill, 1965), Chap. 5.

ponents in the State Department, the proposal failed to arouse equivalent enthusiasm on the continent. Only the Germans were moved to express lukewarm support of the plan, whose virtues were at best debatable. The military utility of the force was never entirely convincing. As a political device for providing America's allies greater access to United States strategic planning, it left something to be desired, for, as Henry Kissinger pointed out, "if joint planning [were] confined to the MLF, it would have been inadequate; if extended to cover all of the alliance's strategic forces, the MLF would have been quite irrelevant." [15]

By 1965 the MLF plan had been quietly dropped by President Johnson. In its place the United States began to promote another method of permitting allied consultation on nuclear questions. In February, 1966, the American, British, German, Italian, and Turkish defense ministers met in what came to be known as the "McNamara Committee" to wrestle with the issues of nuclear deterrence in an international forum. Shortly thereafter the North Atlantic Council established the NATO Nuclear Planning Group as a permanent consultative and planning mechanism for the alliance. The Netherlands and Canada were subsequently added to its membership, and the harmony of the Group's deliberations was facilitated by the departure in 1966 of France from the integrated command and planning organization of the alliance.

The French departure from the NATO organization spurred efforts to modernize the structure of the alliance rather than modify United States strategic doctrine. The headquarters were transferred from Paris to Belgium. A NATO communication satellite system was created in 1967 on an experimental basis to develop more efficient methods of maintaining command control over allied forces. Arrangements for the joint development and production of armaments have been devised. Through the implementation of a force planning exercise, the deployment and design of NATO's defense forces are being rationalized on a long-term basis. Late in 1967 NATO formally altered its basic strategy for the first time in eleven years. The new "flexible response" strategy conforms to that earlier adopted by the United States. The effect of these developments—as well as the intention of the MLF proposal—is that the essential precondition of American-European interdependence, namely, Europe's dependence on American protection, is left fully intact. That interdependence is a basic source of allied cohesion (as well as allied restiveness), and it tends to secure for the United States a measure of influence over political developments on the continent.[16]

With regard to trade as well as defense, the United States began to search in the 1960s for broader communities of cooperation. Since 1945 the United States has cooperated in the general movement

---

[15] *Ibid.*, pp. 140–141.

[16] Notable in this connection is the fact that relatively little encouragement has been given to the promotion of a European nuclear deterrent over which the United States possesses no veto power.

to liberalize trading relations among non-Communist states. As a signatory to the General Agreement on Tariffs and Trade, the United States committed itself to extend "most favored nation" treatment to all other signatories. America displayed little tolerance for preferential trading regimes except where they promised to contribute significantly toward the creation of larger political communities. As previously indicated, the United States warmly endorsed the creation of the European Economic Community. As the Common Market began to erect its external tariff barrier, however, the United States not only was forced to consider more earnestly the possible trade-diversion effects of that customs union, it was moved to create a broader institutional framework for handling commercial relations among all the advanced industrial nations as well. As a first step, the former Organization for European Economic Cooperation (OEEC) was transformed in 1961 into the Organization for Economic Co-operation and Development (OECD). The United States and Canada —and later, Japan—became members. The new organization was to facilitate commercial and financial cooperation and encourage joint planning of external assistance programs in the developing regions. In 1962 the United States passed a Trade Expansion Act, which conferred extraordinary discretionary powers upon the President for the negotiation of reciprocal tariff reductions with other industrial states. Subsequently, in the Kennedy negotiations, which began in 1963 and were consummated in 1967, trade liberalization among the non-Communist industrial states was extended toward its logical conclusion.

Those negotiations, in which the United States bargained with Great Britain, Japan, and the European Economic Community (as a single unit), provided a possible precedent for future discussions of preferential tariff arrangements for the developing countries, the so-called technological gap between Europe and America, and East-West trade. Clearly the United States now seeks to capitalize on such opportunities to promote the "eventual emergence of a looser community of the more developed nations of the world, including not only Japan but also most of the European Communist states, so that the current conflicts among the developed nations can be gradually transformed into the beginnings of cooperation, particularly in regard to the Third World." [17]

Already cooperation among the non-Communist industrial states has yielded substantial benefits. The establishment of mechanisms for assuring such cooperation on commercial matters is no minor political achievement. America's continued willingness to open its financial and capital markets to all, to maintain the stability of the dollar even at the expense of more expansionist domestic monetary and fiscal policies, to provide liquidity for the further growth of world trade by running persistent balance-of-payments deficits, and to press trade liberalization to its logical conclusion even at the

[17] Zbigniew K. Brzezinski, "American Globalism," *Survey* (January 1966), p. 22.

expense of subjecting some domestic producers to severe competitive pressures have all undergirded and sustained the degree of cooperation that has been attained.

The United States has also continued to develop institutional links with states in other regions, particularly in the Western Hemisphere. Hemispheric institutions abound. The Organization of American States is the political expression, the Rio Treaty the military expression, and the Alliance for Progress the socioeconomic expression of the United States desire to create an inter-American system that can assure regional stability and prosperity. Toward somewhat more exclusive regional schemes within the hemisphere, the United States has also adopted a favorable attitude. Thus the United States welcomed the creation of the Central American Common Market and the Latin American Free Trade Area in 1960. In 1967 President Johnson even supplied some of the initiative for the proposal adopted by the heads of state of twenty Latin American republics to establish a Latin American Customs Union by 1980.

With respect to Africa and Asia, the United States has been only peripherally involved in the promotion of regional cooperation ventures. Nevertheless, America provided important financial support for the creation of African and Asian development banks. It has also supported the work of the United Nations economic commissions for each area. In the Middle East and in Southeast Asia the United States has taken the lead in organizing collective defense pacts and has participated in various consortia arrangements for making economic assistance available to several important states.

Nor has the American commitment to regional or functional solutions to pressing international problems excluded a firm devotion to a more universal organization, the United Nations. Having played a seminal role in its creation, the United States has been among the most ardent supporters of the United Nations ever since. Although the United Nations has proved generally to be a rather fragile reed upon which to rely for purposes of maintaining international peace and security, American officials have continuously acknowledged its utility as a debating forum, a symbol of a broader international community, a standing diplomatic conference facilitating constant contact with all important states, and an international executive agency occasionally capable of undertaking collective security functions. The United States contributes 32.02 percent of the United Nations' annual operating budget, a comparable share of the budgets of the specialized agencies, and an even more substantial portion of the voluntary economic assistance programs and the emergency peace-keeping operations.

The strength of America's commitment to the United Nations has varied over time. In the immediate postwar period, substantial voting majorities could be readily mobilized for American initiatives in the General Assembly. Due to the absence of the Soviet delegate from the critical meetings of the Security Council in June, 1950, the

United States was able to gain United Nations authorization for enforcement action against North Korea. Subsequently it sponsored the Uniting for Peace resolution that established the General Assembly's rights to sponsor collective measures for the maintenance of peace in the event of the Security Council's inability to act as a result of the veto power of its permanent members. As the constituency of the General Assembly changed with the demise of colonialism and the creation of new states, the United States looked upon the United Nations as a forum in which sympathy for American policies on East-West issues might be generated. Sensitivity to the views of non-Western statesmen, confidence in the genuine neutrality of Secretary-General Dag Hammarskjold, and a desire to avert the extension of cold war competition into new areas prompted America's warm endorsement of United Nations exercises in "preventive diplomacy" in the Middle East in 1956 and in the strife-torn Congo in 1960. As the size of the Afro-Asian majority in the General Assembly has grown in the 1960s, United States policy-makers have become uneasy about the gap between the capacity of that majority to pass resolutions and its inability to implement them. This has given rise to some renewed interest in the role of the Security Council. It also prompted the United States to abandon its campaign to finance General-Assembly-sponsored peace-keeping operations on the basis of compulsory assessments rather than voluntary contributions.

United States policies toward the United Nations have been neither cynical nor sentimental. They have been marked by a notable pragmatism. As John Stoessinger observed:

> The United States does not have a single undifferentiated philosophical approach toward the international organization... It does not tailor its national interests to fit a general philosophy toward the U.N., but adjusts its "philosophy" to its national interests. When the national interest dictates a larger role for the U.N., the United States favors expanding the roles of the General Assembly and the Secretary-General, urges major peace-keeping operations, and sustains costly economic and social programs. On the other hand, when the American interest dictates a more conservative role for the U.N., the United States has employed the hidden veto, attacked the Secretariat, prolonged the membership stalemate, fought for the exclusion of Red China, withdrawn support from the [International Refugee Organization], by-passed the IAEA, and attacked the unanimity principle of the Special Fund.[18]

It is impossible to generalize about the success or failure of American attempts to institutionalize cooperation with other states,

[18] John G. Stoessinger, *The United Nations and the Superpowers* (New York, N.Y.: Random, 1965), p. 186.

other than to say that some such attempts have been more successful than others—hardly an illuminating observation. Certainly the motives that have inspired such efforts have varied widely. What is clear is that the American approach to the organization of institutionalized cooperation has been shaped by a flair for the practical. A leading member of a host of regional, functional, and universal international organizations, the United States has through such associations linked itself with virtually every member of the world community. This gives the United States multiple diplomatic options for dealing with specific international problems. It also tends to prevent the division of the world into distinct and exclusive groupings. The resulting "cross-cutting" cleavages and overlapping memberships may contribute significantly to the amelioration of interstate conflicts.

Promoting the reconciliation of former foes

The organization of a stable and durable peace has been a central preoccupation of the United States since 1945. It is important to recall, in this connection, that by defining its cold war objective as the *containment* rather than the *liquidation* of expansionist communism, America adopted an aim that did not necessitate perpetual conflict between East and West.[19] Moreover, the original containment policy vaguely anticipated a gradual transformation of the Soviet policy, implying that the basis for a new political relationship would be possible once the Russians abandoned the quest for global dominion.

As long as American policy was based upon a massive confrontation with the Soviet bloc, its reconciling role was confined largely to what in common parlance was known as the Free World. In Europe, the United States encouraged the reconciliation of France and Germany by maintaining a military presence on the continent that was reassuring to both. In Asia, America quietly nurtured emerging ties of friendship between Japan and her former enemies in the Far East.[20] Links with both Greece and Turkey through NATO have permitted the United States to play a helpful mediating role in their repeated conflicts over the disposition of Cyprus since 1960. In the Middle East the United States persistently has implored Arab and Israeli statesmen alike to settle their disputes peacefully. Despite a formal alliance with Pakistan, the United States adopted the stance of a conciliator rather than a fellow belligerent during the India-Pakistan war over Kashmir in 1965.

With respect to the amelioration of cold war animosities, American policies have been directed toward a mitigation of Europe's partition, the containment of the arms race, and the development of fruitful relationships with the government of Mainland China.

---

[19] Brief rhetorical emphasis was given to the "liberation" of the "captive nations of Eastern Europe" during the 1952 election campaign. No overt moves were undertaken to implement that objective.

[20] With the notable exception of China.

Peaceful engagement

Throughout the first two decades of the cold war, America was more preoccupied with the creation of an Atlantic community than with overcoming the schism between East and West. Confrontation and containment rather than reconciliation were the order of the day. This is not to say that the American attitude toward all Communist regimes was one of unremitting hostility. On the contrary, economic assistance was offered to Yugoslavia as early as 1948. Various contacts were established and carefully cultivated with Poland during the 1950s. Cultural exchange agreements with the Soviet Union and other Eastern European countries were negotiated beginning in the late 1950s. Still, the United States concentrated upon building a strong and cohesive community of Western states as a prerequisite to any fruitful negotiations over the stalemated issues of the cold war. Thus the United States fashioned exclusive political, military, and economic associations in the West. Germany was rearmed and integrated organically into NATO. Proposals for disengagement in Central Europe were spurned, and diplomatic recognition of East Germany denied.

Since 1962 the emphasis in America's European policy has changed appreciably. Prompted by the growing evidence of polycentrism in the Eastern bloc and by the catharsis in Soviet-American relations produced by the Cuban missile crisis, "bridge-building" and "peaceful engagement" replaced confrontation and containment as the dominant strains in the policy. This shift was most explicitly enunciated in President Johnson's speech of October 7, 1966. Seeking both to deepen the basis for the East-West détente and to prevent France's President de Gaulle from monopolizing the initiative in advocating remedies for Europe's partition, President Johnson urged the adoption of a number of specific steps toward "peaceful engagement." These included the ratification of a consular treaty, the establishment of a direct air transit link between the United States and the Soviet Union, the adoption of a treaty on the uses of outer space, progress toward agreement on a nonproliferation treaty, an expansion of East-West trade, and a moratorium on the deployment of antiballistic missile defenses. Since then the consular treaty and treaty on the uses of outer space have been ratified, and the air transit link has been established. Mutually acceptable language for the draft of a nonproliferation treaty has been agreed upon. New trade legislation has been introduced to Congress, but is currently stalled in committee. Initial discussions of a moratorium on ABM defenses have been held, and substantive negotiations are now in prospect.

Despite the progress in reinforcing a Soviet-American détente, the United States policy continues to reveal a lingering tension between a desire on the one hand to strengthen allied unity and on the other to promote East-West accord. Attempts have been made to employ NATO as an instrument for coordinating Western initiatives toward Eastern Europe, most notably in the so-called Harmel Exercise conducted throughout 1967. It has proved difficult to preserve the cohesion of a defensive alliance in an atmosphere of lessened tension. Nor has bridge-building proved to be an unmitigated success. Aid and trade concessions have been liberally extended to Poland, which has pursued notably illiberal domestic policies and has acknowledged its residual dependence on the Soviet Union more openly in recent years. Rumania and Czechoslovakia, on the other hand, with whom the United States has enjoyed no significant relations, have been extremely assertive in seeking to establish their independence of Soviet control.

The United States has had limited influence over developments in Eastern Europe. It has lent encouragement to those states seeking a relaxation of Soviet control. It has not intervened to protect them against Russian responses. While bridge-building may have yielded limited concrete benefits, it has encouraged a rethinking of America's European policy. That process of reassessment has produced the conviction that the division of Germany can only be overcome within the context of a general reconciliation of Eastern and Western Europe. Consequently, reunification is no longer seen as the first step in the normalization of East-West relations or as a test of Soviet good faith. It is now viewed as the end product of a long process of overcoming the partition of the continent. To that extent American policy is now more compatible with the West German desire to develop its own "openings to the East" and with the generally shared European desire to end the artificial compartmentalization of the continent into rival blocs.

The arms race

The management of the arms race provides another focal point for converging Soviet and American interests. As early as 1946 the United States sought to introduce limitations on access to and use of nuclear weapons. The Baruch plan, which was the principal United States arms control proposal of the early postwar years, would have subjected all nuclear explosives and fissionable materials to international ownership and control. The impulse to self-abnegation was not so strong as some of the plan's proponents alleged, for had the Soviet Union accepted its terms, the United States would have retained indefinitely its monopoly on industrial and technical experience with the atomic bomb. The proposal never elicited, however, the slightest interest from Moscow.

Once the Russians exploded their first atomic weapon—August, 1949—American interest in disarmament quickly waned. The next few years were dominated by the massive conventional rearmament precipitated by the outbreak of the Korean war and the acceleration of the arms race with the development of thermonuclear weapons. With both sides possessing unprecedented weapon capabilities, mutual distrust became more difficult to dissipate, the problems of inspection became more difficult to resolve, and the costs of "cheating" on an arms reduction agreement became the more difficult to ignore. In any event, American policy-makers could scarcely negotiate seriously about nuclear disarmament at the very moment when the New Look military strategy shifted the emphasis away from a balanced arsenal to a decided reliance upon nuclear weapons to deter a wide variety of threats.

This explains why interest gradually shifted in the late 1950s away from *arms reduction* to *arms control*. Policy-makers were especially eager to ameliorate reciprocal fears of surprise attack, to remove some of the dangers of accidental war, and to pose some checks on the spread of nuclear weapons to "*nth*" countries. The first two problems were explored in technical discussions with the Soviet Union in 1958; the latter concern produced prolonged negotiations that led ultimately to the signing of the Atomic Test Ban Treaty in August, 1963.

In the 1960s continuing efforts to achieve negotiated arms control agreements with the Soviet Union, for example, a non-proliferation treaty, have been supplemented by tacit agreements upon policies of restraint. In recent years strategic policy has been defined with arms control considerations in mind. Thus America's strategic posture has been rendered less accident-prone, less dependent upon tactical warning of an impending attack, more responsive to presidential control, and considerably more flexible. The publication of massive, detailed explanations of American defense policies has been undertaken with one eye on Congress and the other on hopes of engaging the Soviet Union in a "strategic dialogue" in which the common interests of averting a nuclear holocaust, of managing grave international crises, and of arresting the spread of nuclear capabilities may be reflected increasingly in tacitly coordinated policies. Most recently these hopes have focused upon the avoidance of a costly and fruitless race for ABM defenses.

Reestablishing relations with China

In Asia, the building of bridges to Mainland China has scarcely begun. The quest for reconciliation is a distant hope rather than the immediate objective of current policies. For nearly two decades the United States has attempted to contain and isolate Mainland China. Diplomatic recognition has been withheld. The United States regularly has led the fight to deny Mainland China credentials in the United Nations. American policies have aimed at impairing the legitimacy of Mao Tse-tung's regime. American allies and military forces encircle China. A strategic embargo has been maintained to hamper China's economic development.

Despite this pattern of formal hostility, communications with the Peking government were established in the 1950s. Unofficial relations were conducted. More or less regular diplomatic conversations have been carried on through the American Embassy in Warsaw, Poland. Occasional trial balloons for a "two Chinas policy" have been flown. Chiang Kai-shek has been prevented from undertaking overtly provocative moves against the Mainland. The assumption that China's Communist government would be overthrown has been replaced by an evident acknowledgment of that government's permanence. Pessimistic estimates of the possibility of developing fruitful relations with China, along with the strength of the domestic "China lobby," however, have prevented more than minuscule changes in the official attitude toward China.

Since 1966 a new American policy of "containment without isolation" has been evolving. Various steps have been contemplated to expand Sino-American contacts, in anticipation of possibly favorable developments in Chinese policies during or after the long-expected succession of China's aging leaders. The establishment of diplomatic relations with Outer Mongolia, some expansion of Chinese-American commerce, and a relaxation on travel restrictions have all been under consideration. Thus far no basic changes have occurred. The bitterness of Chinese animosity toward the United States, the reinforcement of Chinese-American enmity by the Vietnamese war, and the domestic turmoil in China all make an early thaw in Sino-American relations unlikely.

In the short run, a reconciling role for the United States in Asia seems destined to focus upon the promotion of cordial relations among non-Communist states in that region. Mention has already been made of the mediating role the United States has played in quarrels between Pakistan and India and between Japan and Korea. In Asia, as in Europe, in short, American efforts are being directed toward the development of amicable relations among the non-Communist states in order to create a regional-international system into which a "contained" China may be ultimately integrated. The necessity or the feasibility of this endeavor may be challenged; its consistency with the most basic elements in America's postwar foreign policies is self-evident.

8

Contemporary foreign policy problems

To govern, as someone has said, is to choose. Choice, in the making of foreign policy, entails the allocation of scarce resources among a multitude of competing objectives. Aims must be defined, priorities asserted, means selected. Inevitably such choices engender controversy, for issues are complex, interests legion, uncertainties great, and risks often substantial. The costs and consequences of competing alternative courses of action cannot be specified with precision, for in foreign policy one is seeking (at least marginally) to shape an environment that is beyond the control of any single state. Since divisions within the government on important decisions are frequently close and intense, political courage as well as analytic skill may be essential for wise decisions. In this chapter the emphasis is upon analysis. Problems posed by the development of new military technology, the declining solidarity of the Western alliance, and the prospect of political instability and revolutionary warfare in the Southern Hemisphere will be considered.

The ABM issue: adjusting strategy to the development of novel weapons

In the nuclear age, the problems of defending the American people from destruction in a general war have become virtually insurmountable. Heretofore, foolproof defenses against intercontinental ballistic missiles carrying thermonuclear warheads have not been developed.

Nor have they been considered technically possible. Consequently, the deterrence of war has become the absorbing preoccupation of American strategists, the highest priority aim of American defense policy. "The ultimate deterrent to a deliberate nuclear attack on the United States or its allies," former Secretary of Defense McNamara declared, "is our clear and unmistakable ability to destroy the attacker as a viable society." The maintenance of such a capability requires, in turn, that United States strategic forces be sufficiently protected as to be able to survive an enemy surprise attack and perform their retributive mission against alerted defenses.

American strategic forces may be protected by either active or passive defenses. Whereas active defenses involve direct countermeasures against an attacking force, passive defenses seek to enhance the invulnerability of strategic forces through such measures as dispersal, hardening, concealment, and mobility. Since the late 1950s, the United States has spent billions of dollars securing the invulnerability of its retaliatory forces by deploying hundreds of missiles in dispersed and hardened sites in the continental United States and additional hundreds of missiles on board concealed and mobile Polaris submarines. As the Soviet Union has similarly perfected its strategic forces, a situation of "parity in peril" has emerged in which the reciprocal ability of the superpowers to destroy one another and their inability to prevent such destruction, should war occur, undergirds a relationship of relatively stable mutual deterrence.

A substantial research and development program has been maintained in order that no technical or scientific gaps appear that might disrupt the strategic balance. Research and development work on the Nike-Zeus antimissile missile was begun as early as 1956, before the United States had fired a single intercontinental ballistic missile (ICBM). In the late 1950s an expensive air defense system against the threat of Soviet manned bombers was procured. Few considered the system effective, however, and the concepts of offensive deterrence came to be accepted as virtual articles of faith. From 1960 until 1967 three successive United States Administrations postponed a decision on whether to put various ballistic missile defense systems into production. The Nike-Zeus and later the Nike-X systems were resisted by Secretary of Defense McNamara as technically deficient, excessively costly, and strategically undesirable systems that, in any event, were prone to obsolescence. Such reservations were widely shared within the defense community, though not by members of the Joint Chiefs of Staff. Three developments have forced a reconsideration of the desirability of deploying an antiballistic missile (ABM) system.

First, technical breakthroughs have resolved some of the problems associated with missile defense. A decade of research and development yielded unexpected advances in radar systems, computation devices, high-acceleration missiles, missile guidance, warhead miniaturization, and command and control systems. Above all, weapon-effects test results suggest that the unimpeded radiation released by large warheads exploded in space might dramatically extend the radius of a "kill" by an antimissile missile. This simplifies the problem of distinguishing between incoming offensive warheads and decoys, and permits the destruction of enemy warheads outside the atmosphere, without the necessity of contaminating the atmosphere around one's own cities.

Second, there has been substantial evidence of Soviet interest in the development and deployment of their own ballistic missile defenses. An ABM system has been deployed around Moscow, and ambiguous intelligence reports led many to speculate—apparently prematurely—in 1967 that the so-called Tallinn Line of defenses being established along Russia's northwestern frontier was to provide a wider defensive screen.[1] Anxious not to overreact, President Johnson in January, 1967 proposed negotiations with the Russians directed toward the achievement of a moratorium on ABM deployments. The Soviet response was somewhat cryptic but scarcely enthusiastic. While implying that "we won't build an ABM if you don't," Secretary McNamara announced that the United States was undertaking a number of measures designed to increase its capacity to penetrate Soviet defenses even if the Soviets did procure an ABM system. Thus an improved Poseidon submarine-launched ballistic missile (SLBM) was to replace the Polaris delivery systems, and the development of multiple independently targetable reentry vehicles (MIRVs) "specifically designed for use against targets heavily defended with ABMs" was accelerated.

Third, rapid Chinese progress in developing their own nuclear capabilities provided the prospect of a foe against whom missile defenses might be more confidently constructed. Pentagon officials have estimated that the Chinese might be able to deploy medium-range ballistic missiles (MRBMs) with a 700-mile range within several years, and by the mid-1970s might have enough ICBMs to strike the United States and inflict up to twelve-million casualties.

It seems plausible, moreover, that the backlog of political pressures created by a decade of research and development in ABM defenses provided considerable momentum for a decision to deploy. So, too, did domestic political pressures in 1967 as the President was confronted by more and more public lobbying for a deployment decision by some political advisers, several influential congressional leaders, and all members of the Joint Chiefs of Staff.

On September 18, 1967 Secretary of Defense McNamara announced plans to deploy a "light," Chinese-oriented ABM. The system is to provide a marginal "area defense" of the American populace against the primitive kinds of attack that the Chinese may be able to launch in the 1970s and some "point defense" of American strategic forces against a Soviet counterforce attack.[2] The system, to be known as the Sentinel ABM system, consists of perimeter acquisition radars,

---

[1] Since then a consensus in the intelligence community has come to support the hypothesis that the Tallinn Line was deployed against the expected American procurement of B-70 bombers.

[2] The potential anti-Soviet aspects of the system have been played down in public disclosures about the Sentinel system.

missile site radars, long-range Spartan area-defense missiles, and Sprint local-defense missiles. Approximately twelve Spartan ABMs are planned for exoatmospheric interception and area defense. Half that number of clusters of Sprint missiles for point defense are to be installed. The total cost of the system is estimated to be $5 billion. Such estimates have generally been quite conservative. Much of the equipment is yet untested. It is to be completely deployed within four to six years.

Extremely significant strategic issues are raised by the development of missile defense technology. Nor have these issues been resolved by the Administration's decision. Already (in the summer of 1968), many are calling for the cancellation of the Sentinel deployment.[3] Others favor a heavier anti-Soviet system. Still others prefer the installation of the Sentinel system, possibly as the "foundation" for a more ambitious defense network.

The case for a heavy ABM system

The Joint Chiefs have provided the most consistent and determined advocacy for ABM deployment. For several years they have urged the production of a "heavy" anti-Soviet system whose cost might range from $12 to $40 billion. They favor an area-defense system for much of the country, specifically including ABM sites around the twenty-five most densely populated areas of the United States. They also favor a substantial deployment for point defense of SAC bases and missile sites in the continental United States.

The arguments of the proponents of a heavy ABM system appear orthodox enough. Such a system, they contend, would enhance United States deterrent capabilities by insuring the survival of American retaliatory forces against improved Soviet attacking forces. Should deterrence inexplicably fail, the area defense might save millions of lives. In addition, it would provide insurance against an accidental attack or efforts by intermediate or small states to initiate a "catalytic" war among the superpowers. By offsetting the incipient strategic capabilities of the secondary powers, it would pose, in their view, an additional inhibition against nuclear proliferation. And it would perpetuate indefinitely that strategic superiority essential to sustain the "Cuba power environment in the world." [4] Additionally, those eager to begin immediate deployment of a heavy system see it as a means of forcing the Soviet Union to expend technological and economic resources to counter the American system, of complicating the Russian missile-targeting problem, and of demonstrating to America's adversaries and allies that the United States is not "first-strike" minded.

[3] A bipartisan group of senators sought to deprive the Defense Department funds to implement the ABM deployment decision in June, 1968, but were defeated 52–34 when the matter was brought to a vote.

[4] That nuclear balance that existed in the fall of 1962 and that, in the view of the Joint Chiefs, prevented the Soviet Union from exploiting the Cuban missile crisis for local advantages in Berlin or elsewhere.

The case against the deployment
of a heavy ABM

The case for deployment of an anti-Soviet heavy ABM is questionable on many grounds. In the first place, it is arguable whether such a costly system is necessary for purposes of diminishing Soviet confidence that they could accomplish with impunity a preemptive strike against the United States. To be sure, point defense of missile sites is a logical method of enhancing the invulnerability of American retaliatory forces. But is it "cost-effective" relative to other methods, such as hardening, dispersal, and mobility? By incorporating MIRVs in every missile launcher, the United States "assured destruction" force is to be vastly improved just in anticipation of the possible deployment of a Soviet ABM force. In view of this and other planned countermeasures to increased Soviet offensive and defensive capabilities, the United States would appear to enjoy sufficient insurance against a deliberate Soviet nuclear attack. For the foreseeable future, such an attack can be described only as suicidal.

Second, while an area-defense system might conceivably save some American lives should deterrence fail, its damage-limiting capabilities depend upon the successful operation on the first try of what has appropriately been described as "the most complicated engineering feat ever attempted." On the basis of past experiences with air defenses, it seems doubtful whether one should consider them reliable against a resourceful foe in an age when improvements in offensive capabilities continually overwhelm defensive improvements. In short, a heavy ABM system would be enormously expensive yet terribly prone to obsolescence. As the Director of Defense Research and Engineering stated, "Because of the enormous quantities of equipment involved, and the rapid rate at which the technology changes, to maintain an effective system one would essentially have to turn over the whole system, the whole $20-billion system, every few years." [5] In any event, even the most optimistic claims regarding the extent to which ABM defenses might reduce American casualties in a general war with the Soviet Union would leave casualties at a level that is totally unacceptable.

Third, such area defense as a heavy ABM might provide would presumably be more efficacious against an accidental strike or an attack by a secondary power. Yet neither event is more than the most remote probability. A state can quickly become "insurance poor" if it is prepared to expend extravagant sums protecting against such improbable contingencies. Nor is the ABM likely to be an effective disincentive against additional nuclear proliferation. "Nth" countries currently aspiring to nuclear status have neither the desire nor the capacity to develop nuclear forces that would threaten the United States. Their motivations are rooted in local rivalries and considerations of rank and prestige, neither of which are necessarily affected

[5] Senate Committee on Foreign Relations, *U.S. Armament and Disarmament Problems, Hearings,* 90th Cong., 1st Sess., 1967, p. 15.

by the deployment of ballistic missile defenses in the United States.

American decisions might, to be sure, divert additional Russian rubles into defense spending. It is far from clear that such diversions are calculated to promote political developments in Russia that would reinforce a mellowing of Soviet foreign policy. ABM deployment might also prompt the Russians to devote their energies to the development of more powerful offensive forces, more sophisticated penetration devices, and more refined tactics for striking American cities with bigger and dirtier bombs in the event of war. The cost of the heavy ABM is also exorbitant if the purpose is merely an additional demonstration of America's pacific intentions or the complication of Soviet missile-targeting problems.

It seems difficult to avoid the conclusion that to deploy such a system would accelerate the arms race and substantially increase the level of United States defense spending without measurably increasing American security.

The case for a limited, Chinese-oriented ABM

If the deployment of ballistic missile defenses against the Soviet Union seems inexpedient, what about the case for a more modest system designed to offset Chinese offensive capabilities in the 1970s? The decision to build a Chinese-oriented ABM is based upon several assumptions: (1) such a system is substantially cheaper than an anti-Soviet system; (2) the Chinese are sufficiently irrational as not to be deterred by America's overwhelming offensive capabilities; (3) the prospect of American invulnerability to Chinese countermeasures will make American nuclear guarantees to Asian states threatened by China more credible and will thus serve as reassurance to those states now hesitant about signing the nonproliferation treaty, and (4) an anti-Chinese system can be deployed without arousing the Soviet Union to countermeasures.

In the view of the Defense Department, the Sentinel system will be able to hold American fatalities below one million in the face of the "primitive" attacks China will be able to mount in the coming decade. Further improvements in the Sentinel system are believed to be obtainable with but modest additional outlays in order to limit the Chinese damage-potential well into the 1980s.[6] In addition to providing a measure of insurance against the Chinese, by deploying a "thin" ABM, the United States can hedge against future developments in technology, gain industrial experience with the new defensive capability, and begin to produce a "building block" for a possible future anti-Russian capability. By deploying the Sentinel as a point-defense system as well as an area-defense system, America is able to buy an additional form of invulnerability for its strategic forces at a time when advances in offensive capabilities—for example,

[6] Robert McNamara, *The Fiscal Year 1969–73 Defense Program and the 1969 Defense Budget* (Washington, D.C.: Department of Defense, 1968), p. 63.

progress in satellite reconnaissance, improvements in missile accuracy and terminal guidance, and the development of more powerful warheads capable of "burrowing" to destroy underground targets—conceivably may threaten the defensibility of fixed, land-based missiles, even in superhardened sites.

The case against a limited, Chinese-oriented ABM

On the face of it, it seems curious that American capabilities which are considered sufficient to deter attacks on the United States or its allies by a state as formidable in its military capabilities as the Soviet Union are not considered a reliable deterrent to attacks by an underdeveloped and militarily weak state like China. Pentagon officials have for years been discounting the French *force de frappe* as totally irrelevant vis-à-vis the Soviet Union. Oddly enough, as Bernard Brodie has observed, "when it comes to considering China as a threat against us, comparable insights have tended to give place to the notion that the Chinese are capable of doing just about anything, even if it means their own complete destruction." [1] To justify massive expenditures for a defense against an as-yet-nonexistent Chinese ICBM force seems calculated to enhance China's status in Asia, make their military potential appear far more impressive than it actually is, and frighten precisely those states whose fears an American ABM is designed to assuage.

A Chinese-oriented ABM is perhaps justifiable if the assumption that the Chinese are likely to act in an irrational manner to provoke a nuclear showdown with the United States can be persuasively sustained. No careful appraisal of Chinese behavior—as opposed to an excessive preoccupation with the vituperative political rhetoric which is standard from Peking—will, however provide evidence for the image of irrationality upon which the case is based. In short, the Sentinel system will provide insurance against the most improbable contingency. The Chinese will not be able to deploy an ICBM force for some time; thus there is time to reassess the necessity of developing defenses for any threat they might later pose. They may, moreover, choose to initially deploy an MRBM force with a range sufficient to reach many of their Southeast Asian nations, leaving for later the option of procuring more refined, later-generation ICBMs. This would render the Sentinel system an obsolescent defense against a nonexistent threat. Even if China was foolhardy enough to contemplate a surprise attack against an overwhelmingly superior foe equipped with ballistic missile defenses, what is to prevent them from resorting to other forms of delivery such as nuclear torpedoes against coastal cities or the small nuclear device transported to a major city in a suitcase? But, then, it does take a special form of insanity to

[1] *Los Angeles Times* (September 17, 1967).

direct a surprise attack against an adversary's cities rather than his retaliatory installations! [8]

Is it likely that ballistic missile defenses will enhance the credibility of nuclear pledges to Asian states by limiting the dire consequences of honoring them? Viewed in this light, the Sentinel ABM is a natural complement to the American campaign to arrest the spread of nuclear weapons. Actually, American nuclear guarantees are intrinsically incredible in areas whose security does not bear an organic relationship to the security of the United States. Asians are likely to become more alarmed about their own ability to limit damage and pose deterrent threats than about the American capacity to do so. An American ABM would pose a stopgap at best, unless it were offered to Pacific allies. But providing ballistic missile defenses for others would not only be enormously costly, it would also by no means necessarily head off pressures for offensive nuclear capabilities in India and Japan. In reality, the ABM appears to bear a tenuous relationship to the sort of military threats that China will be able for the foreseeable future to pose for its Asian neighbors; namely, encouragement to revolutionary warfare in which nuclear threats are irrelevant.

Nor is it certain that the deployment of an anti-Chinese ABM can be dissociated from one that possesses anti-Russian potential. Any American ABM complicates the Russians' ability to maintain their retaliatory capability. Thus it will likely elicit some countermeasures. Improvements in the Sentinel will inevitably be interpreted as movements toward a larger anti-Soviet system. As Jeremy Stone has noted, "Sentinel is far more effective in neutralizing overall Soviet capabilities than the primitive Soviet efforts around Moscow are in reducing those of the United States. And consider how much the latter overreacted to the Soviet efforts." [9]

To summarize, the deployment of a limited ABM oriented against China has the advantage of permitting the United States to gain assurance that the Soviet Union does not "steal a technical march" on it, while avoiding an immediate and unlimited acceleration of the Soviet-American arms race. By coupling the decision with renewed exhortations to the Soviet Union to negotiate measures of mutual restraint, some leverage may be gained over future Soviet procurement decisions.[10] But a vigorous research and development effort would appear sufficient to guard against technical surprises. By justifying the ABM decision with reference to China, the Sentinel

---

[8] For thorough analyses of the decision to deploy ABM defenses, see Jeremy J. Stone, "The Case Against Missile Defenses," *Adelphi Papers*, No. 47 (April 1968); and Robert L. Rothstein, "The ABM, Proliferation and International Stability," *Foreign Affairs* 46 (April 1968), pp. 487–502.

[9] Stone, *op. cit.*, p. 10.

[10] The United States is not-so-subtly hinting that should the Russians continue to deploy an ABM system, no efforts will be spared to outstrip them in the subsequent competition. An ABM gap will thus replace the missile gap of the early 1960s.

system has been provided with a basis for continued existence independent of future Soviet progress. That justification meanwhile promises to compound rather than alleviate American political and diplomatic problems in Asia. Also, while some area defense seems feasible against a negligible Chinese ICBM threat, such a deployment may lead to unfortunate arms control implications vis-à-vis the Soviet Union. Finally, the stability of the United States-Soviet strategic balance would seem to depend upon the avoidance of such area defenses as might threaten the second-strike capabilities of either superpower. But in deploying area defenses to guard against a negligible threat from China, the United States may, by threatening to degrade Soviet retaliatory capabilities, unleash a new and costly upward spiraling of defense expenditures.[11]

The case for postponing ABM deployment

Although the decision to deploy the Sentinel system has already been announced, overturning that decision remains an option. The case for immediate deployment of ballistic missile defenses is far from compelling. Moreover, the fiscal pressures created by the Vietnamese war, evidence that the Russians are not rushing the deployment of a wider network of ballistic missile defenses along the Tallinn Line,[12] and indications that the internal turmoil in China has caused serious lags in their schedule for achieving a long-range missile capability all provide grounds for reconsideration. To forego the deployment of an ABM system at this time (summer, 1968) would not appear to entail extraordinary risks for the United States. America can afford such measured forebearance, since it is well ahead in the development of nuclear technology; it is capable of storming the ABM objective with a crash program, should the need arise, and such efforts would doubtless avail in view of the long lead times involved in the deployment of modern offensive and defensive systems. In any event, the measures already taken to offset a possible Soviet ABM will suffice for an interim period to absolutely guarantee the maintenance of a fully adequate assured destruction force. In this connection, it would appear prudent also to limit any increase in American offensive capabilities in order not to appear capable of a surprise attack with relative impunity. Such an appearance might not only be intrinsically destabilizing, but might increase Soviet incentives to build a massive ABM, thus provoking the United States to follow suit. Not only can the United States afford to go to considerable lengths to induce Soviet restraint with respect to ABM procurement, it can scarcely afford not to. The minimal costs of a widespread

---

[11] The Soviet Union's acceptance, in the summer of 1968, of President Johnson's invitation to discuss a wide range of offensive and defensive missile control problems may indicate a mutual desire to avert such an increase in expenditures.

[12] Those are now considered by intelligence analysts to be air defense capabilities erected against the possibility that the United States would produce an improved manned bomber.

defensive system are very high. The development of a real ballistic missile defense would materially increase the level of American defense spending. It is difficult to see how it would appreciably improve America's security position.

It should be evident from this discussion that disciplining the development of technology to the requirements of strategy is no simple task. The basic difficulty derives from the existence of multiple objectives, such as the deterrence of war, the limitation of damage should war occur, the development of force structures that can achieve those two aims without adding unnecessary burdens to the arms race, the management of the arms race in a manner compatible with the maintenance of durable political relationships with allies and adversaries, and the impossibility of calculating precisely which course of action will achieve the optimal results with respect to these competing aims. Given the multiplicity of objectives and the diversity of variables warranting consideration, it is obvious that one's analysis of such questions must be continuously and critically reevaluated in response to new political, military, and technical developments.

Contemporary problems of alliance management *

For nearly two decades, NATO has constituted the bulwark of Western defense and the cornerstone of United States policy in Europe. The success of the Western alliance is easily documented. It closed the door to westward expansion by the Soviet Union. It provided the protection that Europeans considered essential to the confident reconstruction of their economies and societies. It stimulated cooperative endeavors that extended far beyond the organization of collective defense. It has served as a convenient instrument within which Germany's "orderly rehabilitation" could be encouraged. Moreover, it has been "as much a way of handling relations amongst its members as a way of meeting an external threat." [13] By promoting the peaceful settlement of disputes among its members, it has helped perpetuate a relative quiescence in European politics for two decades. As McGeorge Bundy, a prominent adviser to Presidents Kennedy and Johnson, once observed, "NATO is not all of what we care about in Europe, but nothing we care about in Europe is possible without NATO."

* This section was written before the Russian invasion of Czechoslovakia in the summer of 1968 dramatically altered the nature of the debate within and about NATO. Predictably, Soviet military moves in Central Europe have stimulated allied unity. However, the original analysis has been left essentially intact due to the author's conviction that the invasion of Czechoslovakia reveals the political weakness of the Soviet Union in Eastern Europe, not their military aggressiveness toward Western Europe. Thus the basic problems of the NATO alliance are likely to reappear, though in a different politico-military context.

[13] Thomas Schelling, "The Atlantic Alliance," *The Virginia Quarterly Review*, 43 (Winter 1967), p. 23.

For several years, the alliance has found itself in a state of serious disarray. France has withdrawn from the organization for which the O in NATO stands. President De Gaulle has denied the allies regular use of the costly complex of bases, depots, airfields, communication facilities, and pipelines on French soil that formerly constituted a crucial link in the logistic infrastructure of NATO. The command and planning organs of the alliance have been relocated from Paris to Belgium. Other French links with the alliance are being severed. Allied rights to overfly French territory have been restricted. French contributions to NATO's military expenses have been curtailed. French officials continue to assure their allies that their forces and bases will be available in the event of an "unprovoked aggression," but they leave no doubt that the interpretation of what constitutes "unprovoked aggression" will be made by France alone.

The French withdrawal from the integrated military structure of the alliance has been accompanied by public recriminations against American policies in Europe, the Middle East, Africa, and the Far East. Meanwhile, autonomous French decisions have complicated the problems of implementing American-preferred strategies on the continent. By withholding French territory from the alliance, a non-nuclear defense of Europe, as implicitly contemplated in the McNamara strategy of "conventional pauses" and graduated deterrence, is rendered more difficult. The existence of the French *force de frappe* does nothing to facilitate the execution of a "controlled response" strategy in the event that deterrence fails and escalation occurs. Nor have other NATO allies appreciably increased their exertions on behalf of the alliance in order to compensate for France's defection. To be sure, the United States has moved vigorously to "modernize" the structure of NATO, as indicated in Chapter 7. Still, serious doubts persist regarding the adequacy of that response to the new situation. Other problems of adjustment remain to be resolved.

Those changing conditions that have prompted NATO's internal crisis are easily enough enumerated. One may simply recall the chief characteristics of European politics in 1947. The Soviet Union then appeared fully mobilized and militarily aggressive, thus posing a credible conventional invasion threat. The United States was invulnerable to any direct attack by the Russians. Consequently, America could provide absolute protection to those Western European states that were willing to huddle under its atomic umbrella. The Europeans were, with few exceptions, militarily weak, their economies were dislocated, and their political life was marked by instability. The interdependence of American and European security interests was generally acknowledged. The priority of Western Europe in America's concerns was unquestioned. And the European willingness to accept the informal hierarchy embodied in the alliance was enhanced by their preoccupation with lingering colonial involvements.

In 1968 the perception of a Soviet military threat has sharply declined, and the "dialogue of confrontation" has been replaced by the "language of détente." The United States has lost its invulnerability along with its innocence. This has compromised the absolute protection that alignment with the United States once afforded. The Europeans have, meanwhile, overcome their weakness. Economies have been rebuilt, political self-consciousness has been revived, and enervating colonial ventures have been liquidated. Increasing evidence of Soviet moderation calls into question the need for the alliance. American vulnerability raises doubts about the adequacy of the American-preferred NATO strategy. The resurgence of the Western European states has rendered the political arrangements by which the alliance is managed and strategic decisions reached seem anachronistic. The interdependence of European and American destinies is no longer glibly assumed.

Is NATO still necessary?

The perpetuation of NATO is of little value in and of itself. The alliance is an instrument, and its utility depends upon the degree to which its existence and structure contribute to the development of desired political developments on the continent. It is with this in mind that some nurture doubts about the desirability of continuing the alliance in its present form beyond the initial twenty-year term prescribed in the Treaty. Actually, few question the prudence of retaining the Treaty, which links European and American security interests into formal and reciprocal obligations for their collective defense. Doubts about the necessity of integrated command and planning arrangements are more widespread.

The case for dissolving the NATO military structure rests on the premise that the objectives of the alliance (again as an integrated structure for coalition military planning and preparedness) have been achieved. Some believe that it is no longer militarily necessary nor politically desirable. The development of long-range delivery vehicles with thermonuclear payloads has not only rendered war exceedingly remote, it is argued, but makes it unnecessary for the United States to maintain advance bases on the continent. The chief deterrent to war in Europe is the United States strategic nuclear arsenal and not the conventional troops stationed on the continent or earmarked for NATO in case of an emergency. Moreover, the argument goes, in a crisis, troops stationed in the United States could be deployed rapidly on the continent, thus demonstrating American resolve in moments of danger even as the outflow of dollars would be curtailed during more normal times.

The maintenance of an integrated NATO alliance also implies the perpetuation of a Europe fragmented and partitioned into two armed camps. This, it is argued, may now inhibit progress toward the reconciliation of East and West, and place the United States in the position of appearing to resist a desire general among Europeans to overcome cold war divisions. Since the objective is the containment of Russia rather than merely the continued existence of the alliance, why not seek to promote reciprocal Soviet and American disengagement from Central Europe? The withdrawal of Soviet troops from

Eastern Europe would then permit greater freedom of action to the former satellites, permit a normalization of relations between Germany and her neighbors to the east, and facilitate the negotiation of a formal end to the stalemated issues of the cold war. According to this logic, in the interest of widening and deepening East-West détente, the liquidation of NATO and the Warsaw Pact would become a prime objective of policy. They might then be replaced by an exchange of nonaggression pacts or the creation of a more all-embracing European collective security system.

Others dispute this logic. They ask: Has the Soviet threat vanished or has it merely gone underground? Is the relative quiescence of Soviet policy a function of internal and durable transformations of Soviet political life, or is it conditional upon a temporarily unfavorable balance of forces on the continent? If Russian moderation has been prompted by Western countervailing strength, would the dissolution of that strength—represented by the solidarity of the alliance—create tempting vacuums, encourage new adventures, and revive former ambitions? How much should one be prepared to wager upon the state of Soviet internal politics, about which little is yet known? It is well to remember that however greatly the cold war has been diminished on the continent, the unresolved fate of Berlin and Germany poses constant dangers to a precarious stability.

The ultimate deterrent in Europe certainly is the American nuclear guarantee. But how credible would that guarantee be if NATO were dissolved? The alliance provides the legal basis for the stationing of American troops on German soil. The continued presence of those troops, many believe, is a source of reassurance to the Western Europeans that America will honor its commitments to the common defense, and to the Eastern Europeans that a "safety latch" will continue to be imposed on German military power. Supporters of NATO also argue that a withdrawal of United States forces across a 4000-mile ocean barrier would upset the continental military balance, since Soviet forces would remain on the frontier. Somewhat more persuasive is the argument that, in view of the fact that a variety of challenges may yet be posed to Western Europe's territorial integrity and political stability, it is necessary to retain a broad menu of military capabilities and contingency plans. In the absence of such preattack military planning and joint preparedness policies, conflicts of a limited character might more easily escalate into nuclear war. Thus, it is argued, rather than dissolving NATO, maximum efforts must be expended to insure NATO's continued ability to cope with aggression at whatever level it may manifest itself.

Finally, the virtues of collective defense can be easily overlooked. By comparison with the disastrous results of earlier efforts to provide security through unilateral nationalistic efforts, NATO has been an extraordinary success. The record ought to counsel prudence in exchanging the advantages of arrangements that have worked tolerably well for the uncertainties of a fluid political situation on the continent.

NATO continues to retain its utility as a means of expressing

Atlantic interdependence. It may, however, be prudent to shift emphasis from military integration to cooperation in monetary, commercial, and technological matters through other international institutions. A precipitate downgrading of the alliance in American concerns may be less efficacious than efforts to alter its chief functions and its internal political arrangements. Excessive American initiatives in this direction may, however, be unavailing, for they could merely reinforce European suspicions that to the United States the alliance is principally an instrument for managing clients rather than one for confronting common dangers. Restraint is possible, insofar as America needs NATO less for its own security than does any other member. Thus the United States need not assume the risks of dissolving the alliance, but may contemplate changes in its strategy and structure that would render it more relevant to the changing political environment.

Revamping NATO strategy

It is easier to make a case for maintaining NATO than it is to specify how its solidarity might be enhanced. It is no simple matter to sustain cohesion in a defensive coalition of states joining a superpower with allies inferior in size, wealth, scope of interests, and military capabilities—particularly when the consciousness of common danger is gone. The problems are especially acute in view of the divergences that geography introduces into the security calculations of European and American defense planners. These differences have animated a continuing debate on the strategy of the alliance.

To serve a coalition, a strategy must be militarily sound and politically acceptable. Two principal criticisms have been directed at American strategy for Europe in recent years. Both imply that the United States has been more sensitive to the military than the political side of the strategic equation. Some Europeans have harbored doubts about the reliability of American nuclear guarantees in an age of mutual deterrence. Others question the prudence of requests for a European conventional buildup in order to support a strategy positing "conventional pauses" and the limitation of damage if deterrence should fail. The first problem challenges American ingenuity in the delicate "art of commitment"; the second its ability to devise a strategy which satisfactorily meets the Europeans' overriding concern with deterrence without neglecting those interests which geopolitical considerations permit the United States to indulge: the limitation of damage and the quest for victory should deterrence fail. Both are problems of such technical and political complexity that one cannot do justice to them in a brief analysis. Alternative methods of resolving them can but be sketched with a broad brush.

How can the credibility of American nuclear guarantees to NATO allies be sustained in an age of mutual deterrence? Theoretically many answers are possible; practically, a variety of methods have been employed by the United States. First, it is widely acknowledged that the credibility of deterrent threats is above all contingent upon the capacity to execute them. This explains the substantial efforts made in the early 1960s to incline the strategic balance more clearly in America's favor. By procuring a vast missile force, the United States acquired a measure of strategic superiority which doubtless chastened whatever impulses the Soviet Union may have entertained toward adventurism on the continent. It likewise permitted the United States the luxury of a counterforce strategy which promised to blunt Soviet strategic capabilities and thereby limit damage on the United States and Europe should deterrence fail. To America's allies this capability was designed to fortify the credibility of nuclear guarantees by conveying the impression that the costs of implementing them could be confined. It is necessary only to add that the recent buildup of Soviet missile capabilities renders the counterforce or "controlled response" strategy of the early- and mid-1960s increasingly obsolete and enforces a greater reliance upon threats of massive retaliation.

Second, the credibility of nuclear threats presumably can be reinforced by placing the means for implementing them in the hands of those with the strongest incentive for doing so. The MLF was designed to accomplish such a purpose without at the same time encouraging national nuclear weapons development programs. Neither this nor any similar scheme has been able to resolve the host of technical, military, and political problems associated with nuclear sharing. Nor are any such proposals under active consideration by the members of the alliance at the present time. It is, of course, possible that the deterrent capabilities of NATO are enhanced by the existence of multiple centers of nuclear power. Such a possibility is officially denied by American defense leaders, however, and the French *force de frappe* has been developed in spite of American hostility to the program rather than with its encouragement, assistance, and approval.

Third, a rather subtle theory of brinksmanship proposes that the possession of substantial conventional capabilities for dealing with limited European challenges can bolster the credibility of America's nuclear guarantees to NATO allies. According to such strategists as Thomas Schelling, the function of a substantial conventional force in Europe is "to meet a local crisis as effectively as they can, posing the continual threat that if the crisis continues and enlarges, the danger of intercontinental nuclear war continues and enlarges with it." [14] Considerations such as these inspired the campaign of the early 1960s to build up NATO's conventional strength to thirty combat-ready divisions. The effort achieved scant success. The Europeans proved understandably reluctant to rearm at precisely the moment when the general fear of war was declining on the continent and when the Soviet Union was thinning out its troop strength in Central Europe. In some quarters the exhortations for conventional rearmament merely accentuated fears that the United States' primary inter-

---

[14] Testimony of Thomas C. Schelling before the Senate Committee on Government Operations, *The Atlantic Alliance, Hearings*, 89th Cong., 2nd Sess., 1966, p. 97.

est was insuring that if hostilities occurred they would be confined to Europe. Subsequently, pressures for a conventional buildup have been eased, and the tendency to discount the significance of tactical nuclear weapons in "limited" European conflicts appears to have been reconsidered.

Finally, the credibility of American pledges to defend her allies continues to rest upon the deployment of sizable American forces in Europe. Should armed conflicts between the NATO and Warsaw Pact countries occur, America's involvement would be automatic and inevitable. Controversy has periodically raged over the desirable force levels of the American contingent on the continent. Presently, strong pressures are being mounted for a substantial reduction in the size of that force. Former President Eisenhower, Senate Majority Leader Mike Mansfield, and General James Gavin (ret.) have all publicly called for such reductions. A variety of reasons have been adduced to justify such a move. The withdrawal of several American divisions might force Western European states to assume a more significant share in the burdens of the common defense. It would surely alleviate the outflow of dollars from the United States at a time when the balance-of-payments problem is most acute. The partial disengagement of American troops from the center of the continent might induce the Soviet Union to cooperate in a tacit, reciprocal, phased program of troop reductions in Central Europe.

The potential costs of such a step are equally impressive. First, to cut deeply into NATO's conventional strength might compromise its ability to handle limited or ambiguous probes. The long stated requirement of thirty divisions for this purpose was probably exaggerated. Psychological and military judgment are essential to the redefinition of what is minimally required. Second, the timing and manner with which troop withdrawals are carried out is crucial to the effect of such a move. It would be tragically unfortunate if they were handled in such a way as to imply a decisive shift to an "Asia-first" orientation and a general diminution of American concern with European security problems. Third, it is conceivable that unless such withdrawals are managed within the context of reciprocal Soviet and American reductions, they may convince the West Germans that an international settlement of the problem of German reunification is unfeasible, thereby encouraging them to initiate unilateral efforts to revise existing political arrangements. Nor does it seem desirable that such reductions go so far as to reduce the United States presence to a token rather than a fighting force, since the functions that presence serve include the reassurance of Eastern Europe of West Germany's peacefulness, as well as the guarantee to West Germany that its integrity and independence will be defended. It would appear that the somewhat more threatening situation that has emerged in Europe as a result of the Warsaw Pact's invasion of Czechoslovakia has, in any event, rendered the question of troop withdrawals from the continent academic for the immediate future.

In all of these matters, as well as with respect to the questions of nuclear control, appropriate force levels, arms control, and the general evolution of NATO's strategic policy, effective policies must reflect an appreciation of what the Soviet Union and its allies may do, which strategies are politically acceptable to America's European allies, and what price the United States is prepared to pay in economic and social terms for insurance against contingencies whose probability fluctuates with political developments on the continent.

Discovering new roles for an old alliance

The solidarity of the Atlantic alliance has not been enhanced by focusing attention upon the divisive issues of strategy and the intractable problems of nuclear control. This has led many observers to the conviction that some "vast new enterprise" must be discovered to engage the cooperative energies of members of the alliance. Most specific suggestions imply that NATO must develop its potential for making peace rather than for merely deterring or waging war.[15] Senator Frank Church has recommended, for example, that less emphasis be placed upon NATO as a "fort" and more upon its utility as a "forum."

It is less clear which "vast enterprise" might revivify the alliance. Certainly there is little hope of achieving unity by emphasizing the ideological struggle between communism and the free world. That particular definition of the cold war never did arouse the enthusiasm of America's allies. No ideological crusade against communism can evoke more than uneasiness or indifference in states, like France or Italy, in which local Communist parties have long since become an integral part of society and have participated in the governance of union organizations, municipalities, and even the central institutions of the state.

No more promising is the proposal that NATO take a more assertive role in policing the disputes of the Third World. Not only do American and European perspectives on the nature of those conflicts and their significance differ fundamentally; the alliance has never been capable—even during the darkest days of the cold war—of defining a common policy toward the conflicts of the Southern Hemisphere. While it may be desirable to improve the coordination of Western economic assistance programs to underdeveloped states, the more inclusive Organization for Economic Cooperation and Development appears to be a far more appropriate institution in which to promote such coordination. With regard to the disciplining of intra- or interstate strife in the Third World, the Europeans seem willing to leave to the United States the burdens of tranquilizing political forces in the developing areas, reserving for themselves the right to freely criticize those efforts. Nor has the United States been prepared to accept the possible constraints on its freedom of action which the search for a common policy with its NATO allies might entail. If previous attempts to mobilize allied support for American

[15] See, for example, Zbigniew K. Brzezinski, "The Framework for East-West Reconciliation," *Foreign Affairs* (January 1968), p. 273.

policies in Cuba, the Dominican Republic, and Vietnam are indicative of the prospects, the effort is foredoomed to failure.

A third possibility is a renewed effort to achieve the "Grand Design" for Atlantic partnership, proposed during the Kennedy Administration. The vision of the United States harnessing the energies of a united Europe to the tasks of Western defense, the liberalization of Atlantic trade, and the economic development of the Third World was intrinsically appealing to most Americans. The specific policies devised to give substance to Atlantic interdependence—the MLF concept to preserve unity of command in nuclear matters, and support for Britain's application for membership in the Common Market in order to strengthen Europe even as it was given an "outward" and more Atlantic orientation—came to naught, however, and enthusiasm for the Grand Design has gradually waned. Its operational feasibility is hampered by the vigorous resistance offered by General de Gaulle, the remoteness of political unification of Western Europe, and the growing preoccupation with adjustments to the more polycentric Communist system of states in Eastern Europe.

Some suggest that the promotion of a settlement of the German question and the broader problems of European security might provide the hinge for a common policy. It is well to remember, however, that the prospect of a reunited Germany in the center of the continent does not inspire much enthusiasm in either East or West. In any event, there is now general agreement on the proposition that German unification can be achieved and would be tolerable only within the framework of a broader European community capable of absorbing and domesticating such a formidable aggregation of power. This implies in turn that the reunification of Germany must be preceded by a reconciliation of Eastern and Western Europe and the redefinition of political relations between these fragments of a broader European community, on the one hand, and the extra-European powers, America and Russia, on the other.

While the search for a common policy toward the East must be among the highest priority objectives of American policy, the difficulties must not be overlooked. The premises of official French policy tend to foreclose common approaches for the moment. Not only have the West Germans displayed a greater independence in their Eastern policies in recent years, they continue to refuse to candidly identify for their Western partners the price they are prepared to pay for a general settlement of European security questions. In any event, the Russian occupation of Czechoslovakia vividly and starkly reveals the distance to be traveled before the basis for a new European concert can be established.

Finally, there are those who would evade the problems of high policy and concentrate on the promotion of joint programs in the development of technology, the exploration of space, and the reform of educational systems. Such joint ventures might be open to all who wish to participate, thus providing institutional links between Eastern and Western Europe as well as between the Atlantic nations. Indeed the complementarity of these endeavors is important to keep in mind.

If Atlantic solidarity is to be preserved, it seems essential that the gap between Europe and America in the realms of education, science, and technology be narrowed. If the reconciliation of East and West is to be achieved, NATO must probably receive less emphasis as a military coalition preparing for combat and more as a diplomatic constellation seeking to define the terms of a European settlement. If the central emphasis upon the military alliance is to be downgraded, it appears critically important that a variety of new institutional links with the Europeans—both East and West—be established. If American troops are to be withdrawn from the continent, the potential of this bargaining asset should be exploited in order to facilitate fruitful negotiations on the German and European security problems.

Ultimately, of course, it may be impossible to discover—without the assistance of more aggressive policies by the Soviet Union— "vast enterprises" sufficient to ensure Atlantic solidarity. After all, it has always proved more difficult to unite states *for* general and constructive purposes than to unify them *against* a specific threat to the status quo.

This search for "vast enterprises" which might provide orienting objectives for American policy in Europe discloses a variety of conceptual efforts to define a structure of world political arrangements within which American interests can be sustained and American power preserved. Most of these designs are marked by a penchant for symmetry and simplicity. Although George Ball is doubtless correct in his complaint that American foreign policy is marked by an almost doctrinaire pragmatism,[16] it is just possible that the most feasible design for European-American relations is one which will enable the United States to indulge its tendency to "muddle through." In this respect the concept of the Western alliance as a "web of special relationships" certainly has much to commend it. A pluralistic alliance would permit a loose pattern of relationships in which the specific forms of cooperation might vary depending on the issue, "now loose, now tight, now comprehensive, now limited to a core of nations, thereby leaving open the door for such presently unconceived notions as may later emerge for our emerging pluralist yet interdependent world."[17]

The management of military threats to specific segments of the alliance might be delegated to those threatened most directly by Communist provocations in the Baltic, Mediterranean, or central front. Responsibility for managing the nuclear forces of the alliance could be exercised by those enjoying custody over nuclear weapons in consultation with other interested parties.[18] Genuinely integrated

[16] Ball, *The Discipline of Power*, p. 27.

[17] Seyom Brown, "An Alternative to the Grand Design," *World Politics* (January 1965), p. 238.

[18] This describes in essence the present *modus operandi* of the so-called McNamara Committee, in which some interested parties to the alliance participate in the conception, formulation, and elaboration of nuclear strategy in return for their acquiescence in America's unified operational command over the strategic forces.

military planning would be facilitated by the inclusion of only those with a concrete stake in the performance of specific defensive tasks. Such arrangements would demolish the myth of an egalitarian alliance, but the myth never produced equality among unequals anyway. Arrangements would be based upon a variety of "special relationships." Americans have sought carefully to avoid special relationships, but all relationships are special insofar as they are built upon unique constellations of converging and conflicting interests. They would be compatible with the value placed upon pluralism by Americans. They would accord with the American tendency to organize trade, aid, diplomacy, and military policy in institutions that are as inclusive as possible but as exclusive as necessary.[19] And finally they would be consistent with the promotion of an East-West détente, for they would permit a loosening of organizational ties within the Western world and facilitate the inclusion of Eastern European states in cooperative arrangements where mutual interests are sufficient to sustain their participation.

In 1969 NATO will celebrate its twentieth anniversary. A reappraisal of the future of the alliance is long overdue. "The Atlantic alliance has proved its vitality," President Johnson once observed. "We are committed, and will remain firm. But the Atlantic alliance is a living organism. It must adapt to changing conditions." The process of adaptation has begun. The pattern of its future evolution is far from foreordained.

Policing third-world disputes

Many critics of United States foreign policy decry the frequency with which the United States has intervened to shape the outcome of domestic strife in Third-World nations. Spokesmen for the Administration deny the allegation that America covets the role of global policeman. But they readily admit that fostering nontotalitarian patterns of modernization in the developing countries is a cardinal objective of American policy. If they were candid they might concede that upon occasion pursuit of that aim has inspired interventions on behalf of governments whose capacity to establish their authority was more than a trifle dubious, or against revolutionary movements whose character, aims, and international affiliations were at best obscure.

To discuss American policy in terms of a dichotomy between interventionism and noninterventionism is certain to be misleading. Seyom Brown's astute observation that "a posture of nonintervention when the insurgents are losing can be just as much an 'intervention' in the domestic affairs of a given country as is overt intervention to help the government forces reestablish the 'balance' when the insurgents are winning" is a timely reminder of the wisdom of Talley-

[19] See Laurence W. Martin, "The Future of the Alliance," in *Changing East-West Relations and the Unity of the West*, Arnold Wolfers (ed.) (Baltimore, Md.: Johns Hopkins University Press, 1964), pp. 219–38.

rand who considered nonintervention a somewhat metaphysical expression having the same meaning as intervention.[20] The more interesting questions are: What instruments are most likely to be efficacious in particular situations in promoting internal developments in other states that are compatible with American interests? Under what circumstances should the United States contemplate military intervention in the internal disputes of others? To which side ought the United States commit its resources and its prestige in such struggles? How may the United States reconcile its interest in stability with its interest in averting politically and economically costly adventures of the sort experienced in the Bay of Pigs invasion in 1961, the Dominican Republic intervention in 1965, and the deepening involvement in Vietnam since 1961?

One can scarcely answer any of these questions in general, for revolutions tend to be singular and unique in their causes and consequences. Thus it is extraordinarily difficult to define guidelines for an American policy toward interstate and intrastate strife in the developing areas. Indeed it is impossible even to catalogue the problems such conflicts pose for American policy-makers, let alone subject them to any discerning analysis, given the limits of space in a book of this kind. Any such attempt, moreover, would be colored inevitably by judgments about the prudence and the prospects of American policies in Vietnam, whose uncertain outcome will certainly reshape the dimensions of the entire range of problems related to this subject. Consequently, rather than attempt to analyze the costs and consequences of alternative courses of action toward revolutionary movements in the Third World, several observations will be offered that might inform the more detailed analyses of others.

1. It is evident that domestic strife—rebellions, revolutions, secessionist movements, guerrilla struggles, military coups d'états, and so forth—is endemic in the very process of political and economic development upon which most of the Third World states are currently embarked.[21] Violent opposition to governments is predictable when political leadership is considered alien, weak and ineffectual, arbitrary and capricious, or unrepresentative of broad segments of the populace. Little imagination is required to recognize that one or another of these qualities characterize the regimes of many of the fledgling states with which the United States became engaged in collective defense arrangements in the 1950s. The United States may have an obvious interest in seeing the power of these regimes legitimated, but there are surely limits to the contribution that an ally can make to the establishment of another government's authority, particularly in regions where national sentiment is self-conscious and easily inflamed against foreign powers. Nor is authority, once established, necessarily long secure. Insofar as the pace of modernization

[20] Brown, *The Faces of Power*, p. 361.

[21] The point is abundantly documented in Cyril Black, *The Dynamics of Modernization* (New York, N.Y.: Harper, 1967).

is accelerated, the challenges of incumbent leaders multiply. Stable territorial frontiers must be established, strategies of industrialization must be formulated and applied, peoples of disparate ethnic, religious, and cultural backgrounds must be integrated into a national society, demands for popular participation in public policy-making and more equitable distribution of public services must be indulged or parried. All these "crises of development" provide abundant opportunities for convulsive upheavals, as the history of any "developed" country will attest. This is to suggest that there are ample reasons for anticipating that violent disorders will sweep through Latin America, Africa, and Asia in the years ahead. And such a prediction may be hazarded without assigning great significance to the influence either of Communist ideas or Communist *agents provocateurs* in those regions.

2. Although revolutionary potential abounds in the Third World, it is far from clear that Communist movements can effectively exploit such rebelliousness for their own purposes. Certainly International Communism—a euphemism still employed by some to describe an aggregation of states that can neither agree on the definition of communism nor define a common policy on the salient international issues of the day—is not likely to be its prime beneficiary. The weight of historical precedents suggests that Communist movements are viable political forces only in countries in which their leaders have established nationalist credentials, fashioned a political strategy responsive to local political realities, and developed an indigenous constituency. To acquire those attributes essential to local political success is to obtain the capacity to resist efforts by the Chinese or Russians to compromise their independence. Yugoslavia, Albania, China, North Vietnam, Cuba—none has been reduced to the status of a dependent or satellite. Their way of life may be austere, their ideology repugnant, their rhetoric bellicose, but servitude to Moscow's foreign policy designs is conspicuously absent. Under these circumstances the territorial extension of communism would not appear automatically to diminish American security because additional Communist states do not necessarily strengthen a bloc which even now cannot overcome its own divisions or act in unison against the non-Communist world. These comments are not meant to imply indifference toward local Communist successes, but to indicate the global balance of power is not so easily threatened by internal shifts of power in the Third World in an increasingly polycentric international order.

Actually, the prospect of Communist seizures of power in most underdeveloped countries is slight. The struggle against colonialism provided Communist insurgents with their best opportunity to win a broad nationalist following. That opportunity was squandered in most countries of the Third World. The colonialists withdrew with either reluctance or grace or they have been expelled. Local Communists have always had difficulty mobilizing peasant societies to revolt over social or economic issues. Where Communist parties have won a popular following—for example, the Indian state of Kerala, or in

Chile—this reflects either the failure of indigenous elites to provide minimally satisfactory government or an increasingly reformist rather than revolutionary outlook on the part of the Communist leadership. In short, the conditions that nourished the peasant-based, mass-militarized insurrections in China and Vietnam are unlikely to be duplicated in other countries.

There are, consequently, persuasive reasons for doubting the wisdom of considering Vietnam an appropriate "test case" of America's capacity to cope with guerrilla insurgency. In virtually all important respects, Vietnam is unusual and atypical. It is the only country in the world whose people won their release from colonial rule under Communist leadership. The only truly national organizations in Vietnam—bureaucratic, military, and political—are Communist led. President Eisenhower speculated in 1956 that Ho Chi Minh would have garnered 80 percent of the votes had free elections been held in Vietnam. One has difficulty in thinking of another country in the world in which a Communist politician has ever enjoyed such electoral prospects.

Communist *participation* in revolutionary upheavals is predictable.[22] The obstacles to their *controlling* such revolutionary movements are far too often overlooked. Indeed, military coups are more likely than guerrilla wars to disrupt political stability and oust incumbent governments in most developing countries. It is well to note that Communist groups have been notably unsuccessful in penetrating military bureaucracies in most such states. Possibly this is because many Communists have dogmatically clung to the faith that the working classes alone were the vehicles of social change while the military was hopelessly anachronistic, reactionary, and doomed to perish with the rest of the old order. Possibly it is additional evidence of the immunity to infiltration by movements bearing the stigma of foreign attachment enjoyed by military institutions whose entire ethos is nationalistic. It is well to add that the United States has itself been responsible for educating and training many of the most prominent military leaders in non-Western countries through its extensive military assistance program.

All of these considerations suggest that America has no necessary stake in the prevention of revolutions whenever and wherever they may occur, even if they are led by nominal Communists. The axioms of absolute containment are in need of reconsideration.

3. Fears of "indirect aggression" have influenced the definition of America's attitude toward revolutionary situations in the Third World. It appears that the United States has assumed the benign but enormously ambitious role of providing a shield around de-

---

[22] Che Guevara's diaries provide evidence that participation by the established Communist parties of Latin America in guerrilla insurgencies is far from assured. Increasingly, the radical revolutionaries are inclined to view those parties as hopelessly bureaucratic and conservative. See "The Diary of Che Guevara," *Ramparts* (July 27, 1968), *passim.*

veloping countries behind which the traumatic and convulsive shocks of rapid modernization may work themselves out free of external manipulation and control. This role has been rationalized with clarity and candor by Walt W. Rostow.

> Guerrilla warfare, mounted from external bases—with rights of sanctuary—is a terrible burden to carry for any government in a society making its way toward modernization. For instance, it takes somewhere between ten and twenty soldiers to control one guerrilla in an organized operation. Moreover, the guerrilla force has this advantage: Its task is merely to destroy, while the government must build and protect what it is building. A guerrilla war mounted from outside a transitional nation is a crude act of international vandalism. There will be no peace in the world if the international community accepts the outcome of a guerrilla war, mounted from outside a nation, as tantamount to a free election.[23]

Rostow was, of course, deriving generalizations from his own understanding of the character of the conflict then underway in Vietnam. His definition of the Vietnamese struggle contained elements of truth as well as some misleading assertions. There is, and has been from the days of the partition of Vietnam in 1954, an international component to that conflict which also has the attributes of a civil war. Indeed, virtually all internal wars have a tendency to become internationalized to some extent, since guerrillas naturally seek arms, diplomatic support, and sanctuaries abroad even as incumbent governments covet the legitimacy seemingly conferred by international support as well as various forms of foreign assistance of a more material sort.[24]

Nevertheless, there are good reasons for avoiding an excessive emphasis upon the international components of revolutionary wars. Governments plagued by guerrilla insurgents are generally reluctant to admit that rebels may have legitimate grievances against their rule. They are consequently tempted to stigmatize them as the stalking horses of a foreign foe, the agents of a foreign power.[25] By defining the conflict in terms of external aggression or externally supported subversion, such embattled governments hope to confine the popular support of the revolutionaries even as they are attracting foreign support to their cause. Success in countering insurgencies normally requires, however, that the regime address itself to its own

---

[23] Walt W. Rostow, "Guerrilla Warfare in Underdeveloped Areas," *Marine Corps Gazette* (January 1962), pp. 48–49.

[24] See James N. Rosenau (ed.), *International Aspects of Civil Strife* (Princeton, N.J.: Princeton University Press, 1964), esp. pp. 14–44.

[25] Americans are characteristically prepared to think well of indigenous movements of reform, to think ill of movements that plausibly can be represented as the puppets of a foreign government.

deficiencies of political organization and its own impaired authority. The dilemma is not simply resolved. To accord legitimacy to insurgents' demands is further to erode the authority of established governments. To emphasize the foreign character of domestic threats is to dissipate what leverage the United States may possess for redirecting the attention of the regime back to its internal problems of political development.

4. As great as the temptation to overemphasize the international component in revolutionary wars is the difficulty exhibited by many Americans in developing a sufficiently political conception of the problems posed by revolutionaries. The outcomes of mass militarized insurrections, like the present insurgency in Vietnam, are not likely merely to reflect the sentimental attachments of the majority to one or another set of ideas or leaders. Nor do they merely register the balance of coercive capabilities possessed by the antagonists. What is at stake is the right and the capacity of a government to rule; in short, its authority. Consequently, such conflicts are aptly described as "competitive exercises in administration." To pacify a nation fraught with internal war requires the ability to provide security, an aptitude for organizing the populace, and the capacity to induce a measure of consent from the citizenry.

If one seeks to "win the hearts and minds of the people" by distributing services and supplies to the rural populace without reference to the local security conditions, one may wind up subsidizing guerrilla forces that are zealous and efficient in "taxing," or "selling protection" to the peasantry. On the other hand, to address only the military aspects of denying supplies and sanctuaries to local guerrillas without regard to the impact specific military tactics have upon the lives and livelihood of the rural populace may ultimately render the task of pacification all but impossible.

These considerations would suggest that counterinsurgency entails the careful, subtle, and patient *meshing* of political, economic, military, and diplomatic instruments. The integration of policy in these areas requires in turn a common definition of the problem in Washington and a centralization of authority in the field. Neither is easily achieved. It is evident that none of the succession of American ambassadors or commanding generals in Saigon have exercised authority commensurate with that enjoyed by Sir Gerald Templer, the British Director of Operations during the Malayan emergency. It is doubtful whether such centralization is even possible for a government whose internal divisions are regularly transmitted to the field.

5. The pitfalls of faulty timing are particularly acute when military interventions are undertaken in struggles with a substantial domestic component. Insurgency movements are most vulnerable during their formative stages. Guerrilla bands will then be small, their rapport with the masses precarious, their supplies meager, and their discipline erratic. Preventive intervention by external powers to nip incipient insurgencies in the bud may produce temporarily de-

213

cisive military results. They may also eventuate in costly involvements against adversaries whose identity and aims are matters of conjecture only.

To play a waiting game in such situations, however, also has its costs. As Lucian Pye has observed, "The initial decisions of a government confronted with the threat of internal war are usually the most fateful and long-lasting of any it will be called upon to make throughout an insurrection." [26] Much of America's difficulty in Vietnam is attributable to the fact that its aid was channeled for a number of years through a government—Ngo Dinh Diem's—that had earlier defined the issues at stake and the basis for the domestic struggle's termination in a manner prejudicial to subsequent prospects of success whatever the scale of foreign assistance.[27] In short, it is awfully easy to become militarily involved in the revolutionary strife in the Third World either too early or too late.

6. As critical as the timing of intervention is the scale of the assistance provided. On the basis of recent experiences one may assert the hypothesis that the more massive American military involvement becomes in the politics of a relatively underdeveloped country beset by civil disorders, the more likely it is that that presence will threaten indigenous efforts by the local government to establish its integrity and authority. There are several reasons for the plausibility of this hypothesis.

First, the very presence of a large foreign military establishment provides graphic evidence of the weakness of a regime. The more ardent the embrace of the foreign ally, the more surely will the local regime appear as its client, to the detriment of its self-proclaimed image of independence.

Second, if the establishment and maintenance of the local government's authority depends upon its ability to mobilize and control the populace, clearly it must devise political organizations and institutions capable of adaptation to local political realities, that is, ethnic conflicts, regional rivalries, personal political feuds, and so forth. As long as American military and economic assistance to a beleaguered government is kept at reasonably modest levels, the appearance that *they* are fighting *their* war may be sustained and the priorities of the political development tasks may be honored. Once American assistance reaches a certain scale, however, domestic pressures to achieve results swiftly mount in the United Staes. Washington officials far up the chain of command begin to assert a more decisive voice on day-to-day policy decisions. Hardest pressed to produce rapid results, these officials are less likely to possess a detailed, per-

[26] Lucian Pye, *Aspects of Political Development* (Boston, Mass.: Little, Brown, 1966), p. 139.

[27] For example, the Diem government's habit of considering all opponents as Communists to be dealt with harshly tended to force all opposition groups into the hands of the guerrillas. By identifying his opponents as Viet Cong—that is, as *Vietnamese* Communists—Diem conceded them nationalist credentials. The concession proved to be detrimental to his own cause. For other examples, see Bernard Fall, *The Two Vietnams* (New York, N.Y.: Praeger, 1963), *passim.*

sonal, intuitive knowledge of or "feel" for the newly emerging society and government being assisted. The results can be disastrous.

In Vietnam the attempt to create military and civil bureaucracies patterned on the American model and sufficiently centralized and efficient to handle the massive American military assistance program reflects a limited understanding of the fragmented pattern of political life in that anguished country. Evidence of America's willingness to shoulder the major burdens of the fighting in South Vietnam have predictably diminished the zest displayed by the South Vietnamese Army (ARVN) for combat. Ambitious programs for rural reform and revolutionary development which sound impressive in budgetary hearings in Washington rarely meet the test of operational feasibility, since they are geared to standards of administrative competence and political initiative which are in short supply where the programs must be implemented—in the hamlets and villages of Vietnam.

This is by no means an exhaustive inventory of the "cautionary tales" that may be derived from a careful analysis of America's recent experiences in seeking to discipline revolutionary struggles in the Third World. Perhaps it is sufficient, however, to indicate the limited capacity of outsiders to control the diplomatic alignment and internal political processes of fledgling states. If American policies have frequently proved costly or inefficacious in this realm, it is preeminently because courses of action too often have been guided by considerations of global cold war strategy and too little informed by a sense of the local situation. If American interests in the Third World are to be well managed during the turbulent years ahead, two things are required: first, a plausible understanding of local political forces and of the dynamics of modernization in societies with unique cultures and traditions; and, second, a more impressive sense of proportion in order that global interests are kept in balance and external obligations disciplined by a keen sense of the cost of their acquittal. President Kennedy admirably summarized the lessons of his own and previous Administrations when he said:

Experience has taught us that no one nation has the power or wisdom to solve all the problems of the world or manage its revolutionary tides; that extending our commitments does not always increase our security; that any initiative carries with it the risk of temporary defeat; that nuclear weapons cannot prevent subversion; that no free peoples can be kept free without will and energy of their own; and that no two nations or situations are exactly alike.

These, then, are among the problems with which the United States must come to terms in the future. To such problems there are no obvious remedies, only alternative courses of action whose costs and risks can ultimately be ascertained only after the fact. Is American security best preserved through the fullest exploitation of novel weapon technology or through painstaking efforts to manage the arms race with tacit or explicit Soviet cooperation? Will international settlement of the German and European security problems be best facilitated by the continued presence of American military forces on the continent or by the gradual disengagement of American military power and the replacement of the alliances by what General de Gaulle refers to as a European security system? With respect to the revolutionary struggles in the Third World, should America's role be confined to that of interested bystander, active participant, or neutral arbiter? The very character of these dilemmas suggests that United States foreign policy may be subject to rather dramatic changes of direction in the coming years. It is thus to the sources of constancy and change in American foreign policy that attention must again be directed.

9

The United States in world politics

Thirty years ago the United States was a neutralist state on the periphery of the European state system, entertaining few pretensions of world leadership. Today the United States is a global power exercising power and responsibilities on an imperial scale. Few prophesied the drastic changes in the international situation which were to flow from a world war, a cold war, the development of nuclear weapons, and the disintegration of the imperial system. Fewer still predicted the general contours of America's response to these developments.

Surprise occurrences persistently wreck the best laid plans of soldiers and diplomats, thus accounting for the respect the best among them maintain toward the inscrutability of the future. One example may suffice to indicate the pitfalls of predictions in the realm of foreign policy. In 1950 the United States found itself in a war in Korea that it had not anticipated, for which it was ill-prepared, and which had an enormous influence upon the subsequent course of American foreign policy. The Korean conflict aggravated the cold war and deepened American animosity toward Stalinist Russia. It prompted an acceleration of the nuclear arms race. NATO was transformed from a political alliance into a military coalition preparing for imminent conflict in Europe. Adjustment to the Communist seizure of power in China was complicated by the deployment of the Seventh Fleet to Chinese coastal waters to provide a protective screen for Chiang Kai-shek's government on Taiwan. America's expanded procurement of raw materials in anticipation of other local wars artificially improved the terms of trade for exporters of primary products, rendering their economies even more vulnerable to dislocation when the stockpiling program leveled off in subsequent years. At home, too, the war had its effects, as the domestic price included the paranoid anticommunism mobilized by Senator Joseph McCarthy.

These experiences suggest why a certain agnosticism about the future is entirely appropriate. Developments in American foreign policy will occur against the backdrop of changing relations of force, changing historical circumstances, changes in the national situation and the national sociology, and changes in the psychology of the nation's political leadership. A sense of history may help one discern those deep forces that are moving men, challenging states, and changing societies. No detailed forecast of policies is possible. At best one can attempt to identify the forces which may encourage continuity or induce changes in America's future policies.

The United States rank in the international "pecking order"

The United States seems destined to retain its preeminent position as the world's most formidable industrial and military power. Economic, demographic, and technological forecasts provide abundant evidence for this hypothesis. One set of "surprise-free" projections—that is, extrapolations from current tendencies which are also informed by empirical or theoretical considerations that shape expectations—suggests that the United States will continue to nearly double the annual output of its chief industrial rival, the Soviet Union, in the year 2000. Those projections also indicate that it will take the members of the European Economic Community from sixteen to thirty years to achieve the *per capita* income enjoyed by the United States in 1965. The Soviet Union cannot anticipate such levels of affluence before 1990; nor can China before the latter half of the twenty-first century.[1]

Along with this continued growth of the American economy, one can anticipate an expansion of the amount of resources diverted into research and development. Since a high percentage of research and development work is geared to the needs of the military services, it seems likely that the prime source of American military power will be constantly renewed. In the early 1960s it was fashionable for a time to speak of a "scientific and technological plateau," which, having been achieved, permitted—though it did not insure—a stabilization of the arms race.[2] Recent developments in the technology of ballistic missile defense and the innovation of multiple-independently-targetable-reentry-vehicles suggest that, on the contrary, resolutions in

---

[1] See Kahn and Wiener, *The Year 2000*, pp. 149, 159, and *passim*.

[2] See, for example, Jerome Wiesner, *Where Science and Politics Meet* (New York, N.Y.: McGraw-Hill, 1965), pp. 279–296.

military weaponry will probably continue to occur at roughly five-year intervals.[3] Assuming that the United States wishes to preserve a position of strategic superiority or parity with the Soviet Union, there is ample reason to believe that it has the technical and industrial capacity to do so.

Developments in technology promise not merely to increase the amplitude of America's power potential, but to facilitate the projection of that power over vast distances as well. As Albert Wohlstetter has noted, American mastery of transportation and communication technology now places the United States closer in terms of "strategic distance" to the Laos-Thai border than the Chinese. That is to say, the United States can provide four times the logistic support to a military force in Southeast Asia from a distance of 8500 miles than China can from a distance of 450 miles. Similarly, the United States is as close as the Soviet Union to Iran in these terms.[4] It seems probable that advances in technology will continue to modify the former constraints of geography on the range of American influence.

These developments obviously have a bearing on the question as to whether America might in the future confine its interests geographically to a narrow sphere of influence in the Western Hemisphere or the Atlantic community. Nuclear rockets may be rattled from afar. The effort to arrest the spread of nuclear weapons imposes a correlative obligation to provide alternative sources of security to erstwhile aspirants to nuclear status, wherever they happen to be located. In a global diplomatic system, American security interests are and will continue to be affected by changes in the local disposition of forces in all regions of the world.

America's resources of force are likely to become ever more impressive. The future of America's power—that is, its ability to accomplish large purposes and its capacity to induce others to accept the legitimacy of those purposes—is more problematic. Force does not inevitably yield authority. Analysts at the London Institute of Strategic Studies recently concluded that "the most striking phenomenon of the year [1967] was the revelation of the growing divorce between American physical power and American political authority in the world." The United States, they observed, has never been stronger as a military power, and they anticipated further improvements in America's power potential relative to other states.[5] American prestige and moral authority, on the other hand, are jeopardized by the intensifying racial strife at home and the inconclusive attempt to coerce a small Asian state to settle the Vietnamese war on terms favorable to the United States.

It may be argued (plausibly) that American power is likely to decline in the coming years. As political vacuums in the inter-

[3] Kahn and Wiener, *op. cit.*, Chap. 2.

[4] Albert Wohlstetter, "The Illusions of Distance," *Foreign Affairs* (January 1968), p. 244.

[5] Reported in the Los Angeles *Times* (April 16, 1968), p. 18.

mediate zones between the United States and the Soviet Union have been filled by assertive states in both Western and Eastern Europe, and as other continents have awakened from the slumber of colonial dependence, a multipolar international order has begun to take shape. The continued resurgence of Japan, Germany, France, the United Kingdom, and China, as well as the further development of the considerable potential of states like Canada, India, and Italy, will diminish the American capacity to define the terms upon which relationships with allies, adversaries, and neutrals will be established.

The gradual trend toward a stabilization of American-Soviet relations and the emergence of additional centers of power in the world will not alter fundamentally America's preoccupation with the global balance of power. Nor will it render any less acute the desire to avoid general war. But the methods appropriate to the achievement of these objectives will surely be subjected to a searching reappraisal. The pace at which such a reappraisal produces new policies will be contingent upon the extent to which the further industrialization of the Soviet Union prompts internal political developments which further ameliorate cold war animosities, and upon the degree to which the fragmentation of a once-united commonwealth of Communist states is taken by American political leaders as evidence of the fact that America's irreducible national interests are no longer principally threatened by *international* communism.

Although Soviet-American rivalry is likely to persist, as the ideological antagonism between East and West abates, the focus of American foreign policy may possibly continue to shift to the less developed countries in the Third World. The industrialization of those states is destined to unleash turbulence and violence on a wide scale, for internal strife seems endemic in the very process of political and economic development. This is not to say that the East-West conflict will be simply displaced by a conflict between the North and the South, the rich and the poor nations, the haves and the have-nots. The latter possess neither the power nor the unity to wage such a struggle.

The critical questions relate to the manner in which America competes with the Soviet Union and others for influence in the underdeveloped regions. Policies of competitive intervention threaten to embroil both of them in struggles whose course they can not control and from which they stand to gain little. To engage in bilateral policing ventures promises certain advantages but assumes a coincidence of Soviet and American interests in local conflicts which heretofore has been conspicuously absent. To exercise mutual restraint and adopt a hands-off policy toward struggles within or among states in the Third World is to ignore the persistence of historic animosities among some of them (Israel and the Arab states), the legacy of division upon others (Vietnam and Korea), and the revisionist ambitions nourished by still others (Vietnam and China). These brief observations suggest the organic connection between the task of formulating a new framework for North-South relations and the task of redefining political relationships among the states in the industrially advanced regions. In both, America's voice will be one among many, though an influential one to be sure. The actual influence the United States can exert in these matters will surely depend upon the elaboration of relevant concepts to discipline the application of American power, and the development of a more sophisticated understanding of the sociopolitical processes in the less developed states and of tools to shape political developments within those countries. In the future as in the past, American military prowess may be able to foreclose some outcomes to internal or external struggles that are deemed intolerable. A more positive influence upon the process and prospects of modernization by Third World states requires other instruments, not yet impressively developed.

The American liberal tradition in foreign affairs

The American commitment to the ideals of self-government, self-determination, and noninterference in the domestic affairs of other states is genuine and durable. The implementation of those principles depends, however, upon political calculations that change with circumstances. For more than two decades, those calculations have been informed by reflexes deeply rooted in the consciousness of political leaders who endured the trials of the 1930s and the 1940s. The vast enterprise of containment was based upon a series of premises which have, to be sure, undergone continuous modification but which have tended to emphasize the power and aggressiveness of the Russians and Chinese, the monolithicity of the Soviet bloc, and the dangers implicit in any forceful alteration of existing political boundaries between the Communist and non-Communist world.

Sound enough, perhaps, at the time the containment policy was originally conceived and adopted, many of the central assumptions undergirding that policy have become increasingly challengeable in the light of the Sino-Soviet split, the internal turmoil in China, the resurgence of Europe and Japan, and the successful decolonization of most of Africa and Asia. The Vietnamese war has now precipitated a sweeping reassessment of the basic premises behind America's postwar foreign policy. That war has disclosed the limited influence that the Soviet Union posesses over the policy of a small socialist state, exposed the negligible power of the Chinese to control events in even a neighboring region, and revealed the dubious efficacy of American military power in a conflict in which the United States can alter the coercive balance within a society without being able to more than marginally influence the political forces in contention.

Some responsible leaders in both the Democratic and Republican parties have deplored the Vietnamese war and expressed grave reservations toward the logic with which it has been rationalized. Neo-isolationist sentiment is again perceptible in both liberal and conservative circles. The agony of an inconclusive war has diminished the confidence Americans have traditionally displayed in their capacity to master events. It has dimmed the hopes of many that liberal solutions, liberally applied, promise peace "in our time."

Nevertheless, it is not yet possible to perceive how American policies will be revised as a consequence of the war. Much will depend, as William P. Gerberding has noted, upon the way in which the war is brought to an end, upon the results of the 1968 presidential election, upon the extent to which the new man in the White House is committed to revising the premises upon which American policies have been based, and upon his capacity to successfully alter established modes of thought and overcome the inertia of the foreign policy bureaucracies.[6]

It is safe to predict that American policy can never be quite the same again in the light of recent experiences. Equally plausible is the conjecture that the psychological and emotional impact of the Vietnamese war, upon the younger generation especially, may produce future policies based upon analogies as misleadingly applied as that of Munich to the contemporary situation in Southeast Asia.

Whatever the political calculations, the objectives animating American policies and the principles that govern the application of means to their achievement are likely to reveal considerable constancy. For the sake of argument, these predictions may be hazarded. In the future the commitment to *self-government* will likely serve less as a justification for indiscriminate American assistance to regimes confronting internal threats than as a reminder that indigenous measures of *self-help* is the prerequisite of success in counterinsurgency. Belief in the abstract principle of *self-determination* will surely survive the Vietnamese war, but Americans may in the future be more inclined to stand aside and allow historical forces to work themselves out, and more willing to consider the outcome of domestic struggles in the Third World to be a matter of *humane concern* rather than of vital *strategic importance* to the United States. Certainly the war has given rise to a new search for guiding principles that might restrain the urge to intervene in the domestic or interstate struggles of others.

The American community and foreign policy

The content or style of diplomatic-strategic behavior of a state cannot be predicted on the basis of general propositions related to the nature of the polity, the society, or the economy. Despite the popularity of Marxist ideas and Wilsonian theories of war and peace, the American economy—insofar as it is to be considered capitalistic rather than a "mixed economy"—is not bent on conquest; American democracy

[6] See William P. Gerberding, "Vietnam and the Future of United States Foreign Policy," in *The Political Dimension in National Strategy* (Los Angeles, Calif.: UCLA Security Studies Project, 1968), pp. 1–20.

has not prevented occasional expressions of warlike behavior, and American culture has not imposed uniformities in political conduct that are constant over time. American society is far too complex for its behavior in the external realm to respond to the dynamics of some simple and eternal laws.

The American industrial economy will continue presumably to display an enormous productivity. This will insure the availability of resources that may be employed to further America's designs abroad. Study of the American economy is not likely, however, to permit one to predict the way in which such resources may be deployed. Will they be channeled into additional military ventures? Larger aid programs? More substantial levels of private investment abroad? Will the further development of the American economy promote the growing functional interdependence of the industrially advanced states or merely increase the resources that may be placed in the service of *Gross Politik*?

The rapid pace of social change in America may produce discontinuities in the nation's foreign policy. A massive involvement in international affairs has diverted resources from programs of domestic reform. Participation in foreign wars has accentuated Negro demands for full equality at home. The prospect of compulsory involvement in a conflict that many youths deem of dubious morality has heightened the self-consciousness of student groups as forces in American politics. Technology and urbanization have altered the relationship between citizen and government, denying the latter the indifference of the former. National crises have a more direct impact upon individuals who may witness the dizzying pace of events on their television screens. This permits an emotional involvement in national policies that is not matched by any personal ability to affect the decisions of a vast and complex governmental apparatus. At its worst, the combination of a sense of moral outrage and personal impotence is expressed in outbursts of nihilism that threaten the very fabric of society. In its more constructive forms it is being channeled into organizational efforts to bring the dispossessed, the disgruntled, and the disenchanted into a more substantial participation in American politics.

"Participatory democracy" is the aim of the students, the poor, and the Negroes. Their entrance on the scene of American politics may serve to redirect national energies toward the amelioration of poverty, the reconstruction of the cities, and the revitalization of the educational system as vital preconditions of a genuine integration of the races in American society. The effort to grapple with the overriding problems of domestic politics may, in short, bring an "emotional disengagement" from international politics for a season.[7] A desire to insulate a precarious social order at home from additional strains may then result in a neo-isolationist foreign policy. The addition of new participants in the politics of pluralism will also serve to further

[7] William Pfaff, "Why Solutions Elude Super Society," Los Angeles *Times* (June 9, 1968), Part G, p. 2.

complicate the problems of consensus-building, compounding the difficulties of evolving foreign policy decisions that the government can execute and that the public will support.

The outlook is, therefore, inconclusive. The further development of the economy is creating additional means for transmitting American influence and American values abroad. At the same time it is provoking divisive schisms in the American social order that may produce a diminishing emphasis upon foreign affairs or have unpredictable effects upon any continuing effort to sustain massive international commitments.

American political institutions and processes and foreign policy

It is the saving grace of democracy that if policies prove disastrous the men who made them may be replaced. America is the world's oldest democracy, and the certainty of frequent elections permits, though it does not insure, future changes in the basic direction of American foreign policy. Significant limits upon the potential for change are implicit in the widespread diffusion of governmental power. Thus even an activist and innovating Chief Executive will confront a permanent government with a greater attachment to established modes of procedure and ongoing policies. Out of the interplay of these contending forces, incremental changes in policy may be introduced; radical departures are unlikely.

America's "crisis of identity"

Dean Acheson once remarked of the British that they had lost an empire and failed to discover a rôle. Of the United States in the late 1960s it may be said that America's postwar foreign policy has been successful enough that the need to continue it is more and more widely questioned. The expansion of Communist power has been arrested. Communist ideology has become a source of division even in Eastern Europe. The chasm between Russia and China appears unbridgeable. China has been contained and is torn internally by its own cultural revolution. None of the principal Communist states has enjoyed any notable success in promoting or exploiting revolutions in the developing countries. A more or less rigid bipolarity has given way to a multipolar world within which the United States seems destined to maintain its industrial and military ascendancy for the foreseeable future.

These developments have not given rise to rejoicing in America. Rather, they have unleashed an intense and frequently bitter "great debate" on foreign policy. Politicians, publicists, and professors have joined to formulate a reasonably coherent critique of contemporary American policies. Those policies have been defended by others from the same professions.[8] In general, it appears that liberal critics of the Administration dwell on the possibilities of polycentrism or multipolarity and the dangers of American ascendancy, while spokesmen for the Administration have been somewhat more inclined to recognize the potential dangers of polycentrism and to capitalize on the possibilities of American ascendancy.

Those who believe that the cold war has been definitely ended consider American policies in Europe and Asia hopelessly anachronistic and obsolete. They believe that the United States has little to fear from "wars of national liberation," since nationalism is, in their view, more durable and potent than Communism, and because in a world in which the Communist states are no longer unified, Communist revolutionaries are not easily subordinated to the purposes of either Moscow or Peking. They consider a strengthening of NATO somewhat superfluous at a time when Soviet authority in the Eastern camp is declining. In all of this, there is an evident willingness to acquiesce gracefully in a movement toward greater pluralism in world politics and to accept a gradual diminution in the scope of American responsibilities for other people's affairs.

Beyond this optimism that American interests can be secured while the level of American sacrifice for others is scaled down, critics (those mentioned above) of American policy share anxieties about the "arrogance of American power." Doubtful that America is immune from temptations to misuse its unprecedented resources of power, they see as the common thread in the interventions in Cuba, the Dominican Republic, and Vietnam an increasingly cynical disregard for the rights and interests of others. In her zeal to save other people's skins, they fear, America is about to lose her own soul.

American policies in Southeast Asia are denounced for their alleged departure from the principle of self-determination. Manifestations of American hegemony in the affairs of the Atlantic are decried as evidences of an unwillingness to abide genuine expressions of European independence. "Globalism" is considered anathema to the principle of noninterference. Indeed the general magnitude of America's involvement in world politics is considered doubly unfortunate, on the grounds that a diminution in the threat of Russian imperialism makes it unnecessary and the degree to which global involvement absorbs resources and energies demanded by domestic problems makes it unpalatable.

Naturally enough, most of these propositions are challenged by those presently responsible for United States foreign policy. Those officials are perceptibly less enthusiastic about the emerging

---

[8] For statements of dissent from America's current policies, see, especially, William Fulbright, *The Arrogance of Power* (New York, N.Y.: Vintage, 1967); Theodore Draper, *The Abuse of Power* (New York, N.Y.: Viking, 1967); William Pfaff and Edmund Stillman, *Power and Impotence* (New York, N.Y.: Random, 1966), and Ronald Steel, *Pax Americana* (New York, N.Y.: Viking, 1967). President Johnson's policies have been defended in the speeches and essays of such men as General Maxwell Taylor, Presidential Assistant Walt W. Rostow, and Professor Zbigniew K. Brzezinski.

polycentrism in world politics. In a bipolar world, the threats to American security were less ambiguous, United States responsibilities clearer cut. Moreover, to those responsible for shaping the world in such a way as to enhance America's security and prosperity, there is a natural reluctance to promote trends that seem likely to diminish American influence. Those officials are, further, inclined to consider the principles that have guided American policy in the recent past "tried and tested" rather than "hopelessly obsolete." Finally, there is an understandable reluctance to discount threats that in the past have supplied the cohesion for positive ventures in the Atlantic world. Whatever the difficulties posed by present policies, they have at least the virtue of being reassuringly familiar.

Much of the debate over the future directions of America's foreign policies has focused upon the dichotomy between intervention and isolation. The issue, however, is more subtle. What concept may serve as an organizing principle for the myriad relationships that the United States is destined to maintain with the world? The difficulties of choice are compounded by the variety of available concepts. Some hope that the Soviet Union might be persuaded to participate in a dyarchical rule of the world, with the two superpowers jointly controlling the arms race and developing and policing the non-Western countries. Others are attracted by the prospect of a more organic link between the advanced industrial states in the West in some sort of federal or functional Atlantic community. Still others would prefer a structuring of the world along regional lines, with the United States resuming its benevolent paternalism in the Western Hemisphere. A host of other concepts have their advocates.

It is, of course, possible—even likely—that American policies will not be dominated by any single concept to the extent that they have been disciplined to the tasks of containment during the past two decades. As previously suggested, American policies are likely to evolve in incremental steps. In 1947 radical departures were facilitated by the appearance of dangers that were novel, obvious, and ominous. Today the world is becoming increasingly complex, the threats to American security more subtle and indirect, the nature of America's interests increasingly ambiguous, and the responsibilities for preserving world order somewhat more diffuse. In the face of such uncertainties, policy innovations are likely to be tentative and halting. Such marginal shifts are likewise all that can be accommodated by a government as complex as that of the United States. If more dramatic revisions are forthcoming they will likely reflect convulsive changes in America's domestic situation.

Such a prediction may be too heavily influenced by the internal controversies unleashed by the Vietnamese war. But what appears to be at stake is America's capacity to develop a foreign policy that is again responsive to recent changes in the international environment and also compatible with America's image of herself as a liberal nation. That historic dilemma will have been given an excruciating twist should the effort to uphold the principle of self-determination in the uncertain terrain of Vietnam occasion the destruction of a liberal policy at home. That such an outcome can even be conceived is evidence enough of the intimate relationship that exists between foreign and domestic politics.

Chapter 1. Introduction

Aron, Raymond, *Peace and War: A Theory of International Relations.* New York: Praeger, 1967.

Block, Joseph and Kenneth Thompson, *Foreign Policies in a World of Change.* New York: Harper, 1963.

Brzezinski, Zbigniew K. and Samuel P. Huntington, *Political Power USA/USSR.* New York: Viking, 1965.

Farrell, Barry, ed., *Approaches to Comparative and International Politics.* Evanston, Ill.: Northwestern University Press, 1966.

Frankel, Joseph, *The Making of Foreign Policy.* London: Oxford University Press, 1963.

Liska, George, *Imperial America: The International Politics of Primacy.* Baltimore: Johns Hopkins University Press, 1967.

Rosenau, James N., ed., *Domestic Sources of Foreign Policy.* New York: Free Press, 1967.

Seabury, Paul, *Power, Freedom, and Diplomacy.* New York: Random, 1963.

Waltz, Kenneth N., *Foreign Policy and Democratic Politics.* Boston: Little, Brown, 1967.

Chapter 2. Capabilities

Hitch, Charles and Roland McKean, *The Economics of Defense in the Nuclear Age*. Cambridge, Mass.: Harvard University Press, 1960.

Kahn, Herman and Anthony Wiener, *The Year 2000*. New York: Macmillan, 1967.

The Military Balance 1968–69. London: Institute for Strategic Studies, 1968.

Chapter 3. Beliefs and traditions

Carleton, William G., *The Revolution in American Foreign Policy*. New York: Random, 1963.

Gilbert, Felix, *To the Farewell Address*. Princeton, N.J.: Princeton University Press, 1961.

Kennan, George F., *American Diplomacy 1900–1950*. New York: Mentor, 1952.

Leopold, Richard W., *The Growth of American Foreign Policy*. New York: Knopf, 1962.

Lippmann, Walter, *Foreign Policy: Shield of the Republic*. Boston: Atlantic–Little, Brown, 1943.

Loewenheim, Frances L., ed., *The Historian and the Diplomat*. New York: Harper, 1967.

Marshall, C. B., *The Limits of Foreign Policy*. New York: Holt, 1954.

———, *The Exercise of Sovereignty*. Baltimore: Johns Hopkins University Press, 1965.

Osgood, Robert E., *Ideals and Self-Interest in America's Foreign Relations*. Chicago: University of Chicago Press, 1953.

Pfaff, William and Edward Stillman, *Power and Impotence*. New York: Random, 1966.

Thompson, Kenneth W., *Political Realism and the Crisis of World Politics*. Princeton, N.J.: Princeton University Press, 1960.

Chapter 4. Political culture

Boorstin, Daniel, *The Genius of American Politics*. Chicago: University of Chicago Press, 1953.

Galbraith, John K., *The New Industrial State*. New York: Houghton Mifflin, 1967.

Hoffmann, Stanley, "Restraints and Choices in American Foreign Policy," *Daedalus* (Fall 1962), pp. 668–704.

———, "The American Style: Our Past and Our Principles," *Foreign Affairs* (January 1968).

Kissinger, Henry, "Domestic Structure and Foreign Policy," *Daedalus* (Spring 1966), pp. 503–530.

Lindblom, Charles E., *The Intelligence of Democracy*. New York: Free Press, 1965.

Price, Don K., *The Scientific Estate*. Cambridge, Mass.: Belknap Press, 1965.

Chapter 5. Political institutions

Cater, Douglass, *Power in Washington*. New York: Vintage, 1965.

Hilsman, Roger, *To Move a Nation*. Garden City, N.Y.: Doubleday, 1967.

Neustadt, Richard E., *Presidential Power*. New York: Wiley, 1960.

Reston, James, *The Artillery of the Press*. New York: Harper, 1967.

Sapin, Burton, *The Making of United States Foreign Policy*. New York: Praeger, 1966.

Schlesinger, Arthur, Jr., *A Thousand Days*. New York: Houghton Mifflin, 1965.

Scott, Andrew and Raymond Dawson, eds., *Readings in the Making of American Foreign Policy*. New York: Macmillan, 1965.

Sorenson, Theodore, *Kennedy*. New York: Harper, 1965.

Chapter 6. Political processes

Almond, Gabriel, *The American People and Foreign Policy*. New York: Praeger, 1960.

Huntington, Samuel P., *The Common Defense*. New York: Columbia University Press, 1961.

Jackson, Henry, ed., *The National Security Council*. New York: Praeger, 1965.

Montgomery, John, *The Politics of Foreign Aid*. New York: Praeger, 1962.

Schilling, Warner, Paul Hammond, and Glenn Snyder, *Strategy, Politics, and Defense Budgets*. New York: Columbia University Press, 1962.

Wicker, Thomas, *JFK and LBJ*. New York: Morrow, 1968.

Chapter 7. Recent foreign relations

Beloff, Max, *The United States and the Unity of Europe*. New York: Vintage, 1963.

Brown, Seyom, *The Faces of Power*. New York: Columbia University Press, 1968.

Brzezinski, Zbigniew K., *An End to Partition*. New York: Harper, 1965.

Kaplan, Lawrence, ed., *Recent American Foreign Policy*. Homewood, Ill.: Dorsey, 1968.

Kennan, George F., *Memoirs 1925–50*. Boston: Atlantic–Little, Brown, 1967.

Montgomery, John, *Foreign Aid in International Politics*. Englewood Cliffs, N.J.: Prentice-Hall, 1967.

Spanier, John, *American Foreign Policy Since World War II*, 3rd ed. New York: Praeger, 1968.

Stoessinger, John, *The United Nations and the Superpowers*. New York: Random, 1965.

Chapter 8. Foreign policy problems

Aron, Raymond, *The Great Debate*. Garden City, N.Y.: Doubleday, 1965.

Ball, George W., *The Discipline of Power*. Boston: Atlantic–Little, Brown, 1968.

Draper, Theodore, *The Abuse of Power*. New York: Viking, 1967.

Fall, Bernard, *The Two Viet-Nams*. New York: Praeger, 1963.

Gerberding, William, *United States Foreign Policy*. New York: McGraw-Hill, 1966.

Kissinger, Henry A., *The Necessity for Choice*. New York: Harper, 1960.

———, *The Troubled Partnership*. New York: McGraw-Hill, 1965.

Schelling, Thomas, *Arms and Influence*. New Haven, Conn.: Yale University Press, 1966.

Spanier, John and Joseph Nogee, *The Politics of Disarmament*. New York: Praeger, 1962.

Stone, Jeremy J., *Containing the Arms Race*. Cambridge, Mass.: M.I.T. Press, 1966.

Index